# REGIONALIZATION AND LABOUR MARKET INTERDEPENDENCE IN EAST AND SOUTHEAST ASIA

# Regionalization and Labour Market Interdependence in East and Southeast Asia

Edited by

## Duncan Campbell
*Senior Research Officer*
*Task Force on Industrial Relations*
*International Labour Office*

## Aurelio Parisotto
*Research Officer*
*International Institute for Labour Studies*

## Anil Verma
*Professor*
*Faculty of Management*
*University of Toronto*

and

## Asma Lateef
*Consultant*
*International Institute for Labour Studies*

Foreword by Padmanabha Gopinath

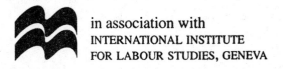 in association with
INTERNATIONAL INSTITUTE
FOR LABOUR STUDIES, GENEVA

First published in Great Britain 1997 by
**MACMILLAN PRESS LTD**
Houndmills, Basingstoke, Hampshire RG21 6XS and London
Companies and representatives throughout the world

A catalogue record for this book is available from the British Library.

ISBN 0–333–67431–6

First published in the United States of America 1997 by
**ST. MARTIN'S PRESS, INC.,**
Scholarly and Reference Division,
175 Fifth Avenue, New York, N.Y. 10010

ISBN 0–312–17703–8

Library of Congress Cataloging-in-Publication Data
Regionalization and labour market interdependence in East and
Southeast Asia / edited by Duncan Campbell . . . [et al.].
p. cm.
Includes bibliographical references and index.
ISBN 0–312–17703–8 (cloth)
1. Labor market—East Asia. 2. Labor market—Asia, Southeastern.
3. Industrial location—East Asia. 4. Industrial location—Asia,
Southeastern. 5. East Asia—Economic conditions—Regional
disparities. 6. Asia, Southeastern—Economic conditions—Regional
disparities. 7. International division of labor. I. Campbell,
Duncan C.
HD5826.A6R44 1997
331.12'095—dc21 97–18984
CIP

This book is printed on paper suitable for recycling and made from fully managed and
sustained forest sources.

10  9  8  7  6  5  4  3  2  1
06  05  04  03  02  01  00  99  98  97

Printed in Great Britain by
The Ipswich Book Company Ltd
Ipswich, Suffolk

# Contents

**Part IV Labour Policy**

# List of Figures and Tables

## Figures

## Tables

# Foreword

In recent years, the International Institute for Labour Studies has addressed the social and labour market implications of globalization. It has taken, as its point of departure, the growing disparity between the international level, at which economic activity is increasingly organized, and the national level, at which social and labour market institutions are traditionally structured. The trend towards greater integration and wider geographical networks of production and distribution has had a direct impact on labour. The deregulation of trade and investment regimes and the expansion of market horizon have accelerated a shift in investment patterns, which has impacted on the quantity, quality and location of jobs in industrialized and developing countries alike.

The process of global integration is particularly apparent of the regional level through the emergence of regional trading blocs, and the clustering of foreign direct investments (FDIs) around the core economies of the European Union (EU), Japan and the United States. A distinct process of regional economic integration has taken place in the rapidly growing economies of East and Southeast Asia (ESEA). Intra-ESEA trade and FDI is one of the most dynamic vehicles in the world economy today, resulting in the establishment of regionally integrated production and distribution networks, driven by an increasingly important regional market.

Much of the current literature has emphasized the macroeconomic aspect of these changes. The Institute has attempted to fill a gap by focusing explicitly on the micro-organizational dimensions of globalization and regionalization. The contributions in this volume reflect that emphasis. The focus is on the production and investment strategies of enterprises, and their correlation to labour market variables. The process of regional integration is not viewed simply as an automatic response to macroeconomic 'fundamentals', but as responding to a range of factors – such as business ties and geographical and cultural proximity – which play an important role in shaping production and trade linkages across locations. Such a perspective facilitates identification of the microeconomic channels through which labour market interdependence is established.

This volume highlights the main labour market implications of regionalization in ESEA. Jobs move with goods and capital across national borders and create new patterns of interdependence between previously insulated labour markets. Employment levels, wages, working conditions and labour management relations in a given location come under the influence of decisions and events taking place elsewhere. As a result, national autonomy in the formulation of labour market policies may be diminishing. Furthermore, the integration of ESEA economies in the international division of labour has had variables effects on workers. Some have derived benefits while others have been left out in the process of transition and change. These emerging realities have several policy implications. They require governments, business and labour to come together to influence labour market outcomes in terms which are relevant both to national and to regional needs. In addition, unless labour markets are managed so as to create sustainable competitive advantage while bringing benefits to the majority of workers, progress will be undermined by social unrest and economic discontinuities. It is the aim of this book to begin the exploration of policy options appropriate to these new developments.

PADMANABHA GOPINATH
*Director, International Institute*
*for Labour Studies*
*Geneva*

# List of Abbreviations

| | |
|---|---|
| AFTA | ASEAN Free Trade Area |
| ANIE | Asian newly industrializing economy |
| ASEAN | Association of Southeast Asian Nations |
| BDDC | buyer-driven commodity chain |
| DRPK | Democratic People's Republic of Korea |
| EC | European Community |
| EOI | export-oriented industrialization |
| EPZ | Export-Processing Zone |
| ESEA | East and Southeast Asia |
| EU | European Union |
| FDI | foreign direct investment |
| GATT | General Agreement on Tariffs and Trade |
| GDI | gross domestic investment |
| GDP | gross domestic product |
| GNP | gross national product |
| GOCC | government-owned and controlled corporation |
| GSP | Generalized System of Preferences |
| IC | integrated circuit |
| ILO | International Labour Organization |
| IMF | International Monetary Fund |
| ISI | import-substitution industrialization |
| MFA | Multifibre Arrangement |
| MFN | most favoured nation |
| MITI | Ministry of Trade and Industry (Japan) |
| NAFTA | North American Free Trade Agreement |
| NIE | newly industrializing economy |
| NTB | non-tariff barrier |
| OBM | original brandname manufacturing |
| OCW | overseas contract worker |
| OECD | Organization for Economic Cooperation and Development |
| OEM | original equipment manufacturing |
| OJT | on-the-job training |
| OPEC | Organization of Petroleum-Exporting Countries |
| PDCC | producer-driven commodity chain |
| PRC | People's Republic of China |

| | |
|---|---|
| SEC | Securities and Exchange Commission |
| SEZ | Special Economic Zone |
| SIJORI | Singapore–Johor–Riau growth triangle |
| SME | small and medium-sized enterprise |
| TNC | transnational corporation |
| TQC | total quality control |
| UNDP | United Nations Development Programme |
| WTO | World Trade Organization |

# Notes on the Contributors

**David E. Bloom**   Deputy Director, Harvard Institute for International Studies (HIID), Cambridge, MA, USA.

**Duncan Campbell**   Senior Research Officer, Task Force on Industrial Relations, ILO (formerly Senior Research Officer, International Institute for Labour Studies), Geneva, Switzerland.

**Voravidh Charoenloet**   Associate Professor, Faculty of Economics, Chulalongkorn University, Bangkok, Thailand.

**Andres J. Dinglasan**   Congressman, House of Representatives, Manila, Philippines.

**Francisco R. Floro**   Vice-President, Philippine Chamber of Commerce and Industry, Manila, Philippines.

**Gary Gereffi**   Professor, Department of Sociology, Duke University, Durham, NC, USA.

**Jeffrey Henderson**   Professor of International Economic Sociology, Manchester Business School, University of Manchester, England.

**Asma Lateef**   Consultant, International Institute for Labour Studies, Geneva, Switzerland.

**Waseem Noor**   Department of Economics, Columbia University, New York, USA.

**Aniceto C. Orbeta, Jr**   Research Fellow, Philippine Institute of Development Studies, Manila, Philippines.

**Aurelio Parisotto**   Research Officer, International Institute for Labour Studies, Geneva, Switzerland.

**Maria Teresa C. Sanchez**   Research Associate, Philippine Institute of Development Studies, Manila, Philippines.

**Niphant Simakrai**   Regional Manager for West Asia, Singer Nikko Co. Ltd, Bangkok, Thailand.

**Ronald Skeldon**   Professor, Department of Geography and Geology, The University of Hong Kong, Hong Kong.

**Min Tang**   Senior Economist, Programs Department (West), Asian Development Bank, Manila, Philippines.

**Myo Thant**   Senior Economist, Economics and Development Resource Center, Asian Development Bank, Manila, Philippines.

**Anil Verma**   Professor, Faculty of Management, University of Toronto, Toronto, Canada.

**Susumu Watanabe**   Professor, Tokyo International University, Kawagoe-shi, Japan.

**Sakool Zuesongdham**   President, The Federation of Bank and Financial Workers' Unions of Thailand, Bangkok, Thailand.

# Introduction

## Aurelio Parisotto and Duncan Campbell

The emergence of new, highly dynamic industrial players from East and Southeast Asia has been a major factor of change in the world economy and a main source of the intensification of competitive pressures during the past two decades. It has generated an enormous interest in industrialized countries concerning its implications for unemployment and industrial restructuring and, in developing countries, as a model to achieve rapid industrialization, growth and the generation of jobs. The attention focused initially on macroeconomic stabilization and aggressive outward orientation as the main recipe for success. Subsequently, the focus shifted to those fundamental features that supported growth of productivity and effective management of the economy, such as the role of the state and state incentives, the quality of human resources, the institutional and cultural basis, and the relations between governments, employers and labour. Each of these factors is likely to have played a role in the 'Asian miracle'. In spite of some similarities, however, in comparing the experiences of the different national contexts there appears to be no Asian model but, rather, different patterns of growth embedded in country-specific systems.

Less attention has been given to the economic interdependencies that exist across countries of the region, in spite of the fact that these interdependencies are important in explaining economic and labour market outcomes. The creation of production networks that span the whole region and take advantage of the varying assets of different countries has been an important element in fostering the competitiveness of firms producing in Asia – by lowering their costs, enhancing their flexibility in responding to changes in world markets, and broadening the scope for product specialization and industrial upgrading. Economic integration through foreign direct investment (FDI) and trade linkages also helped to generate foreign exchange earnings and employment and spread technical and organizational knowledge to a growing number of adjacent locations, thereby creating opportunities to support growth of exports and the creation of employment within the region as a whole.

The complex intra-regional division of labour and technology, therefore,

1

can be a useful starting point to understand more fully some of the reasons of economic success in East and Southeast Asia. The degree of integration in this division of labour shapes the context in which firms and governments frame their strategies. It provides the necessary background against which to assess prospects for industrial development, highlight policy options at the national level and project schemes for policy cooperation at the regional level. More importantly for the purposes of this volume, such a perspective can shed light on a broad range of labour market issues.

Distinctive labour market consequences arise from the different ways in which economies in the region participate in the international/regional division of labour, in terms of the number of jobs generated, their quality and their location. As will be seen throughout this volume, simple integration through the export of basic items assembled by unskilled labour, for instance, may help to generate large numbers of new, poor quality jobs, and activate significant rural migration to those sites that successfully link up with regional and international markets. Deeper integration is more likely to come with better wages, higher demand for skills and changes in labour relations. But the labour market is not only the privileged place to look for the consequences of economic integration and regionalization. Labour market policies, institutions and regulations have a bearing on cross-border trade flows, capital mobility and labour mobility. They influence the pace at which economic integration proceeds and the extent to which countries can benefit from it. 'Managing' the labour market in conjunction with technology and industrial policies is becoming increasingly important in moving from a competitive position based on comparative advantages, such as low wages and ineffective unions, to one based on less fleeting competitive advantages, such as high productivity, innovation capacities, high skills and decent wages. Capital and labour mobility, i.e. integration, renders such managing not only more important but also much more complex in a context in which traditional protective instruments are less and less effective and feasible.

The various 'downstream' implications of the intra-regional division of labour for labour markets and labour policies in the ESEA region are the subject matter of the contributions that make up this volume. Before introducing them, it is useful to review 'upstream' developments, in particular the current trends towards regionalization.

## THE GEOGRAPHICAL DIVISION OF LABOUR AND THE SCOPE OF REGIONAL INTEGRATION

For the purposes of this volume, East and Southeast Asia (ESEA) is defined to comprise a set of economies characterized by extraordinary industrial dynamism during the past two decades. They include: Japan; the four Asian NIEs (Hong Kong, Republic of Korea, Singapore and Taiwan, China); the ASEAN-4 (Indonesia, Malaysia, the Philippines and Thailand); and China. These ten economies are usually grouped in three distinctive tiers, according to their relative level of development and the degree of diversification of their industrial structure. Altogether, they can be seen as a regional compact characterized, in economic terms, by complementary, if not hierarchical, 'vertical' relationships between economies in different tiers, and competitive 'horizontal' relationships within each tier.

Regionalization in ESEA is a relatively new phenomenon, having been preceded by the region's globalization, i.e. the growth of ESEA exports of consumer goods to markets external to the region. Since the 1970s, openness to foreign capital, cheap labour, and the 'export platform' function in simple, labour-intensive manufacturing provided the initial stimulus for the rapid integration of the NIEs in the global economy. This initial configuration changed mainly through a 'cascading' pattern of trade and FDI flows that reflected shifts in comparative advantage (mainly the cost of labour) across the region. Intra-regional integration developed primarily along vertical lines, i.e. from the top economic player in the region, Japan, down to the NIEs, and from Japan and the NIEs, once these were under pressure to develop new factors of competitive advantage, to the ASEAN-4 and China. A fourth layer is currently emerging, comprising countries such as Vietnam, Laos and Cambodia.

Three main features in the process of regionalization are worth noting. First, the FDI activities of firms were a main driver of integration. Although the rapid growth of intra-regional trade is commonly used as an indicator of greater regional economic interdependence, arm's-length trade was not the single most important integrating factor. Highly dynamic components of intra-regional trade were generated to a large extent by capital movements and evolved largely under the organizational governance of firms situated outside the borders of a given exporting economy. This was particularly evident in a few highly globalized industries that largely accounted for the export drive in the region. Electronics and textiles and garments, for instance, accounted in 1994 for over 30 per cent of total commodity exports in seven of the ten economies, and 20 per cent in the remaining three. Both industries are significantly characterized by intra- or inter-firm arrangements within global production and distribution networks, or 'chains', driven by multinational producers and buyers. Beyond factors that favoured the function of coordinating geographically dispersed production networks, such as the presence of overseas Chinese communities, similarities in business practices and geographical and cultural proximity played a major role in forging linkages across locations participating in the process of integration within the region.

It may be tempting to interpret an FDI-led pattern of integration as the product of hierarchical economic relations. Indeed, the dependency of the economies in the lower tiers on foreign capital, technology, and sourcing – in particular from Japan – has been noted by a number of observers (Wilkinson, 1994). However, broadening diversification of exports, growing organizational skills, specialization in new and more sophisticated market niches and the development of endogenous tech- nological capacities attest to a more complex and dynamic pattern than one simply based on either complementary or 'dependency' relations. This is best exemplified by Korean and Taiwanese firms, which are now establishing their own proprietary brand names in a growing range of increasingly sophisticated product lines and compete on a par with Japanese and Western firms on markets both outside and within the region.

Second, economic integration in the ESEA region evolved in the absence of across-the-board preferential trading arrangements such as the NAFTA and the European Single Market. Indeed, trade and FDI across the NIEs and the ASEAN-4, in particular in consumer goods for domestic markets, remained quite limited. If not policy-led, the process of integration was policy-guided. National policy frameworks allowed and encouraged trade and FDI inflows from upper tier econ- omies, or FDI outflows down to locations in the lower tier, as long as these were functional to the restructuring of domestic firms and their successful positioning in international competition. But fully fledged policy cooperation in FDI, trade and labour matters was rather cir- cumscribed. ASEAN aside, the main exception is represented by forms of integration at the subregional level, of which the linkages between Hong Kong and Coastal China and the Singapore–Johor–Riau (SIJORI) growth triangle are the most significant examples. These evolved along the vertical lines described below and seem strongly characterized by the attempt to attract and retain foreign and local capital through the creation of an integrated setting in which an advanced commercial and logistical bases – Hong Kong or Singapore – is complemented by cheaper labour and factory space in the 'hinterland' areas – Coastal China or the Riau province of Indonesia and the Johor state of Malaysia.

Finally, the ESEA region is becoming a major centre of growth in its own, particularly if China is considered. Although the final markets in industrialized countries still represent the main destination of exports from the region, the rising affluence and importance of domestic markets is a dynamic element likely to account for a change in the configuration. In short, the main direction for change is likely to be a shift from vertical to deeper horizontal integration. Such a move should receive further impetus by the recent launch of the ASEAN Free Trade Agreement (AFTA) and the implementation of the Uruguay Round Agreements, which are expected to reduce considerably tariffs and other barriers to trade between developing countries. Nevertheless, the political understanding that is needed for further integration and horizontal policy cooperation at the regional level will be very difficult to achieve in the immediate future.

## THE INTERDEPENDENCE OF LABOUR MARKETS?

The disparate opportunities and outcomes that characterize the individual livelihoods of 'workers in an integrating world' were persuasively illustrated in a 1995 report of that title by the World Bank (1995). It is a rhetorical term worth borrowing to capture how the evolution of the international organization of production radically transforms the lives of individuals in today's economy when compared with the stable, national systems of the past. Consider, for example, the auto worker who worked on the assembly line of the Ford Motor Corporation in Michigan in the mid-1960s. Production was largely destined for the expanding domestic market and, while the job was narrowly defined and monotonous, his wages were sheltered from domestic competition because of the oligopolistic structure of the domestic auto industry and the encompassing nature of labour market institutions which so effectively took wages out of competition that even relatively unskilled work in the auto industry paid at well above the manufacturing industry average. His pay and job security were also protected by the Keynesian demand management policies of the time that served to smooth over the vicissitudes of the business cycle. And with the exception of a small-car niche in the market that domestic producers did not at all perceive as a competitive threat, foreign competition was virtually non-existent because of tariff barriers, restrictions on the mobility of capital, the smaller spread of multinational corporations in general (and, in particular, of those non-US in origin) as well as a variety of other conditions that made national economies more sheltered then than now.

The trend toward regionalization described above, and the factors that underpin this trend, contrast sharply with this earlier world of production. Indeed, a similarity with the past would seem to emerge only through the migration to the ESEA region of what remains a largely Fordist organization of work in low skilled, labour-intensive production. In this volume's discussion, the worker is often a women, employed, for example, on the assembly line in a Thai subsidiary of a large Japanese consumer electronics firm, and engaged in the relatively unskilled and repetitive work of the auto worker more than a generation ago. The circuit boards she assembles are exported daily to other locations in the company's regional network. In fact, the pace of production is altered more than once on a given day, and the demand for her and her coworkers' output has little to do with conditions in the domestic market, but with production needs elsewhere in the firm's Asian network. She is young, as are her largely female colleagues, has no union to represent her, and earns the minimum wage. Work like hers can be performed at other locations in the region. Her wage, although the minimum, is now beginning to appear high in comparison to those in China and Vietnam. Aside from labour, the subsidiary relies on few other inputs from the local economy.

What has changed in the years intervening between these stories is the rise of economic interdependence. The focus on the phenomenon of interdependence – or emerging regionalization within ESEA – would seem unusually appropriate to the region, as it evokes comparison with earlier theory on the 'wild geese flying' pattern of complementary development, elaborated by the Japanese economist, Akamatsu, in the early 1960s.[1] In his view, industries that lost comparative advantage would migrate to lower cost locations, while higher skill-, capital-, and technology-intensive industries would replace the initial sources of comparative advantage in higher cost locations. Yet the interdependent nature of the growth of the region's economies has largely been a subordinate theme in a debate that has turned more often on the question of the 'state' versus the 'market' as exclusive sources of explanations for the region's success (Gore, 1996). Ultimately, the national level of analysis is essential for the identification of strategies and policy instruments most likely to yield effective developmental outcomes. Again, however, the national level alone is an inadequate vantage point if the aim is to assess the contribution of regional economic interdependence to national patterns of growth, as these rely *inter alia* on industry dynamics and the evolving regional organization of production. The dynamics of this cross-national organization of production, then, link the many 'local' labour markets in the region, and the jobs and wages they provide. The linkages are varied and cannot be understood at too aggregate a level: they create interdependencies that are something more than the outcome of the 'market's' free hand. But they are also something beyond the sole determination (and regulatory authority) of the state: with regionalization, 'national' labour market outcomes are increasingly contingent on the cross-border production relationships in which workers participate.

## Interdependence and Integration

As implied by the activity of the Thai assembly worker, it is the complementarity between FDI and trade – the organized activities of major firms, their affiliates and contractors between the region's major capital-sending and capital-receiving countries – which is behind the construction of a regional organization of production. Characteristic of the emerging web of the regional economy is the spatial distance between various production activities and the final markets for which they are destined and, in consequence, the emergence of a host of interdependencies across labour markets which accompany the process of regionalization. Bloom and Noor define 'interdependence' in Chapter 1 as occurring when events in one national market send 'perturbations' through other national markets. As such, interdependence falls short of full 'integration', which may be more characteristic of international financial markets. Interdependence, however, has several implications for the quantity, quality and location of employment and work in the emerging regional division of labour which the chapters in this volume address. 'Interdependence' suggests that these labour market outcomes are to some extent contingent on a range of developments and behaviours outside of the national markets in which they occur.

## Quantity of Jobs

As to the quantity of jobs generated by rising regional interdependence, there can be little doubt that trade, FDI and contractual ties across firms from different countries have expanded formal sector employment in the region. As higher costs have eroded comparative advantage in labour- and low skill-intensive stages of production in Japan and the Asian NIEs (or ANIEs), for example, the substantial relocation to the ASEAN-4 countries has, in regional terms, expanded both output and employment. As Skeldon shows in Chapter 5, total manufacturing employment by Hong Kong firms in 'greater Hong Kong', i.e. including Hong Kong firms' direct investments in Chinese coastal provinces, is several times greater than the Colony's original manufacturing employment base. Accessing labour supply in neighbouring lower cost regions, moreover, has been one strategy by which higher cost countries, such as Singapore, have been able to retain a stake in industries in which comparative cost advantages have been lost. The complementary alignment of stages of production in vertically integrated industries at the cross-border, but subnational level is the principal aim of the 'growth triangle' concept, as outlined in by Tang and Thant in Chapter 6. Nevertheless, the complementary expansion of employment at the regional level need not always imply a seamless and smooth adjustment. Watanabe's discussion in Chapter 4 reflects the rising pitch of debate in Japan on the 'hollowing out' of the Japanese industrial base and 'zero-sum' concerns that employment gains elsewhere in the region could be at the expense of rising unemployment in Japan.

**Quality of Jobs**

Regional interdependence also bears on the quality of the jobs created, and through several channels. At the level of the firm, some chapters support the well established finding that employment within multinational corporations is frequently superior to local labour market alternatives, where such exist. At the macro level, however, concerns do arise over the disparity in time between a location's loss of comparative advantage and the capacity to upgrade human resources. East Asia is widely known as home to economies that have successfully upgraded their participation in international markets in part through a determined focus on education and training. Charoenloet's discussion in Chapter 7, however, highlights dilemmas a country such as Thailand can face when an initial comparative advantage in labour-intensive, light industry begins to erode. The best medium-term strategy is to support a tendency toward industrial upgrading which appears to be occurring in some instances. This, however, presupposes an investment in human resources which the author finds lacking: 80 per cent of manufacturing employees have no more than a basic education. In such a situation, there is a risk that short-term strategies acquire greater appeal, as when pressure mounts against raising the minimum wage as anti-competitive, or freedom of association is actively discouraged in export processing zones, as Orbeta and Sanchez discuss in Chapter 8. All are efforts to 'restore the initial conditions' of factor-cost advantage, as Verma takes up in Chapter 9, his Conclusion to the volume. They are particular features of the lower (and more directly competitive) end of the region's complementary organization of production, and are largely unsustainable given the rising availability of ever-lower cost locations and the high degree of 'locational elasticity' that characterize this form of comparative advantage.

As the above example implies, power imbalances also characterize interdependence. There are clearly leaders and followers, greater or lesser degrees of dependence, stable and less stable platforms for participation in the regional organization of production. From within the conceptual framework of the 'commodity chain', Gereffi argues in Chapter 2 that an inverse relationship exists between locational dependence and the quality of employment, as reflected in the relative stability of employment, skills, wages and potential for upgrading. He suggests a taxonomy of 'export roles', ascending stages through which locations may pass in their participation in a cross-border chain of production, from mere assembly to control over design, marketing, and brand name. Skills are a key ingredient both for job quality and for increasing the range of export roles that a location can play. On the other hand, they appear to be a necessary but not sufficient ingredient. A range of state policies also applies. Henderson in Chapter 3 considers the role of the state's industrial policies as a key determinant of whether industrial upgrading becomes embedded and self-sustaining or remains reliant on foreign infusions of capital and know-how. In the Philippines, meanwhile, the high quality of labour supply has historically surpassed the demand for its use, according to Orbeta and Sanchez, and the situation has begun to change only in the 1990s. As the Philippines becomes better integrated in the regional economy, the country's traditionally high proportion of overseas contract workers (OCWs) may diminish and its composition change, external migration increasingly affecting only the more skilled.

## Location of Jobs

Regional interdependence, finally, influences patterns in the location of jobs, and this influence is reflected in two sets of concerns in the volume. The first centres on the extent to which capital and contracts flow to developing locations in the region, thereby generating employ-ment opportunities linked to participation in the regional economy. The second (conversely) focuses on the migration of labour to sources of employment, and consequently on patterns of internal as well as exter-nal migration. The growth of East Asia has been characterized by the emergence of labour shortages in Japan as well as in the ANIEs, and the region has seen a substantial rise in legal and illegal migration from labour-surplus to labour-shortage areas, both in the Northeast and the Southeast, e.g. Indonesian migration to Malaysia, or Burmese to Thailand. As both Skeldon (Chapter 5) and Tang and Thant (Chapter 6) discuss, patterns of internal and external migration are direct conse-quences of regionalization, whether in China or the SIJORI growth triangle. Indeed, the SIJORI triangle is among other things a deliber-ate internal labour migration strategy for Indonesia. For the most part, however, the chapters in this volume address not the issue of the mi-gration of people to jobs, but of jobs to people as a consequence of the mobility of investment capital and contracts. As such, the main emphasis here is on how the complementarity of FDI and trade link-ages which constitute the motor force of regional interdependence ren-ders labour the immobile if interdependent factor of production.

The East Asian experience can in many ways be viewed as excep-tional. The rising global phenomenon of labour market interdependence, however, is not. In the climate of slow growth in the West, a particu-lar facet of the interdependence of labour market outcomes has occa-sioned intense debate in recent years – the extent to which trade with developing countries may be held responsible for job displacement, the erosion of the wages of the low skilled, and widening wage equal-ity. The majority of academic opinion on this 'zero-sum' view of labour market interdependence doubts the magnitude of its negative effect with-out, however, doubting that employment loss and employment gain must increasingly be understood in a framework of cross-national in-terdependence. The principal argument of the present volume is that labour market interdependence also characterizes East Asian regional-ization, even if the issues appear to be different than those usually framed in terms of the Western debate. The sheer variety of ways in which 'perturbations' across national labour markets arise as ever closer trade and investment linkages integrate the regional economy argues strongly for a broader, more comprehensive view of both positive and negative consequences of interdependence on the quantity, quality and location of jobs. This book is a contribution to that broader debate.

## ORGANIZATION OF THE VOLUME

The volume is structured in four parts. Part I presents an overview of integration in the region. The main purpose is to document and evaluate patterns of regionalization and changes in the main channels for cross-border integration and labour market interdependence – trade, capital and labour mobility.

Part II takes a closer look, mainly from an industry perspective, at the organization of production across firms and how this shapes the international and regional divisions of labour. The concept of global commodity chains, or the sequence of firms encompassing suppliers, manufacturers, and distributors, clustered around a given final product or service, is introduced by Gereffi in Chapter 2, with a particular focus on Asia's important apparel industry, the archetype of a labour-intensive, export-oriented consumer goods industry. In Chapter 3, Henderson also evokes the chain perspective to illustrate the evolution of the international division of labour in the electronics industry and Asia's fit within this global industry.

Part III reviews the main poles of integration at the regional and subregional levels. The objective is to identify the economic and policy drivers of integration and analyze the consequences for labour markets. By Watanabe's Chapter 4, examines the leading role played by Japan in establishing the region's trade and investment linkages. In Chapter 5, Skeldon traces the linkages between Hong Kong and Coastal China, while Tang and Thant, evaluate in Chapter Six the growth triangle concept as a form of policy coordination and its viability as an economic model in various subregional locations.

Part IV considers the outlook for national development and labour policy formulation in Thailand and Philippines, countries that have only recently embarked on their export-oriented programmes. Both in Voravidh's Chapter 7 and in Orbeta and Sanchez's Chapter 8 the major concern is the need to abandon the traditional path of industrialization, based on foreign investment in labour-intensive and low tech manufacturing activities, and to move rapidly into higher value added activities by expanding the scope for linkages between foreign and local firms. Given differences in educational attainment and in different histories of political stability between the two countries, the strategic challenge may be common, but the different starting points suggest a difference in policy choices.

The final chapter is Verma's overview of the main issues discussed throughout the volume, the lessons learned, and directions for policy formulation. These underscore the centrality of skill development and the means through which this objective is attained as the core requisite of development.

**Note**

1. Akamatsu's theory of complementary development is discussed in Gore (1996).

**References**

Gore, C. (1996), 'Methodological Nationalism and the Misunderstanding of East Asian Industrialization,' United Nations Conference on Trade and Development, *Discussion Paper*, 111 (January).
Wilkinson, B. (1994), *Labour and Industry in the Asia-Pacific: Lessons from the Newly Industrialising Countries* (Berlin: de Gruyter).
World Bank (1995), *Workers in an Integrating World, World Development Report 1995* (New York: Oxford University Press).

# Part I

# Overview of Integration

# 1 Is an Integrated Regional Labour Market Emerging in East and Southeast Asia?*

David E. Bloom and Waseem Noor

Economic growth is the leading concern of macroeconomic policymakers. In traditional macroeconomic models, the main factors that promote economic growth are labour force growth, physical and human capital accumulation, changes in the allocation of resources across economic sectors and technological advancement. All these factors are influenced by the integration of national economies, a process that has gained considerable momentum in recent years because of the erosion of economic and institutional barriers to an integrated world economy (see Bloom and Brender, 1993; Ehrenberg, 1994; World Bank, 1995).

Discussing the integration of *particular* factor and product markets is commonplace. The movement of labour between countries is the standard indicator of international labour market integration. Similarly, cross-national mobility of physical or financial capital is the standard indicator of international capital market integration, while trade is the standard indicator of international product market integration. However, integration of particular markets occurs not only through international transactions involving corresponding factors or products, but also through transactions involving other factors or products. Indeed, a fundamental premise of economic theory holds that the labour markets in two countries effectively become integrated when there is trade, capital mobility, or labour mobility between them.

Capital mobility typically represents jobs searching for workers, which is closely related to labour mobility, which represents workers searching for jobs. For example, when a Japanese company establishes an auto assembly plant in Indonesia, it expresses a demand for Indonesian labour in Indonesia. Labor market integration between the two countries takes place when the Japanese set up factories in Indonesia just

15

as when Indonesian workers migrate to Japan to work in Japanese factories. Both cases involve international labour market transactions, with
Indonesian workers selling labour services to Japanese firms.

National labour markets may also become integrated though trade.
When a country exports a good it implicitly also exports the labour
services embodied in producing that good. For example, the export of
domestically produced electronic goods from Singapore to Malaysia is
roughly equivalent, from the standpoint of labour utilization, to the export of Singaporean capital and labour to Malaysia where they are used
to produce the same goods for local sale. Transportation and other
costs of labour, capital, and product mobility are key determinants of
which option Singaporean firms choose for supplying electronic goods
to Malaysian consumers.

The purpose of this chapter is to examine labour market integration
as it has been achieved through labour mobility, capital mobility, and
trade in East and Southeast Asia (ESEA). We do this by examining
aggregate data on each of these three related channels of integration
during the 1980s, leaving to this volume's other contributors the task
of exploring the microeconomic aspects of labour market integration,
such as vertical integration of private industries between countries (Gereffi,
1995) and the emergence of 'growth triangles' (Teal, 1995; Tang and
Thant, 1995; Than *et al.* 1994). We compare integration within ESEA
with integration involving ESEA and other regions. We also assess the
relative contributions of labour mobility, capital mobility, and trade to
labour market integration within the region. In addition, we discuss the
pattern of regional labour market integration during the 1980s in the
light of changes that occurred in incentives for integration and in various
institutional and economic barriers to integration. We conclude by specu-
lating on the prospects for, and the implications of, further integration.


CONCEPTUAL FRAMEWORK

We begin by distinguishing between the concepts of labour market interdependence and labour market integration. 'Labour market interdependence' refers to the extent to which perturbations in one country's
economy are felt in other countries' labour markets. Interdependence is
thus promoted by the absence of barriers to factor mobility and trade.
These barriers may be purely economic, for example, transportation
costs, or they may be institutional, as in the case of legal restrictions
on labour mobility and technology transfer or tariffs and quotas.

By contrast, 'labour market integration' refers to the extent of factor mobility and trade between two or more economies. Thus, even if two economies are not integrated, perhaps because the structure of their economies is so similar that it eliminates the possibility of gains to factor mobility and trade, they may still be interdependent in the sense that a shock experienced in one economy creates incentives for integrated economic activity.

Much has been written about the causes and consequences of international labour mobility (see ILO, 1992; Macmillen, 1982; UN, 1992c), with most researchers viewing migration as a response to spatial differences in labour market conditions (see Abella and Mori, 1994; Borjas, 1990; Stark, 1991). Similarly, spatial arbitrage is the core idea in most studies of capital market integration, with these studies focusing primarily on four areas: (a) the magnitude of total capital flows (see Chen, 1992, 1993; Ruffin, 1993; Yue, 1993); (b) the resulting parity of interest rates across integrated areas (see Haque and Montiel, 1991; Mishkin, 1984); (c) the correlation between investment rates and domestic savings rates (Feldstein and Horioka, 1980; Frankel, 1984) and (d) the intertemporal behavior of individuals in different countries through tests of Euler equations for consumption (Obstfeld, 1986). Montiel (1994) presents a detailed comparison of these different indicators of capital market integration.

International trade is driven by comparative advantage, which in turn, according to the standard Heckscher–Ohlin trade model, is determined by the relative stocks of production factors across countries. Countries export goods in which they have a comparative advantage, resulting in the equalization of product and factor prices between trading partners. Assuming that production technologies are identical for all trading partners, a powerful implication of the Heckscher–Ohlin model is that trade can lead to full integration of product, capital, and labour markets even in the absence of international factor movements. Razin and Sadka (1992) point out that international factor mobility reinforces the integrating effects of trade on factor and product markets.

In addition to the integration of markets, free international trade also results in increased income for all trading partners as well as improvements in their welfare. Recently some industrial countries have argued that many domestic, labour-intensive jobs have been 'siphoned' away by newly industrializing countries in ESEA. Baldwin (1995) reviews studies of the impact of changing trade patterns on domestic labour markets. He concludes that changes in employment and relative wages are generally not attributable to evolving trade conditions. Despite employment loss in particular industries, the employment-creating effects of trade have outweighed the employment-displacing effects.[1]

Even though economic theory suggests that trade alone can potentially substitute for capital and labour mobility in integrating markets between trading partners, empirically this situation is rarely found. Rather, high levels of factor flows are typically associated with high levels of trade flows (Riedel, 1992). Note also that labour mobility does not have the same social or political implications as capital mobility, especially when there are religious, ethnic or racial differences between migrants and the host country population. Thus, while movements of labour and capital have similar effects in promoting factor market integration, they should not be viewed as perfectly interchangeable. Finally, it is worth noting that at a global level, integration appears thus far to be more an industrial country than a developing country phenomenon, contributing significantly to income growth in the industrial countries and reducing disparities in their *per capita* incomes (Bloom and Brender, 1993).

### EMPIRICAL RESULTS

Previous empirical work on the topic of economic integration in ESEA has looked mainly at the growth of capital movements and trade. Yue (1993) and Chen (1993) both document the increased scale of foreign direct investment (FDI) in ESEA, although they do not distinguish between intra- and inter-regional investment. Jha (1994) analyzes the growth of intra-regional trade, but does not compare his findings with the amount of trade carried out with the rest of the world. Riedel (1992) investigates the link between trade and capital movements within ESEA, and finds evidence of a strong positive association between trade and capital movements. The present analysis builds on these studies by examining intra-regional labour mobility in addition to intra-regional trade and capital mobility, and also by assessing the relative contributions of each mechanism to labour market integration in ESEA since the early 1980s. For empirical purposes, ESEA comprises ten economies: China, Hong Kong, Indonesia, Japan, Republic of Korea, Malaysia, Philippines, Singapore, Taiwan and Thailand. Kampuchea, Laos and Vietnam are excluded because of a lack of data.

### Movements of Labour

The labour migration data analyzed in this section were obtained from various International Labour Organization (ILO) publications and through

*Table* 1.1  Level and growth of outmigration from ESEA's major labour-sending countries,[a] by destination region, 1980–91

| | Share | | Growth[b] |
| Region | 1980–2 | 1989–91 | 1980–91 |
| --- | --- | --- | --- |
| Total ESEA[d] | 9.0[c] | 30.3 | 0.180 |
| Other industrial countries | 1.9 | 5.4 | 0.153 |
| Non-industrial countries | | | |
|   Other Asia | n.a. | n.a. | n.a. |
|   Africa | 0.4 | 0.3 | 0.014 |
|   Middle East | 88.3 | 62.2 | 0.003 |
|   Western Hemisphere | n.a. | n.a. | n.a. |
| Other Europe, USSR, and non-aligned | n.a. | n.a. | n.a. |
| Total | 99.7 | 98.2 | 0.042 |

*Notes*:
[a] Only the major labour-sending countries of the region (Indonesia, Philippines, Thailand and Korea) are included.
[b] The growth rates are slope coefficients from regression equations of the following form: $\log X_t = \alpha_0 + \alpha_1 t$, where $X_t$ is the number of migrants for the relevant regional grouping in year t.
[c] All numbers are in percentages. The shares may add to less than 1 because of migration to non-specified areas.
[d] Because of a lack of consistent data for the entire time period, three of the regions have been combined. All countries in Asia are contained in ESEA. Countries in both the Western Hemisphere and Other Europe are included in the Other Industrial Countries category, and countries in Sub-Saharan Africa are included in the Middle East category. The term 'n.a.' reflects this agglomeration.
n.a. Not applicable.

*Sources*: ILO (1990) and personal correspondence with the Bangkok Office of the ILO.

personal correspondence with ILO staff in Bangkok. Unfortunately, the data refer only to the number of documented migrants from the major labour-sending countries of ESEA. The difficulty in assembling reliable data on total labour migration is widely recognized, and is due to both a lack of coordination between labour-sending and labour-receiving countries and to substantial flows of undocumented migrants (see Athukorala 1993; UNDP/ILO, 1993).

Table 1.1 shows the distribution of labour migrants from Indonesia, Korea, Philippines, and Thailand – ESEA's major labour-sending countries

– among groups of destination countries. Also reported are average annual growth rates for total numbers of migrants from the four labour-sending countries to each destination. The growth rates are estimated by regressing the natural logarithm of annual migration outflows on a simple time trend. For the four countries as a whole they show a 4.2 per cent rate of annual increase. However, the number of outmigrants destined for ESEA countries grew more than four times as fast (18 per cent per year), outpacing the growth of migration to all other destination groups in the table. Thus, inter-country labour mobility within ESEA appears to have increased sharply during the 1980s.

By far, the dominant share of outmigrants from the four ESEA labour-sending countries moved to the Middle East throughout the 1980s, but this share fell precipitously from 88 to 62 per cent between 1980–2 and 1989–91 as falling oil prices resulted in essentially zero growth in the number of Middle East migrants from ESEA. By contrast, the share of ESEA migrants destined for other Asian countries more than trebled, another indication of sharply increased intra-regional labour mobility.

Table 1.2 reports the distribution of destinations for labour migrants from Indonesia, Philippines and Thailand. Examination of these distributions reveals that virtually all migrants from these three countries moved to countries with higher *per capita* income. This migration pattern is consistent with the most basic economic model of migration, in which labour mobility is driven by the search for higher wages. Unfortunately, the main implication of this model – the fall in *wage* differentials as labour markets become more integrated – is not testable here because of a lack of appropriate data. An analysis of cross-country differentials in income *per capita* reveals increased inequality from 1979 to 1987 and declining inequality through 1992, with a small net increase for the overall period.[2] However, as *per capita* income reflects hourly wages, hours worked, and unearned income and is subject to many influences not controlled for, this finding does not necessarily contradict the hypothesis that integration promotes convergence in wages across countries.

Most labour experts believe that ESEA's reported labour migration omits a large flow of undocumented migration. Rough estimates place the level of undocumented migrants at 40–50 per cent of total migration, suggesting that the true flow of intra-regional migrants could be as much as double the figures reported in Table 1.2. Available evidence indicates that most of ESEA's documented intra-regional migrants are unskilled and low skill workers, a pattern that would almost certainly

*Table* 1.2   Outmigrants from Indonesia, Philippines and Thailand, by destination country/region, 1991

| Region | Indonesia | | Philippines | | Thailand | |
|---|---|---|---|---|---|---|
| | Number | Share (%) | Number | Share (%) | Number | Share (%) |
| Total ESEA | 53 224 | 42.2 | 121 843 | 26.4 | 29 172 | 47.8 |
| China | 1 | | – | | 134 | |
| Hong Kong | 1 079 | | 50 652 | | 8 431 | |
| Indonesia | n.a. | | – | | 146 | |
| Japan | 873 | | 57 344 | | 6 263 | |
| Korea | 426 | | 193 | | – | |
| Malaysia | 40 715 | | 5 741 | | 2 473 | |
| Philippines | – | | n.a. | | – | |
| Singapore | 9 937 | | 7 697 | | 9 488 | |
| Taiwan | 190 | | 43 | | 2 237 | |
| Thailand[a] | 3 | | 173 | | n.a. | |
| Other industrial countries | 4 645 | 3.7 | 26 529 | 5.8 | 3 227 | 5.3 |
| Non-industrial countries | | | | | | |
| Other Asia | 1 474 | 1.2 | 10 112 | 2.2 | 8 877 | 14.6 |
| Africa | 17 | 0.0 | – | – | 35 | 0.1 |
| Middle East | 66 884 | 53.0 | 302 825 | 65.6 | 19 660 | 32.2 |
| Western Hemisphere | – | | – | | – | – |
| Other Europe, USSR, and non-aligned | 1 | 0.0 | – | – | – | – |
| Total | 126 245 | 100.0 | 461 309 | 100.0 | 60 971 | 100.0 |

*Notes:*
[a] For Thailand, the migration to Libya and Algeria are included in the Middle East region.
– Indicates that no migration was reported to this destination.
n.a. Not applicable.

*Source:* ILO Bangkok Office.

be accentuated if data were available on the skill distribution of undocumented migrants.

Intra-regional labour migration flows are quite small in relation to
the overall size of the labour force in the major labour-receiving economies of ESEA (that is, Hong Kong, Japan, Malaysia, Singapore and
Taiwan). Even doubling the reported numbers as a crude adjustment
for undocumented migration suggests there were only 470 000 intra-
regional migrants in 1991, about 0.6 per cent of the total work force
in these countries. Although the necessary data are not available, this
percentage would be even smaller if one were able to measure net
migration. Even if one assumes that migrants stay about five years,
total labour migration would only account for about 2 per cent of the
total labour force in ESEA's labour-receiving countries.

Although foreign workers accounted for a relatively small share of
work force size in the labour-receiving countries of ESEA, labour migration accounted for a relatively large share of labour force growth in
those countries. Documented migrants alone constituted about one-third
of labour force growth in 1991. To the extent that undocumented migrants are counted as part of the labour force (assuming a doubling of
documented migrant numbers), total labour migrants, averaging roughly
200 000 workers per year in ESEA's labour-receiving countries during
the 1980s, would account for the bulk of work force growth. Thus,
intra-regional labour mobility in ESEA, although it is not a large share
of the total labour force, appears to contribute significantly to annual
labour force growth in the labour-receiving countries of ESEA.[3] Among
the labour-sending countries, outmigration reduced labour force expansion
by about 13 per cent between 1990 and 1991, thus serving to even
out, albeit slightly, the supply of labour across countries within ESEA.

Worker remittances are another mechanism through which national
economies may become integrated. Remittances may be used to finance investments in human or physical capital or to increase consumption of domestically produced goods. Provided the net flows are
from capital-rich to labour-rich countries, remittances will also promote
factor price equalization, the hallmark of full integration. Nominal remittances increased for Filipino, Indonesian and Thai workers worldwide at the modest rate of 6 per cent per year from 1981 to 1991. This
figure exceeds the 4.2 per cent rate of increase in the number of those
workers, but by less than the rate of price inflation, providing evidence of declining real remittances per migrant (assuming the average
length of stay was stable during this period). Among Filipino, Indonesian and Thai workers in Singapore, total remittances increased during

1981–91 at a rate of just 4 per cent per year, well below the 25 per cent rate of increase in the number of migrants. Thus, there is little evidence that worker remittances were an important mechanism of economic integration in ESEA during the 1980s.

## Movements of Capital

International capital mobility takes a variety of forms. It divides naturally into the mobility of public capital and the mobility of private capital. Public investment includes grants and loans from multilateral and bilateral organizations. Private investment includes direct foreign investments, whereby investors in one country acquire equity interests and direct managerial influence in enterprises located in another country. Private investment also includes investments in foreign financial instruments, such as stocks and bonds.

To gauge the extent of capital movements, we examine the amount of foreign direct investment (FDI) from ESEA countries to countries within and outside the region.[4] Table 1.3 reports growth rates of intra- and inter-regional direct foreign investment for ESEA's major capital-sending countries, namely Hong Kong, Korea, Japan, Taiwan and Singapore, during the 1980s. Because data are not available for a consistent set of years, estimates are reported separately for each economy.

FDI from Japan, ESEA's dominant exporter of capital, increased at an average annual rate of 21 per cent during 1980–92. The rate of increase accelerated in the mid-1980s, following the sharp appreciation of the yen against the dollar triggered by the 1985 Plaza Accord. Japan's FDI to other ESEA countries, which grew at an average annual rate of 15 per cent from 1980 to 1992, also accelerated in the mid-1980s. This acceleration is consistent with the view that yen appreciation led Japan to invest in lower wage countries in ESEA in an attempt to remain competitive in international product markets.

For Hong Kong and Korea, the 1980s growth rates of FDI within ESEA were greater than outside ESEA. They were lower for Japan, Taiwan and Singapore. With the exception of Korea. ESEA's share of FDI declined among all of ESEA's major capital-sending countries. Thus, capital mobility furthered ESEA's regional integration in the 1980s, but not as rapidly as it promoted ESEA's integration with the rest of the world.

Table 1.4 reports levels of foreign investment by Taiwan and Japan in the ESEA region, divided into capital movements to current capital-sending countries (Japan, Korea, Hong Kong, Singapore and Taiwan)

*Table* 1.3   Distribution and growth of FDI among ESEA's major capital-sending countries,[a] by destination region, c. 1980–90

| Region/Year | Hong Kong Shares (%) | | Growth[b] | Korea Shares (%) | | Growth | Japan Shares (%) | | Growth |
|---|---|---|---|---|---|---|---|---|---|
| | 1984–6 | 1987–9 | 1984–9 | 1981–3 | 1988–90 | 1981–90 | 1980–2 | 1990–2 | 1980–2 |
| Total ESEA | 67.5 | 59.4 | 0.280 | 16.5 | 31.0 | 0.380 | 27.3 | 14.2 | 0.151 |
| Rest of world | 32.5 | 40.6 | 0.102 | 83.5 | 69.0 | 0.287 | 72.7 | 85.8 | 0.224 |
| World total | 100.0 | 100.0 | 0.267 | 100.0 | 100.0 | 0.302 | 100.0 | 100.0 | 0.209 |

| Region/Year | Taiwan Shares (%) | | Growth | Singapore Shares (%) | | Growth |
|---|---|---|---|---|---|---|
| | 1980–2 | 1990–2 | 1980–2 | 1980–92 | 1987–9 | 1980–9 |
| Total ESEA | 70.0 | 70.3 | 0.119 | 73.3 | 61.4 | 0.041 |
| Rest of world | 30.0 | 29.7 | 0.163 | 26.7 | 38.6 | 0.127 |
| World total | 100.0 | 100.0 | 0.126 | 100.0 | 100.0 | 0.068 |

*Notes*:

[a] Only major capital exporters are included in the data (Hong Kong, Korea, Japan, Taiwan and Singapore).

[b] The growth rates are slope coefficients from regression equations of the following form: $\log X_t = \alpha_0 + \alpha_1 t$ where $X_t$ is the amount of FDI for the relevant regional grouping in year $t$.

*Sources*: Japan: OECD (various years); Korea, Singapore, Hong Kong: OECD (1993); Taiwan: Ministry of Economic Affairs (various years).

*Table* 1.4   Total foreign investment by Japan and Taiwan in ESEA, selected years

|  | 1983–5 | | 1990–2 | |
| Region | Amount (US$ million) | Share (%) | Amount (US$ million) | Share (%) |
| --- | --- | --- | --- | --- |
| To ESEA's capital-sending countries (Japan, Hong Kong, Korea, Singapore, Taiwan) | 2 691 | 55.2 | 7 632 | 39.2 |
| To ESEA's capital-receiving countries (China, Indonesia, Malaysia, Philippines, Thailand) | 2 183 | 44.8 | 11 831 | 60.8 |
| Total | 4 874 | 100.0 | 19 463 | 100.0 |

*Sources*: Japan: OECD (various years); Taiwan: Ministry of Economic Affairs (various years).

and to current capital-receiving countries (China, Indonesia, Malaysia, Philippines and Thailand). The share of investment directed toward the capital-receiving countries rose from about 45 per cent in the early and mid-1980s to 61 per cent by the early 1990s. This shift supports the 'flying geese' description of capital investment in the region, according to which industry is dynamically relocated to suitable lower wage economies to maintain international competitiveness (see Tang, 1994). Further analysis is needed to assess whether this description also fits patterns of foreign investment among the NIEs, a 'cascading' pattern of intra-regional capital mobility.

## Movement of Goods

Table 1.5 documents the rapid growth of trade within ESEA and between ESEA and the rest of the world during the 1980s, by reporting growth rates of exports. The figures in the column (1) are average annual rates of growth of ESEA exports to different country groups during 1979–92. Column (2) shows growth rates of total exports from ESEA and non-ESEA countries. The reported growth rates are the coefficients of linear trend terms in simple regression models in which the dependent variable is the natural logarithm of the nominal value of exports (converted to US dollars using period average market exchange rates).

Table 1.5 indicates that the current dollar value of ESEA's intra-regional exports during 1979–92 grew at an average annual rate of

*Table* 1.5   Growth rates[a] of exports, 1979–92

| Region | ESEA exports to (1) | World exports from (2) |
|--------|--------------------|-----------------------|
| Total ESEA | 0.122 | 0.104 |
| Rest of world | 0.094 | 0.060 |
| Total | 0.104 | 0.068 |

*Note*:

[a] The growth rates are slope coefficients from regression equations of the following form: $\log X_t = \alpha_0 + \alpha_1 t$, where $X_t$ is the nominal value of exports for the relevant regional grouping in year 1.

*Sources*: IMF (various years); Taiwan Council for Economic Planning and Development (1994).

12.2 per cent, about one-third faster than the 9.4 per cent growth rate of ESEA's inter-regional exports, almost double the growth rate of exports from non-ESEA industrial countries (7.3 per cent), and more than double the growth rate of exports from all non-ESEA countries (6.0 per cent). Thus, in terms of trade growth, ESEA countries outperformed non-ESEA countries, with the growth of ESEA's intra-regional trade outpacing the growth of its inter-regional trade, which implies even faster integration within ESEA than between ESEA and the rest of the world.

Table 1.6 looks at the growth of trade in terms of changes in its distribution among country groups. Column (1) reports shares of ESEA exports. Columns (2) and (3) present the shares of total world exports and world GNP for different regions. From 1979–81 to 1990–2, ESEA countries increased their share of world exports from 15 to 22 per cent, outpacing the growth in their share of world GNP, which increased from 17 to 22 per cent. Equally impressive was the growth in the share of ESEA exports going to ESEA countries during this same period: from 33 to 41 per cent.[5]

Table 1.7 reports the 1992 level and the 1979–92 growth rates of trade between ESEA countries. The growth rates are calculated using export data for the endpoints of the time interval. Although Japan is the region's dominant trading partner, China and Hong Kong have the largest country-to-country trade flow in ESEA. Overall, 61 per cent of exports that stayed within ESEA in 1992 were accounted for by Japan (31 per cent), Hong Kong (15 per cent), and China (15 per cent), with an additional 17 per cent attributable to Taiwan (9 per cent) and Korea (8 per cent). The rapid growth of trade between Hong Kong and China

*Table 1.6* Distribution of ESEA exports, and world exports, by Region, 1979–92 (per cent)

| Region | ESEA exports to (1) | | World exports from (2) | | Share of world GNP (3) | |
|---|---|---|---|---|---|---|
| | *1979–81* | *1990–2* | *1979–81* | *1990–2* | *1979–81* | *1990–2* |
| Total ESEA | 32.9 | 41.0 | 14.7 | 21.8 | 16.9 | 22.2 |
| Other industrial countries | 42.9 | 46.9 | 58.4 | 61.3 | 66.1 | 63.1 |
| Other non-industrial Asia | 4.1 | 2.8 | 1.1 | 3.2 | 2.1 | 1.7 |
| All other countries | 18.8 | 8.8 | 25.7 | 13.8 | 14.8 | 13.1 |

*Note:*
The sum of the shares is less than 1 because of trade to non-specified areas.

*Sources:* IMF (various years); Taiwan Council for Economic Planning and Development (1994); World Bank (1994).

Table 1.7 Levels, 1992, and average annual growth rates, 1979–92, of trade within ESEA

| | | | | | Exports from: | | | | | |
|---|---|---|---|---|---|---|---|---|---|---|
| | China | Hong Kong | Indonesia | Japan | Korea | Malaysia | Philippines | Singapore | Taiwan | Thailand |
| To China | – | 35 412 | 1 613 | 11 967 | 2 654 | 772 | 146 | 1 124 | n.a. | 386 |
| | | (41.7)ᵃ | (62.0) | (9.5) | (76.0) | (11.8) | (8.4) | (15.6) | n.a. | (13.2) |
| Hong Kong | 37 464 | – | 869 | 20 779 | 5 909 | 1 549 | 426 | 4 591 | 15 415 | 1 507 |
| | (20.5) | | (18.2) | (14.3) | (20.4) | (17.6) | (7.9) | (12.8) | (22.2) | (14.5) |
| Indonesia | 471 | 734 | – | 5 582 | 1 935 | 506 | 40 | n.a. | 1 215 | 283 |
| | (29.6) | (5.2) | | (7.8) | (19.3) | (6.1) | (-1.1) | | (8.9) | (3.1) |
| Japan | 11 691 | 6 262 | 11 607 | – | 11 599 | 5 401 | 2 020 | 2 813 | 8 894 | 5 686 |
| | (11.7) | (14.9) | (3.8) | | (10.0) | (5.8) | (4.0) | (5.7) | (11.2) | (13.3) |
| Korea | 2 435 | 1 938 | 1 385 | 17 786 | – | 1 389 | 27 | 1 626 | 1 150 | 533 |
| | (137.1) | (18.9) | (10.4) | (8.4) | | (15.5) | (-12.0) | (16.2) | (15.8) | (19.9) |
| Malaysia | 645 | 832 | 534 | 8 128 | 1 136 | – | 208 | 5 699 | n.a. | 842 |
| | (10.8) | (13.8) | (17.4) | (13.9) | (22.0) | | (10.5) | (8.2) | n.a. | (10.4) |
| Philippines | 209 | 1 108 | 176 | 3 520 | 746 | 477 | – | 684 | 1 023 | 155 |
| | (3.4) | (11.5) | (0.5) | (6.2) | (15.8) | (7.6) | | (8.5) | (13.3) | (22.1) |
| Singapore | 2 029 | 3 130 | 2 878 | 12 981 | 3 222 | 9 391 | 251 | – | 2 876 | 2 823 |
| | (15.9) | (13.0) | (3.0) | (13.0) | (24.0) | (12.9) | (10.9) | | (15.9) | (15.1) |
| Taiwan | n.a. | 4 219 | 1 345 | 21 166 | 2 262 | 1 270 | 283 | 1 545 | – | 618 |
| | n.a. | (18.1) | (12.6) | (13.0) | (22.5) | (15.6) | (11.4) | (16.7) | | (18.6) |
| Thailand | 893 | 1 059 | 335 | 10 384 | 1 532 | 1 490 | 109 | 2 700 | 1 810 | – |
| | (11.7) | (15.0) | (18.5) | (14.9) | (22.3) | (19.4) | (14.4) | (12.1) | (19.1) | |

Notes:

ᵃ The percentage growth rate from 1979 to 1992 is reported in parentheses below the 1992 level of exports in million current US dollars. The growth rate is calculated as the average percentage increase in export value from 1979 to 1992. The rate is calculated since 1980 for Korean exports to China, Malaysian exports to Philippines, and Chinese exports to Indonesia; since 1981 for Indonesian exports to China; and since 1990 for Chinese exports to Korea, because exports were not reported for these pairs in 1979.

n.a. These countries did not report exports to the respective partner countries from 1979 to 1992.

– Not applicable.

Sources: IMF (various years); Taiwan Council for Economic Planning and Development (1994).

and of exports from Japan to Hong Kong, Korea, and Taiwan account
for 41 per cent of the growth of intra-regional trade.

## ACCOUNTING FOR LABOUR MARKET INTEGRATION IN ESEA

The foregoing analyses provide evidence that the mechanisms of labour
mobility, capital mobility, and trade have all contributed to labour market integration in ESEA. The purpose of this section is to measure the
overall pace of labour market integration and to assess the relative importance of each mechanism to the overall process. We do this by converting the amount of trade and capital mobility within ESEA into
units of equivalent labour migration, an exercise that necessitates estimating: (a) the amount of labour mobility between all pairs of countries
in ESEA that would replace actual flows of capital between the countries,
in a way that accounts for differences between the length of the working life of capital and the duration of stay of labour migrants; and (b)
the amount of labour services embodied in ESEA's intra-regional trade.[6]

To calculate the labour migration equivalent of capital movements,
we begin by estimating the ratio of total labour force to capital stock
for each country (see Table 1.8). Following Leamer (1982), the capital
stock of a country is assumed to be the accumulated gross domestic
investment (GDI) since 1970, assuming an average ten-year life span
for capital due to depreciation.[7] As one might expect, Table 1.8 indicates that the labour: capital ratios for Thailand and Indonesia are much
higher than the ratios for Japan or Singapore, and that the ratios declined over time as more capital was accumulated while population
levels stabilized.[8]

For the next stage of the exercise, we conduct the following though
experiment: If there are two countries, (relatively capital-rich) country
A and (relatively labour-rich) country B, how much labour would need
to flow from B to A to have the same amount of production as would
result from a capital flow from A to B? The answer is the number of
labour migrants from country B that would have worked with the capital had it remained in country A. We estimate this number – that is,
the labour mobility equivalent of a given capital inflow – under two
assumptions. First, we assume that people's productivity depends on
their location (the low estimate). Thus, workers migrating from country B to country A exhibit the productivity levels of country A's workers. In this case, we calculate the labour mobility equivalent of a capital
inflow by multiplying a country's total capital exports by the labour:

*Table* 1.8  Ratio of total labour force to total capital stock in ESEA, selected years (workers/US$ 1 million)

| Country | 1980 | 1986 | 1991 |
|---|---|---|---|
| China[a] | 881 | 519 | 429 |
| Hong Kong | 88 | 62 | 36 |
| Indonesia | 881 | 519 | 429 |
| Japan | 42 | 29 | 14 |
| Korea, Rep of | 206 | 127 | 54 |
| Malaysia | 223 | 131 | 116 |
| Philippines | 491 | 498 | 518 |
| Singapore | 64 | 32 | 22 |
| Taiwan[b] | 127 | 118 | 59 |
| Thailand | 745 | 549 | 234 |

*Notes*:
[a] Data on China's investment patterns is not available so we assume that the ratios are similar to Indonesia (the most labour-abundant country).
[b] For Taiwan, gross fixed capital formation was used instead of GDI.

*Sources*: Taiwan Council for Economic Planning and Development (1994); World Bank (1994).

capital stock ratio of the *capital-sending* country. Under the second assumption (the high estimate), people's productivity is inherent to them. Now country *B* workers moving to country *A* will have the same productivity as they did in country *B*, because their productivity is a function of their education and other personal characteristics. With this assumption, the labour mobility equivalent calculation involves multiplying a country's total capital exports by the labour: capital stock ratio of the *capital-receiving* country. Both estimates are calculated as they provide an upper and lower bound for labour mobility equivalents.

The final step in this exercise involves accounting for the fact that capital is long-lived. Suppose, for example, that some piece of capital depreciates fully when it becomes *t* years old and that it works with *n* people (for simplicity, in both the capital-receiving and capital-sending countries). In this example, the labour mobility equivalent of moving this piece of capital would be *n* workers per year, or *nt* workers over the *t*-year life of the capital. We assume that *n* workers moving for each of *t* years is the same as *nt* workers moving for one year.

As we assume that capital has a ten-year life span and depreciates linearly, a unit of FDI can only be used to full capacity during its first year. By the next year, it will retain only a fraction of its full value, and even less of its value by the second year. Thus, one unit of capital moving to a country for ten years is equivalent to five $(5 = \int_0^{10} (1 - x/10)dx)$ units of capital moving to a country for one year. To complete the capital conversion, we multiply the labour mobility equivalent by five to express capital mobility in person-years of labour migration.[9]

To convert trade among ESEA countries to equivalent units of labour migration, we estimate the amount of labour embodied in exports – that is, the number of workers involved in producing exports. As mentioned earlier, instead of trading with a partner, a country could simply export the capital and labour necessary for production and produce the good in the country's trade partner. The number of workers contributing to the production of exports is estimated by finding the share of workers in the economy contributing to exports and multiplying this by the total labour force.[10] Assuming the share of labour in gross national product (GNP) equals the share of labour in exports, the number of workers contributing to the export sector is simply the percentage of exports in total production times the total labour force:[11]

$$\text{Labour mobility equivalent of trade} = \frac{\text{Value of exports}}{\text{GNP}} \times \text{Total labour force}$$

Table 1.9 reports our calculations of equivalent units of labour migration associated with intra-regional trade and capital mobility in 1980 and 1990. The first row presents the documented number of migrants within ESEA multiplied by the number of years, on average, migrants reside in the host country – four (low estimate) to six (high estimate) years.[12] The labour mobility equivalents for capital and trade (as calculated above) are reported in the next two rows. Both calculations for converting capital flows to labour mobility equivalents are provided. The sum of total labour mobility equivalents is presented in the last row.

The estimates show that trade was overwhelmingly the largest contributor to labour market integration in ESEA throughout the 1980s. For example, trade embodies a labour flow that is one–two order of magnitude greater than that embodied in DFI and direct labour movements.[13] The results also show that capital mobility contributed more to regional labour market integration than did labour mobility.

The figures in Table 1.9 also reveal that labour market integration increased sharply among ESEA countries in the 1980s. Nearly 9 per cent of ESEA's labour force participated, either directly via labour

*Table* 1.9   ESEA labour, capital and trade movements in units of labour mobility equivalents, selected years (person-years)

|  | 1980 | | 1990 | |
|---|---|---|---|---|
|  | *Number* | *Share (%)* | *Number* | *Share (%)* |
| *I. Low estimate* | | | | |
| Labour migration | 95 672 | 0.28 | 677 628 | 0.94 |
| Capital movements | 525 377 | 1.55 | 706 371 | 0.97 |
| Trade | 33 327 383 | 98.17 | 71 068 372 | 98.09 |
| *Total* | 33 948 431 | | 72 452 371 | |
| *II. High estimate* | | | | |
| Labour migration | 143 508 | 0.33 | 1 016 442 | 1.28 |
| Capital movements | 9 904 695 | 22.83 | 7 607 193 | 9.55 |
| Trade | 33 327 383 | 76.83 | 71 068 372 | 89.18 |
| *Total* | 43 375 585 | | 79 692 007 | |
| Labour force of ESEA | 731 865 936 | | 903 994 242 | |
| GNP *per capita* of ESEA (US$) | 1 208 | | 2 693 | |

mobility or indirectly via capital mobility or trade, in cross-national labour market transactions in 1990, up from just 5.2 per cent in 1980.

CONCLUSIONS

We have two main results to report: first, the 1980s saw rapid integration of the labour markets of ESEA countries; and, second, the integration was achieved mainly through the sharp increase in intra-regional trade, with a relatively small contribution from intra-regional capital mobility and an even smaller contribution from direct labour mobility.

Notwithstanding the considerable integration of ESEA labour markets that has already occurred, the prospects for further integration are quite strong. Much of the regional integration that occurred within ESEA during the 1980s seems to go hand in glove with ESEA's integration with the rest of the world (also accomplished mainly through sharply rising trade and increased capital mobility). With the end of the Uruguay Round of the GATT and the establishment of the World Trade Organization (WTO), mutual trade barriers are likely to diminish, thereby promoting further expansion of trade.

If ESEA's historical response to growing extra-regional demand for

*Table* 1.10   Measures of tariff restrictions

| Region | Lee index[a] (1) | Average tariff rates (%)[b] (2) |
|---|---|---|
| Total ESEA | | |
| China | n.a. | n.a. |
| Hong Kong | 0.000 | 0.2 |
| Indonesia | 0.016 | 32.6 |
| Japan | 0.003 | 4.0 |
| Korea | 0.029 | 23.5 |
| Malaysia | 0.015 | 25.0 |
| Philippines | 0.036 | 29.2 |
| Singapore | 0.005 | 6.4 |
| Taiwan | 0.018 | 22.8 |
| Thailand | 0.046 | 30.7 |
| Other industrial countries | 0.010 | n.a. |
| Non-industrial countries | | |
| Other Asia | 0.057 | n.a. |
| Africa | 0.038 | 30.5 |
| Middle East | 0.029 | 7.0 |
| Western Hemisphere | 0.036 | 24.3 |
| Other Europe, USSR, and non-aligned | n.a. | n.a. |

*Notes*:
[a] The Lee index is calculated by making the following calculation:
Tariff restriction = $[0.528 - 0.026 * \log (AREA) - 0.096\log(DIST)] * \log (1 + OWTI)$ where $AREA$ = size of the country, $DIST$ = average distance to capitals of the world's twenty major exporters, and $OWTI$ = own import weighted tariff rates on intermediate inputs and capital goods.
[b] The aggregate measures are calculated by taking the average of the country rates in the region.

*Sources*: The Lee index of tariff restrictions is calculated in Lee (1993) and is part of the Barro and Lee data set available from the National Bureau of Economic Research in Cambridge, MA. The average tariff rate figures for ESEA are from Riedel (1992), while the regional aggregates are from Erzan and Karsenty (1989). The rates for the regions are based on a sample of countries in the region.

its goods and services continues, one may expect further integration within the region. Indeed, as Table 1.10 shows, the integration ESEA achieved in the 1980s occurred in the presence of non-zero tariff barriers. Column (1) in Table 1.10 presents an index of tariff restrictions estimated by Lee (1993) for different countries. The estimates for the regional aggregates are simple averages of the Lee figures for countries within the region. Although some countries in ESEA did have large protection indexes, for example, Thailand (0.046) and Philippines (0.036), the region as a whole had a lower level of tariff restrictions than other regions. Similarly, in column (2), average tariff rates for ESEA countries were, in general, lower than the rates for African countries and about equal to those for Latin American countries.[14]

Corresponding to possible further reductions of trade barriers is the considerable scope for further capital market integration. Negative attitudes and other institutional deterrents to the movement of capital decreased during the 1980s. For all the countries in the region, recent legislation has provided for increased incentives to attract foreign investment, and barriers to capital mobility have diminished significantly since the late 1980s (UN, 1992a). For example, China has slowly been phasing in legislation to allow greater domestic capital ownership by foreign-owned firms. In contrast to capital mobility, there is no indication that ESEA countries are dissatisfied with their immigrant or emigration flows or that changes in their immigration and emigration policies are likely (UN, various years). We may reasonably expect cross-country migrant labour flows to continue at about the same pace for the next decade. Thus, trade will probably continue as the main driving force behind integration, followed by capital mobility (which may increase in importance), and then by labour mobility.

Further declines in the costs of international transportation and communication and the increased prominence of integrative economic institutions within the region, such as the Asia-Pacific Economic Cooperation Council (APEC), are likely to promote further integration. Also, given its economic position and geographic proximity to ESEA. Australia is likely to become more integrated with the ESEA countries, a development that has already begun. Australia's exports to ESEA countries (8.2 per cent) grew at almost twice the rate of Australia's trade with the rest of the world (4.6 per cent) during 1979–92. Similarly, Australia's imports from ESEA countries also grew at a rate almost 1.5 times as large as its imports from the rest of the world.

### Notes

* The authors would like to thank Dr Min Tang, Dr Pasuk Phongpaichit, Dr Duncan Campbell, Mr Aurelio Parisotto, and other participants at an International Labour Organization conference in Bangkok for helpful discussions and comments. The authors would also like to thank Mr Pracha Vasuprasat

and Mr Manola Abella for help in accessing labour migration data, and the ILO's International Institute for Labor Studies for financial support.

1. Along with the standard effects of trade and factor mobility, economic integration also spreads the cost of economic shocks across integrated markets. For example, the economic consequences of a fall in the demand for one country's timber because of growing environmental awareness can be diminished by the outmigration of forestry workers from that country.
2. We computed Gini coefficients using *per capita* income data for the ESEA countries. The estimates increased from 0.51 to 0.56 from 1979 to 1987, but fell to 0.54 in 1992.
3. In terms of direct evidence, the foreign-born share of the Japanese population was a paltry 0.6 per cent in 1980 and consisted mostly of Koreans. The foreign-born share increased only slightly during the 1980s, reaching 0.7 per cent in 1990. Although Japan is perhaps an extreme example, these figures provide little evidence that the integration of Japanese and other ESEA country labour markets was achieved through labour mobility. Unfortunately, similar data are not available for other countries in ESEA.
4. FDI is usually defined as total paid up shares of foreign subsidiaries that are owned by domestic companies (OECD 1994). Although data on the total amount of direct investment into ESEA are readily available, data on the sources of this investment are not. Portfolio investments would be a reasonable alternative indicator of private capital movements, but the source countries for these capital movements are even more difficult to ascertain.
5. See Jha (1994) for an especially lucid and detailed analysis of the growth of intra-regional trade in ESEA and south Asia.
6. An alternative method for calculating labour migration equivalents of capital mobility and trade involves assuming some production function and then using estimated parameters to map FDI and export values into labour equivalents. We did not adopt this approach in our analysis because of the difficulty involved in assembling estimates of the necessary parameters for the different countries within ESEA.
7. Because of a lack of data on GDI for Taiwan, we estimate Taiwan's capital stock from data on gross fixed capital formation. GDI equals gross fixed capital formation *plus* changes in inventory.
8. Investment figures for China are not available, so we assume that China's labour: capital ratio is the same as Indonesia (the most relatively labour-abundant country).
9. Improving upon this calculation would require data on lagged numbers of ESEA's inter-country migrants, which are unfortunately not available.
10. To avoid the potential problem of double counting, the value added contribution of trade should only be used in these calculations; unfortunately such a data set is not available. By using the total value of exports we are potentially biasing upward the labour mobility equivalent of trade. For example, if Indonesia exports raw timber to Philippines, and then Philippines re-exports manufactured goods using this timber to Indonesia, then our analysis would wrongly consider the total value of Philippine export as trade's labour migration equivalent. However, if the exports that are sent to another country for processing are then re-exported to other parts

of the world and not back to other ESEA countries, then our analysis is still correct. For example, Gereffi's (1995) 'triangle manufacturing', where textiles are imported by Hong Kong or Korea from China and Indonesia and then the finished product is re-exported to the USA and Europe, is a case where our analysis does not overestimate the effects of trade.

11. The assumption that the labour share in exports is equivalent to the labour share in GNP is strong and perhaps unrealistic. Unfortunately, it is almost impossible to find out for certain what labour's share of trade is in different countries. For example, one may conjecture that for more labour-abundant countries like China, Indonesia and Philippines, labour's share of trade is higher than labour's share of GNP, whereas in more capital-abundant economies like Japan, Taiwan and Singapore, the share of labour in their exports is probably lower than labour's share of GNP. Because the statistics on labour's share are unavailable, we assumed that for the ESEA region the shares of different countries balanced out, thus giving *on average* equal shares in trade and GNP. To test how critical this assumption is to our results we carried out a sensitivity analysis under two extreme scenarios. The first scenario is that labour's share of exports is twice as large as labour's share in GNP, and the second is that labour's share of exports is half as large as labour's share in GNP. The first assumption would serve to increase the labour equivalent of trade in Table 1.9, while the second assumption would tend to diminish the labour equivalent. The analysis reveals that trade's share of labour mobility equivalents rises to more than 99 per cent under the first assumption and drops to 62 per cent under the second assumption. We see that even under the extreme conditions of the second assumption, trade is still the predominant factor of integration, accounting for upward of 60 per cent of labour market transactions in the region.

12. These figures are based on discussions with Manola Abella at the ILO office in Geneva. Given the changing composition of labour migrants in the region, accurately estimating duration of stay is difficult. The four–six year range is based on the idea that it takes approximately this many years in order to recoup the investment of migration.

13. An interesting question is whether this strong position for trade will still be true once Hong Kong and China are no longer separate economies. Although the trade between Hong Kong and China is large, there are significant capital flows between these two regions as well, and one would assume significant labour flows (although we do not have the data on labour flows out of China). Assuming a post-1997 world, it may be true that that the importance of trade in relation to capital may decline, because the trade flow between the two countries would no longer be incorporated in the above calculation. But as the total capital flows between the two countries would also be excluded from the calculation, the relative importance of trade after 1997 should be the same.

14. These arguments do not imply that reducing tariff barriers is a sufficient condition for promoting growth in the region. Indeed, Rodrik (1994) shows that some ESEA countries grew rapidly despite strong trade policy intervention by their governments.

# References

Abella, M. and H. Mori (1994), 'Structural Change and Labour Migration in East Asia', paper presented at the OECD Conference on Development Systems, Employment, and International Migration. (11–13 July) (Paris).

Authukorala, P. (1993), 'Statistics on Asian Labour Migration: Review of Sources, Methods and Problems', in ILO and Asian Regional Team for Employment Promotion (eds), *International Labour Migration Statistics and Information Networking in Asia* (New Delhi, India: ILO).

Baldwin, R.E. (1995), 'The Effects of Trade and Foreign Direct Investment on Employment and Relative Wages', National Bureau of Economic Research, *Working Paper*, 5037 (Cambridge, MA: NBER).

Bloom, D.E. and A. Brender (1993), 'Labor and the Emerging World Economy', *Population Bulletin*, 48 (2) (Washington DC: Population Reference Bureau).

Borjas, G.J. (1990), *Friends or Strangers* (New York: Basic Books).

Central Bank of China, Taiwan (various years), *Financial Statistics.*

Chaponniere, J.R. (1992), 'The Newly Industrialising Economies of Asia: International Investment and Transfer of Technology', *STI Review* (April).

Chen, E.K.Y. (1992),'Changing Pattern of Financial Flows in the Asia-Pacific Region and Policy Responses', *Asian Development Review*, 10(1): 46–85.

Chen, E.K.Y. (1993), 'Foreign Direct Investment in East Asia', *Asian Development Review*, 11 (1): 24–59.

Ehrenberg, R.G. (1994), *Labor Markets and Integrating National Economies* Washington, DC: Brookings Institution).

Erzan, R. and G. Karsenty (1989), 'The Profile of Protection in Developing Countries', *UNCTAD Review*, 1 (1): 51–74.

Feldstein, M. and C. Horioka (1980), 'Domestic Saving and International Capital Flows', *Economic Journal*, 90 (June): 314–29.

Frankel, J.A. (1984), 'International Capital Mobility and Crowding Out in the US Economy: Imperfect Integration of Financial Markets or of Goods Markets?', National Bureau of Economic Research, *Working Paper*, 1772 (Cambridge: MA: NBER).

Gereffi, G. (1995), 'Global Commodity Chains and Third World Development', paper presented at a Conference organized by the International Institute for Labour Studies and the ILO Regional Office for Asia and the Pacific (23–26 January) (Bangkok, Thailand).

Haque, N. and P.J. Montiel (1991), 'Capital Mobility in Developing Countries: Some Empirical Tests', *World Development*, 10(10): 1391–8.

International Labour Organization (ILO) (1992), *World Labour Report* (Geneva: ILO).

International Labour Organization (ILO) (1990), Regional Office for Asia and Pacific, *Statistical Report 1990: International Labour Migration from Asian Labour-Sending Countries* (Bangkok: ILO).

International Labour Organization (ILO) (1993), Asian Regional Program on Labor Migration, 'Newspaper Clippings and Reprints of Periodicals' (May) (Bangkok: ILO).

International Monetary Fund (IMF) (various years), *Direction of Trade Statistics Yearbook* (Washington, DC: IMF).

Jha, S.C. (1994), 'International Trade in Asia: Current Trends and Prospects', paper presented at 1994 *Financial Times* Conference on the Asian Capital Markets (28–29 April) (London).

Leamer, E.E. (1982), *Sources of International Comparative Advantage: Theory and Evidence* (Cambridge, MA: MIT Press).

Lee, J.W. (1993), 'International Trade, Distortions and Long-run Economic Growth', *IMF Staff Papers* (June) (Washington, DC: International Monetary Fund).

Lim, L. *et al.* (1992), *Foreign Direct Investment and Industrialisation in Malaysia, Singapore, Taiwan and Thailand*, Development Studies Centre (Paris: OECD).

Macmillen, M.J. (1982), 'The Economic Effects of International Migration: A Survey', *Journal of Common Market Studies*, 20(3): 245–67.

Mishkin, F. (1984), 'Are Real Interest Rates Equal Across Countries? An Empirical Investigation of International Parity Conditions', *Journal of Finance*, 39: 1345–58.

Montiel, P.J. (1994), 'Capital Mobility in Developing Countries: Some Measurement Issues and Empirical Estimates', *World Bank Economic Review*, 8 (3): 245–67.

Obstfeld, M. (1986), 'How Integrated Are Capital markets? Some New Tests', National Bureau of Economic Research, *Working Paper*, 2075 (Cambridge, MA: NBER).

Organization for Economic Cooperation and Development (OECD) (1993), *Foreign Direct Investment Relations between the OECD and the Dynamic Asian Economies* (Paris: OECD).

Organization for Economic Cooperation and Development (OECD) (1994), *International Direct Investment Statistics Yearbook* (Paris: OECD); also personal communication for Japan between 1980 and 1992.

Razin, A. and E. Sadka (1992), 'International Migration and International Trade', National Bureau of Economic Research, *Working Paper*, 4230 (Cambridge, MA: NBER).

Riedel, J. (1992), 'Intra-Asian Trade and Foreign Direct Investment', *Asian Development Review*, 10 (2): 111–46.

Rodrik, D. (1994), 'King Kong Meets Godzilla: The World Bank and the East Asian Miracle', (New York, NY: Columbia University) (mimeo).

Ruffin, R.J. (1993), 'The Role of Foreign Investment in the Economic Growth of the Asian and Pacific Region', *Asian Development Review*, 11(1): 1–23.

Stark, O. (1991), *The Migration of Labor* (Cambridge, MA: Basil Blackwell).

Taiwan Council for Economic Planning and Development (1994), *Taiwan Statistical Data Book, 1994* (Republic of China).

Taiwan Investment Commission, Ministry of Economic Affairs (various years), *Statistics on Overseas Chinese and Foreign Investment* (Republic of China).

Tang, M. (1994), 'Recent Development on Capital Flows to the Asian and Pacific Developing Countries' (Manila: Asian Development Bank) (mimeo).

Tang, M. and M. Thant (1995), 'Growth Triangles in International Perspective', paper presented at a Conference organized by the International Institute for Labour Studies and the ILO Regional Office for Asia and the Pacific (23–26 January) (Bangkok, Thailand).

Tang, M. and J. Villafuerte (1995), 'Capital Flows to Pacific Developing Countries: Recent Trends and Future Prospects', Statistical Report Series No. 18 (Manila: Asian Development Bank).

Teal, G. (1995), 'The JSR (Johor–Singapore–Riau) Growth Triangle', paper presented at a Conference organized by the International Institute for Labour Studies and the ILO Regional Office for Asia and the Pacific: A New Approach to Regional Economic Cooperation (23–26 January) (Bangkok, Thailand).

Thant, M., M. Tang and H. Kakazu (1994), *Growth Triangles in Asia* (Hong Kong: Oxford University Press.

Union of International Associations (1994), *Yearbook of Organizations, Vol. 1, Organization Descriptions and Cross-References* (Munich: K.G. Saur).

United Nations (UN) (1989), Department of International Economic and Social Affairs, *Trends in Population Policy, Population Studies*, 114 (New York: United Nations).

United Nations (UN) (1992a), *World Investment Directory 1992: Foreign Direct Investment, Legal Framework and Corporate Data, Vol. 1, Asia and the Pacific* (New York: United Nations).

United Nations (UN) (1992b), Department of Economic and Social Development, *Global Population Policy Database, 1991* (New York: United Nations).

United Nations (UN) (various years), Department of International Economic and Social Affairs, *World Population Monitoring Report* (New York: United Nations).

United Nations Development Programme (UNDP/ILO) (1993), Asian Regional Programme on International Labour Migration, *Regional Seminar on International Labour Migration Statistics and Information Networking in Asia: summary of Proceedings* (New Delhi, India: ILO).

World Bank (1994), *World Tables* (Baltimore, MD: Johns Hopkins University Press).

World Bank (1995), *World Development Report 1995* (Washington, DC: World Bank) (mimeo).

Yue, C.S. (1993), 'Foreign Direct Investment in ASEAN Economies', *Asian Development Review*, 11(1), pp. 60–102.

# Part II

# Organization of Production

# 2 The Reorganization of Production on a World Scale: States, Markets and Networks in the Apparel and Electronics Commodity Chains

Gary Gereffi

Over the past several decades, the world economy has undergone a fundamental shift toward an integrated and coordinated global division of labour in production and trade. In the 1950s and 1960s, production tended to be organized within national boundaries. International trade consisted, to a large degree, of raw materials flowing from the periphery to the industrialized core of the world economy, while manufactured exports were sent by American, European, and Japanese firms from their home bases to all corners of the globe. Foreign Direct Investment (FDI) in manufacturing emerged as a response to the protectionist policies implemented by core and peripheral nations alike that wished to diminish the foreign exchange drain of an excessive reliance on imports and augment the employment benefits from locally based production.

Today the most dynamic industries are transnational in scope. Modern industrialization is the result of an integrated system of global trade and production. Open international trade has encouraged nations to specialize in different branches of manufacturing and even in different stages of production within a specific industry. This process, fuelled by the explosion of new products and technologies since the Second World War, has led to the emergence of a global manufacturing system in which production capacity is dispersed to an unprecedented number of developing as well as industrialized countries. 

New patterns of specialization between countries entail the

fragmentation and geographic relocation of manufacturing processes on a global scale in ways that slice through national boundaries. As almost every factor of production – money, technology, information, and goods – moves effortlessly across borders, the very idea of distinct American, German, or Japanese economies is virtually meaningless. In an era where products consisting of many components are made in a wide variety of countries, what is an 'American' computer, a 'German' car, a 'Japanese' camera, a 'Korean' microwave oven or a 'Taiwanese' bicycle? Corporations are becoming increasingly disconnected from their home nations as manufacturers, traders, bankers, and buyers simultaneously scour the globe for profitable opportunities.

The newly industrializing economies (NIEs) of East Asia – South Korea, Taiwan, Hong Kong, and Singapore – have been the focus of considerable attention by academics and policymakers alike for their outstanding economic record over the past four decades. Explanations of how the East Asian NIEs attained and sustained their competitive advantage, and the implications for other developing countries, are diverse. Neoclassical economists focus on low wages as the initial stimulus for labour-intensive export industries, coupled with government policies that have created free markets, stability, and openness to trade. The latter position is challenged by statist interpretations, which argue that significant government intervention is a key feature of East Asia's export success. The World Bank (1993) has tried to steer a middle course in this debate by claiming that East Asia has pursued 'market friendly' economic growth, which combines an adherence to macroeconomic policy fundamentals with selective state intervention. While the neoclassical and statist perspectives show that labour costs and government policies are key factors in the early stages of export-oriented development, they are not sufficient to account for the many changes that have occurred during the recent evolution of East Asia s export industries.

In an effort to move beyond the 'state versus markets' debate, this chapter focuses on the organization of production as a major determinant of industrial transformation in East Asia. During the past several decades, East Asia's export industries have become increasingly diversified, internationalized, and regionally integrated. Whereas industrial upgrading from labour-intensive to capital- and technology-intensive industries has clearly occurred within Japan and the East Asian NIEs, by itself the industrial upgrading concept is inadequate because it retains the national economy as the central unit of analysis. The successful export industries of Japan and the East Asian NIEs are part of a broader process of globalization in which international production and trade networks create hierarchical divisions of labour within and between regions. East Asian firms have mastered the art of using networks as a strategic asset. The technological and organizational learning that occurs within these networks is an essential feature of East Asia's ability to endogenize its international competitive edge.

The structure of the chapter is as follows. First, recent production and trade trends in a variety of Third World regions are analyzed, which underscore the existence of a dynamic global manufacturing system anchored by the NIEs of East Asia. Second, a global commodity chains perspective is introduced that reconceptualizes the linkages between firms, industries and countries. A distinction is drawn between producer-driven and buyer-driven commodity chains. These contrasting forms of international economic organization coexist in the international economy, they are sectorally differentiated, and they have very different implications for national and regional development. Third, five export roles are identified that tie Third World regions to the world economy. Developing nations have evolved through particular sequences and combinations of these roles, with varying consequences for national development. Fourth, in an effort to show the interplay of economic, political, and sociocultural dimensions of international competitiveness, the chapter focuses on the contrasted regional divisions of labour in the apparel and electronics industries of East Asia. Even after considering the role of low wages, quotas and other government policies and product cycles, I conclude that organizational variables (such as types of commodity chains, the structure of networks, organizational learning and conventions) are significant determinants of export growth, industrial upgrading, and other aspects of economic performance in East Asia.

## THE CONTEMPORARY ERA OF ECONOMIC GLOBALIZATION

Economic globalization has forged a complex interdependence of nations at all levels of development. Three specific trends in the international economy serve to illustrate the nature of the contemporary global manufacturing system in greater detail: (1) the spread of diversified industrialization to large segments of the Third World; (2) the shift toward export-oriented development strategies in peripheral nations, with an emphasis on manufactures; and (3) high levels of product specialization in the export profiles of most Third World countries, along with continual industrial upgrading by established exporters among the NIEs. The impact of these processes of change in the Third World is highly uneven, with some nations improving their position in the global economy and others becoming marginalized from it.

## Worldwide Industrialization

A new global division of labour has changed the pattern of geographic specialization between countries. The classic core–periphery relationship in which the developing nations supplied primary commodities to the industrialized countries in exchange for manufactured goods is outdated. Since the 1950s, the gap between developed and developing countries has been narrowing in terms of industrialization. As developed economies shift overwhelmingly toward services, vigorous industrialization has become the hallmark of the periphery. This can be seen by taking a closer look at production and trade patterns within the Third World.

Industry outstripped agriculture as a source of economic growth in all regions of the Third World. From 1965 to 1990, industry's share of gross domestic product (GDP) grew by 13 per cent in East and Southeast Asia, by 10 per cent in sub-Saharan Africa, 5 per cent in South Asia, and 3 per cent in Latin America. Agriculture's share of regional GDP, on the other hand, fell by 16 per cent in East and Southeast Asia, 11 per cent in South Asia, 8 per cent in sub-Saharan Africa, and 6 per cent in Latin America (World Bank, 1992: 222–3).

Manufacturing has been the cornerstone of development in East and Southeast Asia. In 1990, 34 per cent of the GDP of East and Southeast Asia was in the manufacturing sector, compared with 26 per cent for Latin America, 17 per cent for South Asia, and only 11 per cent for sub-Saharan Africa. The manufacturing sector's share of GDP in some developing nations, such as China (38 per cent), Taiwan (34 per cent), and South Korea (31 per cent), was even higher than Japan's manufacturing/GDP ratio of 29 per cent. These differences in performance are corroborated over time as well. The manufacturing sector exhibited much greater dynamism in East and Southeast Asia than anywhere else in the Third World. Between 1965 and 1990, manufacturing increased its share of GDP in these two regions by 10 per cent points, compared to net sectoral growth rates of 4 per cent in sub-Saharan Africa and 2 per cent in South Asia and Latin America.

## Diversified, Export-oriented Industrialization

World trade expanded nearly 30-fold in the three decades after 1960. Manufactured goods as a percentage of total world exports increased from 55 per cent in 1980 to 75 per cent in 1990. Furthermore, the share of the NIEs' manufactured exports that can be classified as 'high tech' soared from 2 per cent in 1964 to 25 per cent in 1985, and those embodying 'medium' levels of technological sophistication rose from 16 to 22 per cent during this same period (OECD, 1988: 24).

Hong Kong and China topped the list of developing country exporters in 1993 with $135 and $92 billion in overseas sales, respectively, followed by Taiwan ($85 billion), South Korea ($82 billion) and Singapore ($74 billion). In the next tier, several of the Southeast Asian nations (Malaysia, Thailand and Indonesia), along with Brazil and Mexico, all generated substantial exports, ranging from $30 to $47 billion. Exports accounted for 24 per cent of GDP in East and Southeast Asia, in contrast to an export: GDP ratio of 23 per cent for sub-Saharan Africa, 16 per cent for the advanced industrial nations, 11 per cent for South Asia, and 10 per cent for Latin America and the Caribbean. Saudi Arabia illustrates the declining fortunes of the world's major oil-exporting states. Its 1993 export total of $41 billion, while double that of its nearest Middle East competitor, the United Arab Emirates, is less than 40 per cent of Saudi Arabia's 1980 exports (Table 2.1).

In exports as in production, manufactures are the chief source of the Third World's dynamism. In 1993, manufactured items constituted well over 90 per cent of total exports in three of the four East Asian NIEs, and they were approximately three-quarters of all exports for the entirety of Asia. In Brazil and Mexico, the share of manufactures in total exports is over one-half, while in sub-Saharan Africa the manufacturing figure is nearly one-quarter of all exports (Table 2.1). There is a strong 'South Africa effect' on sub-Saharan Africa's regional total, however. If we exclude South Africa, which accounts for just 7 per cent of sub-Saharan Africa's population but 38 per cent of its overall exports and 74 per cent of its manufactured exports, the manufacturing share in the region's total exports falls from 24 per cent to 10 per cent. In every region of the world, the relative importance of primary commodities in exports as well as GDP has decreased, usually quite sharply, since 1970. Asian nations have moved fastest and furthest toward manufactured exports during this period. Sub-Saharan Africa and Latin America are still mostly primary commodity exporters, although to a lesser degree than in the past and with substantial subregional variation (Table 2.2).

*Table* 2.1    Growth of exports in major world regions, 1980–93

| Region/Country | Exports (US$ billions) | | Exports; GDP (%) | | Manufactured exports: total exports (%) | |
|---|---|---|---|---|---|---|
| | 1980 | 1993 | 1980 | 1993 | 1980 | 1993 |
| Advanced industrial | | | | | | |
| countries | n.a. | 2 896.8 | n.a. | 16 | n.a. | 82[a] |
| USA | 216.7 | 464.8 | 8 | 7 | 68 | 82 |
| Germany | 192.9 | 380.2 | 24 | 20 | 86 | 90 |
| Japan | 129.2 | 362.2 | 12 | 9 | 96 | 97 |
| East and Southeast Asia | n.a. | 308.1 | n.a. | 24 | n.a. | 74[a] |
| Hong Kong | 19.7 | 135.2 | 97 | 150 | 93 | 93 |
| Taiwan | 19.8 | 84.7 | 48 | 39 | 91 | 93 |
| South Korea | 17.5 | 82.2 | 30 | 25 | 90 | 93 |
| Singapore | 19.4 | 74.0 | 185 | 134 | 54 | 80 |
| Malaysia | 13.8 | 47.1 | 58 | 73 | 19 | 65 |
| Thailand | 6.5 | 36.8 | 19 | 29 | 29 | 72 |
| Indonesia | 21.9 | 33.6 | 31 | 23 | 2 | 53 |
| Philippines | 6.0 | 11.1 | 17 | 21 | 37 | 76 |
| China | 18.3 | 91.7 | 8 | 22 | 47 | 81 |
| South Asia | n.a. | 34.0 | n.a. | 11 | n.a. | 73[a] |
| India | 6.7 | 21.6 | 5 | 10 | 59 | 75 |
| Pakistan | 2.6 | 6.6 | 12 | 14 | 50 | 85 |
| Bangladesh | 0.8 | 2.3 | 7 | 9 | 66 | 82 |
| Latin America and | | | | | | |
| Caribbean | n.a. | 135.0 | n.a. | 10 | n.a. | 38[a] |
| Brazil | 20.1 | 38.6 | 10 | 9 | 39 | 60 |
| Mexico | 15.3 | 30.2 | 9 | 9 | 39 | 53 |
| Argentina | 8.0 | 13.1 | 6 | 5 | 23 | 32 |
| Sub-Saharan Africa | n.a. | 61.7 | n.a. | 23 | n.a. | 24[a] |
| South Africa | 26.1 | 22.9 | 35 | 22 | 54 | 73 |
| Nigeria | 26.0 | 11.9[a] | 29 | 40[a] | 1 | 2 |
| Kenya | 1.3 | 1.4 | 22 | 29 | 16 | 29[a] |
| Tanzania | 0.5 | 0.4 | 12 | 20 | 16 | 15[a] |
| Middle East | n.a. | n.a. | n.a. | n.a. | n.a. | n.a. |
| Saudia Arabia | 109.1 | 40.9 | 95 | 34 | 0 | 9 |
| United Arab Emirates | 20.6 | 20.5 | 69 | 59 | n.a. | 4[a] |
| Iran | 13.5 | 16.7 | n.a. | 16 | 1 | 4 |

Notes:
[a] 1992
GDP Gross domestic product
n.a. Not available.

*Sources*: World Bank (1982: 114–15, 124–5; 1983: 166–7; 1995: 166–7, 186–7). The 1980 data for Taiwan are from Council for Economic Planning and Development, *Taiwan Statistical Yearbook* (1991: 23, 199, 208), while the 1993 calculation for exports/GDP is from Republic of China, 1994: 27, 190).

The maturity or sophistication of a country's industrial structure can be measured by the complexity of the products it exports. Here again, the East Asian NIEs are the most advanced. In Singapore and South Korea, overseas sales of machinery and transport equipment, which utilize capital- and skill-intensive technology, grew as a share of total merchandise exports by 44 and 36 per cent, respectively, from 1970 to 1993. Taiwan's exports in this category increased by 23 per cent and Hong Kong's by 12 per cent. In Southeast Asia, Malaysia (39 per cent) and Thailand (28 per cent) have been strong performers in this sector, while in Latin America, Mexico (20 per cent) and Brazil (17 per cent) also made machinery and transport equipment a dynamic export base (Table 2.2).

**Geographic Specialization and Export Niches**

While the diversification of the NIEs' exports toward non-traditional manufactured items is a clear trend, less well recognized is the tendency of the NIEs to develop sharply focused export niches. In the footwear industry, for example, South Korea has specialized in athletic footwear, Taiwan in vinyl and plastic shoes, Brazil in low priced women's leather shoes, Spain in medium priced women's leather shoes, and Italy in high priced fashion shoes. Mainland China traditionally was a major player in the low priced end of the world footwear market, especially in canvas and rubber shoes. Because of its low wages and vast production capacity, however, China now has displaced Taiwan and South Korea from many of their mid-level niches, and it is challenging Brazil, Spain, and even Italy in the fashionable leather footwear market (Gereffi and Korzeniewicz, 1990). Today China is the world's foremost volume exporter of inexpensive consumer goods, such as clothing, footwear, toys and bicycles.

Similar trends are apparent for many consumer items and even intermediate goods, such as semiconductors. South Korea, for instance, has focused on the mass production of powerful memory chips; Taiwan, by contrast, makes high value designer chips that carry out special functions in toys, video games and electronic equipment. Singapore has upgraded its activities from the assembly and testing of semiconductors to the design and fabrication of silicon wafers, while Singapore and Malaysia produce the majority of hard disk drives for the world's booming personal computer market. Although the location of hard disk drive production in Singapore and Malaysia reflects efforts by multinational enterprises (MNEs) to reduce manufacturing costs,

Table 2.2  Structure of merchandise exports, by type of industry, 1970–93

| Region/Country | Primary commodities | | Textile fibres, textiles, and clothing | | Machinery and transport equipment | | Other manufactures | |
|---|---|---|---|---|---|---|---|---|
| | 1993 | Δ1970–93[c] | 1993 | Δ1970–93 | 1993 | Δ1970–93 | 1993 | Δ1970–93 |
| Advanced industrial countries[a] | 18 | –9 | 5 | –1 | 43 | +8 | 34 | +2 |
| USA | 18 | –12 | 3 | 0 | 49 | +7 | 30 | +5 |
| Germany | 10 | –1 | 5 | –1 | 48 | +1 | 37 | 0 |
| Japan | 3 | –4 | 2 | –11 | 68 | +27 | 27 | –13 |
| East and Southeast Asia[a] | 26 | –41 | 20 | +7 | 25 | +19 | 30 | +16 |
| Hong Kong[a] | 5 | +1 | 40 | –4 | 24 | +12 | 31 | –9 |
| Taiwan | 7 | –17 | 15 | –14 | 40 | +23 | 38 | +8 |
| South Korea | 7 | –17 | 19 | –22 | 43 | +36 | 32 | +4 |
| Singapore | 20 | –50 | 4 | –2 | 55 | +44 | 21 | +7 |
| Malaysia | 35 | –58 | 6 | +5 | 41 | +39 | 18 | +13 |
| Thailand | 28 | –64 | 15 | +7 | 28 | +28 | 30 | +30 |
| Indonesia | 47 | –51 | 17 | +17 | 5 | +5 | 31 | +30 |
| Philippines | 24 | –69 | 9 | +7 | 19 | +19 | 49 | +43 |
| China[b] | 19 | –9 | 31 | +1 | 16 | 0 | 34 | +8 |
| South Asia[a] | 27 | –26 | 41 | +13 | 5 | +2 | 28 | +11 |
| India | 25 | –23 | 30 | +3 | 7 | +2 | 38 | +18 |
| Pakistan[b] | 15 | –22 | 78 | +22 | 0 | 0 | 7 | 0 |
| Bangladesh[a] | 18 | –18 | 72 | +23 | 0 | –1 | 9 | –6 |

*% share of merchandise exports*

| | | | | | | | |
|---|---|---|---|---|---|---|---|
| Latin America and Caribbean[a] | 62 | −26 | 3 | +2 | 14 | +12 | 21 | +13 |
| Brazil | 40 | −46 | 4 | −5 | 21 | +17 | 35 | +33 |
| Mexico | 47 | −21 | 3 | −8 | 31 | +20 | 18 | +7 |
| Argentina | 68 | −18 | 3 | −5 | 11 | +7 | 18 | +16 |
| Sub-Saharan Africa[a] | 76 | −7 | 2 | +1 | 3 | +1 | 19 | +5 |
| South Africa | 27 | −32 | 3 | −3 | 8 | +1 | 63 | +35 |
| Nigeria | 98 | 0 | 0 | −2 | 0 | 0 | 2 | +1 |
| Kenya[a] | 71 | −16 | 3 | +2 | 10 | +10 | 16 | +5 |
| Tanzania[a] | 85 | −2 | 7 | +5 | 1 | +1 | 8 | −3 |
| Middle East | n.a. | n.a. | n.a. | n.a. | n.a. | n.a. | n.a. | n.a. |
| Saudi Arabia | 91 | −9 | 0 | 0 | 2 | +2 | 7 | +7 |
| United Arab Emirates[a] | 96 | 0 | 0 | 0 | 1 | 0 | 2 | 0 |
| Iran | 96 | 0 | 4 | 0 | 0 | 0 | 0 | 0 |

*Notes:*
[a] The data are for 1992 and Δ1970–92.
[b] The data are for Δ1970–92.
[c] Δ1970–93 Increase or decrease in percentage share of total exports, 1970–93.
n.a. Not available.

*Source:* World Bank (1994: 190–1; 1995: 190–1).

these nations were chosen as export sites primarily because of their skilled labour, well developed transportation and communication infrastructures, and appropriate supporting industries (such as precision tooling).

The global production systems discussed in this chapter raise a host of questions for Third World development. How can countries ensure that they enter the most attractive export niches in which they have the greatest relative advantages? To what extent is a country's position in the global manufacturing system structurally determined by the availability of local capital, domestic infrastructure, and a skilled work force? What are the range of development options available to Third World countries? While these queries cannot be answered fully here, various implications of current global changes for Third World development will be suggested.

## GLOBAL COMMODITY CHAINS

Global commodity chains (GCCs) are rooted in transnational production systems that link the economic activities of firms to technological, organizational and institutional networks that are utilized to develop, manufacture and market specific commodities. In global capitalism, economic activity is not only international in scope, it also is global in organization. Although 'internationalization' refers simply to the geographic spread of economic activities across national boundaries, 'globalization' implies a degree of functional integration between these internationally dispersed activities. What is novel about GCCs is not the spread of economic activities across national boundaries *per se*, but rather the fact that international production and trade are increasingly organized by industrial and commercial firms involved in strategic decisionmaking and economic networks at the global level.

Globalization is not a frictionless web of arm's-length market transactions, as neoclassical economics might assert. Countries are incorporated into the global economy through international production, trade and financial networks that are dominated by foreign capital. Globalization requires the agency of three kinds of international capital: (1) industrial capital – i.e. vertically integrated transnational corporations that establish international production and trade networks through the activities of overseas subsidiaries; (2) commercial capital – i.e. large retailers, merchandisers of brandname products, and trading companies that create and control global sourcing networks typically headquartered in developed countries, coordinated from semiperipheral locations (the NIEs), and with production concentrated in the low wage periphery; and (3) finance capital – i.e. commercial banks, official international lending institutions (such as the World Bank and the International Monetary Fund) and, to a lesser degree, portfolio investors that supply the short-term funds used to finance global production and trade.

Industrial and commercial capital have promoted globalization by establishing two distinct types of international economic networks, which we call 'producer-driven' and 'buyer-driven' commodity chains (Gereffi, 1994). 'Producer-driven commodity chains' are those in which large, usually transnational, manufacturers play the central roles in coordinating production networks (including their backward and forward linkages). This is characteristic of capital- and technology-intensive industries such as automobiles, aircraft, computers, semiconductors and heavy machinery. The automobile industry offers a classic illustration of a producer-driven chain, with multilayered production systems that involve thousands of firms (including parents, subsidiaries and subcontractors). The average Japanese auto maker's production system, for example, comprises 170 first-tier, 4700 second-tier, and 31 600 third-tier subcontractors (Hill, 1989: 466). Florida and Kenney (1991) have found that Japanese auto manufacturers actually reconstituted many aspects of their home-country supplier networks in North America. Doner (1991) extends this framework to highlight the complex forces that drive Japanese auto makers to create regional production schemes for the supply of auto parts in half a dozen nations in East and Southeast Asia. Henderson (1989), in his study of the internationalization of the US semiconductor industry, also supports the notion that producer-driven commodity chains have established an East Asian division of labour.

'Buyer-driven commodity chains' refer to those industries in which large retailers, designers and trading companies play the pivotal role in setting up decentralized production networks in a variety of exporting countries, typically located in the Third World. This pattern of trade-led industrialization has become common in labour-intensive, consumer goods industries such as garments, footwear, toys, housewares, consumer electronics and a variety of hand-crafted items (e.g. furniture, ornaments). Production is generally carried out by tiered networks of Third World contractors that make finished goods for foreign buyers. The specifications are supplied by the large retailers or designers that order the goods.

One of the main characteristics of the firms that fit the buyer-driven model – including retailers like Wal-Mart, Sears Roebuck, and J.C.

Penney, athletic footwear companies like Nike and Reebok, and fashion-oriented apparel companies like Liz Claiborne and The Limited – is that these companies design and/or market, but do not make, the branded products they order. They are part of a new breed of 'manufacturers without factories' that separate the physical production of goods from the design and marketing stages of the production process. Profits in buyer-driven chains derive not from scale, volume and technological advances as in producer-driven chains, but rather from unique combinations of high value research, design, sales, marketing and financial services that allow the retailers and designers to act as strategic brokers in linking overseas factories and traders with evolving product niches in the main consumer markets.

Profitability is greatest in the relatively concentrated segments of GCCs characterized by high barriers to the entry of new firms. In producer-driven chains, manufacturers making advanced products like aircraft, automobiles, and computers are the key economic agents, not only in terms of their earnings but also in their ability to exert control over backward linkages with raw material and component suppliers, and forward linkages into distribution and retailing. The transnationals in producer-driven chains usually belong to global oligopolies. Buyer-driven commodity chains, by contrast, are characterized by highly competitive and globally decentralized factory systems. The companies that develop and sell brandname products exert substantial control over how, when, and where manufacturing will take place, and how much profit accrues at each stage of the chain. Thus, whereas producer-driven commodity chains are controlled by industrial firms at the point of production, the main leverage in buyer-driven industries is exercised by retailers and branded merchandisers at the marketing and retail end of the chain.

The main characteristics of producer-driven and buyer-driven commodity chains are highlighted in Table 2.3. Producer-driven and buyer-driven chains are rooted in distinct industrial sectors, they are led by different types of transnational capital (industrial and commercial, respectively), and they vary in their core competencies (at the firm level) and their entry barriers (at the sectoral level). The finished goods in producer-driven chains tend to be supplied by core country transnationals, while the goods in buyer-driven chains are generally made by locally-owned firms in developing countries. Whereas transnational corporations establish investment based vertical networks, the retailers, designers, and trading companies in buyer-driven chains set up and coordinate trade based horizontal networks.

*Table* 2.3   Main characteristics of producer-driven and buyer-driven GCCs

|  | Producer-driven commodity chains | Buyer-driven commodity chains |
|---|---|---|
| Drivers of GCCs | Industrial capital | Commercial capital |
| Core competencies | Research and Development; Production | Design; Marketing |
| Barriers to entry | Economies of scale | Economies of scope |
| Economic sectors | Consumer durables Intermediate goods Capital goods | Consumer non-durables |
| Typical industries | Automobiles; Computers; Aircraft | Apparel; Footwear; Toys |
| Predominant ownership pattern at finished production stage | Foreign firms | Local firms |
| Main network links | Investment based | Trade based |
| Predominant network structure | Vertical | Horizontal |

## EXPORT ROLES AND NATIONAL DEVELOPMENT

Economic globalization has heightened the role of trade, especially of manufactures, in the world economy. In absolute terms, most countries now are significant exporters. In 1992, two-thirds of the nations for which data were available (78 out of 117) had exports of $1 billion or more (World Bank, 1994: 186–7). Furthermore, there has been a tendency for dynamic world regions to upgrade their exports with higher levels of local value added, thereby amplifying the domestic multiplier effects of trade. In relative terms, exports in 1992 accounted for two-fifths of GDP in East Asia (excluding China), nearly one-quarter in Southeast Asia and sub-Saharan Africa, one-sixth in the advanced industrial countries, and one-tenth in Latin America and South Asia (see Table 2.1).

Countries are connected to GCCs through the goods and services they supply in the world economy. These trade linkages can be conceptualized as a set of five major export roles: (1) primary commodity exports; (2) export-processing (or in-bond) assembly; (3) component-supply subcontracting; (4) original equipment manufacturing (OEM);

*Table* 2.4   Export roles in the global economy occupied by major Third
World regions, 1965–95

| | Primary commodity exports | Export- processing assembly | Component- supply subcontracting | Original equipment manufacturing (OEM) | Original brandname manufacturing (OBM) |
|---|---|---|---|---|---|
| East Asia | X | X | X | X | X |
| Southeast Asia | X | X | X | | |
| Latin America and Caribbean | X | X | X | | |
| South Asia | X | X | | | |
| North Africa | X | X | | | |
| Sub-Saharan Africa | X | | | | |
| Middle East | X | | | | |

and (5) original brandname manufacturing (OBM).[1] Each type of manufactured exporting (roles (2)–(5)) is progressively more difficult to establish because it implies a higher degree of domestic integration and
local entrepreneurship. Therefore, industrial development is enhanced
as countries move from option (2) to option (5).

These export roles are not mutually exclusive. In fact, most nations
are tied to the world economy in multiple ways. The East Asian NIEs
employed all five export roles from the 1950s to the mid-1990s, although they currently are focusing almost exclusively on component-
supply subcontracting, OEM, and OBM. Most of the countries in
Southeast Asia and Latin America are involved in the first three roles.
The bulk of exports in South Asia and sub-Saharan Africa fit the first
two roles, with many African nations limited only to primary commodity exports (Table 2.4). An overview of the principal export roles
in the Third World is provided next, emphasizing their institutional
foundations and development trade-offs.

## Primary Commodity Exports

Primary commodity exports have been an important feature in the economic growth of every Third World region, but all substantially reduced their reliance on this type of export between 1970 and 1992
(see Table 2.2). In general, this reduction has been a conscious deci-
sion because raw materials have well known disadvantages as an export base. The disadvantages multiply when, as is frequently the case,
a country relies heavily on a single primary commodity.

Commodity exporters confront several problems. First, the prices of primary goods are highly volatile. This volatility arises in part from the concentrated pattern of production, where a few countries control a relatively high percentage of world output. A fall in production in a single location – because of labour problems, weather or natural disaster – can cause sharp price changes around the world. Over-supply or international recession may have similar effects. A second (very controversial) problem is the alleged tendency for the terms of trade for primary products to deteriorate. Despite evidence against the claim of a long-term decline, it seems clear that such problems can wreck havoc on primary product exporters over shorter periods. Thus, non-fuel primary producers' terms of trade have fallen substantially over the last twenty years. Other problems relate to particular products. For example, agricultural productivity in most parts of the Third World is very low, while mineral extraction has high productivity but often little spillover to the rest of the economy.

Various solutions to these problems have been tried. In the 1970s, following the success of the OPEC cartel in raising oil prices, attempts were made to form other producer groups to regulate output and thus control prices. These have not proved successful and, in any case, go against the market-oriented policies that many Third World governments have adopted in the past decade. The use of futures and options has gained some adherents, but the requirements for participating in these markets are so stringent that most Third World countries have shied away from them. Perhaps the most successful strategy has been to upgrade primary production, either by shifting to 'non-traditional' products (e.g. the export of exotic fruits and vegetables to developed-country markets) or processing raw materials more before selling them (e.g. furniture rather than logs, or steel rather than iron ore). Nonetheless, most Third World regions continue to rely heavily on traditional primary exports. Sub-Saharan Africa still earns three-quarters of its export revenues this way, while Latin America and Southeast Asia mix primary commodity and industrial exports.

## Export-processing Assembly

The export-processing role emphasizes the labour-intensive assembly of simple manufactured goods from imported components, typically in foreign-owned plants. Often special zones are created with incentives for foreign capital to locate in a designated set of industries, such as apparel, electronics, and other light manufacturing sectors. The main advantages of export-processing zones (EPZs) for the host country are jobs and foreign exchange earnings. Since they rely on cheap labour with minimal skills, EPZs represent the first stage of export-oriented industrialization (EOI) for most Third World countries. Although every region of the Third World has some experience with EPZs, these zones tend to migrate from the more advanced to the least developed nations.

The first EPZs were set up in the 1960s in Asia and Mexico; in the latter case, they were part of a border industrialization programme based on export-oriented *maquiladora* factories (Sklair, 1993; Chen, 1994a). In the East Asian NIEs, EPZs have been declining since the mid-1970s in response to spiralling labour costs and the systematic efforts of these nations to upgrade their mix of export activities by moving toward skill- and technology-intensive products. As East Asia's NIEs abandoned the export-processing role, it was occupied by neighboring low wage areas such as China, Southeast Asia and South Asia. Many countries, including Mexico, which has the world's largest export-processing sector with 550 000 employees, have extended the benefits of EPZs to all export-oriented firms without requiring them to be located in special zones.

The steep hierarchy among world regions in terms of their labour costs has influenced the location of export-processing activities. The East Asian NIEs are by far the most expensive production sites in the Third World. Labour costs decrease sharply as one moves from East Asia to Latin America, Southeast Asia, South Asia and China. In 1991, India, China, Pakistan, Philippines, Indonesia and Honduras had apparel labour costs of under US$0.50 per hour. Indonesia's labour cost of US$0.18 per hour was less than one-twentieth Taiwan's cost (US$3.74) and nearly one-fortieth that of the USA (US$6.77) (O'Rourke 1992: 116–18). This explains the appeal of particular Third World export sites in global sourcing arrangements. From the vantage point of developing nations, however, low wages provide only a transient competitive edge because they can fluctuate rapidly and are relatively easy to duplicate elsewhere.

Most Third World export industries are characterized by a pronounced gender division of labour. The majority of workers in low wage industries like apparel, electronics, toys and footwear are young unmarried women, who constitute a 'part-time proletariat' that frequently combines home based work with jobs in formal and informal factories. The prevailing patriarchal order in these societies reinforces the traditional roles of wives and mothers, and militates against organized resistance by women to improve their working conditions. As industrial labour in the NIEs has become costly and relatively scarce, however, male and older female factory workers are more prevalent. Today at least 25 per cent of the labour force in Hong Kong's apparel industry are men, and nearly one-third of the managers and one-quarter of the assembly workers are over 40 years of age (Hong Kong Government Industry Department, 1992: A17). This changing composition of the work force is likely to alter the social dynamics in some export-oriented industries, especially if male workers galvanize the sporadic efforts to unionize export sectors. So far, the unionization of export-oriented factories has progressed the furthest in South Korea, where the class consciousness of workers has been sharpened by harsh employer practices and low wages in large-scale factories in the auto, steel and textile industries (Deyo, 1989).

Sub-Saharan Africa lags behind the other Third World regions in terms of its limited number of EPZs, largely because of the inadequate transportation and communication infrastructure in many parts of the African region, its shortage of concentrated pools of low wage labour, and a difficult political and cultural environment for foreign investors. Nonetheless, there are a few successful EPZs in Africa that have flourished due to special external conditions. One such case is Mauritius, an island of 1.1 million people located east of Madagascar off the southern coast of Africa. The EPZ sector in Mauritius, which is dominated by textiles and clothing, has been the focal point of the country's development strategy in the 1980s and 1990s. Between 1982 and 1990, the number of EPZ firms increased nearly five-fold from 120 to 570, and employment in these companies quadrupled from 20 000 to 80 000. About 70 per cent of the island's EPZ exports, which totalled over $770 million in 1990, went to the European Community (EC) where Mauritius has privileged access. The disadvantages of Mauritius' location in cost terms have been offset by a concentration on high unit value products, such as 'Scottish' knitwear (mainly jerseys and pullovers). Labor productivity in Mauritius, where most workers are immigrants from India, is regarded as significantly higher than in the Caribbean. The largest source of foreign capital in the EPZs is Hong Kong entrepreneurs, who came to the island because of political uncertainties about the future of Hong Kong, but the political stability and favorable tax treatment offered by Mauritius also make it an attractive site for Indian and now South African investors (Fowdar 1991).

**Component-supply Subcontracting**

'Component-supply subcontracting' refers to the manufacture and export of component parts in technologically advanced industries in the NIEs, with final assembly usually carried out in the developed countries. The primary advantage of this export role is that it can facilitate industrial upgrading and technology transfer in the NIEs, and it may generate significant backward linkages to local suppliers. A potential liability is that these economic networks often are controlled by TNCs, which subordinate national development criteria to their own objectives of global profitability and flexibility.

The component-supplier role has been a major niche for the Latin American NIEs' manufactured exports during the past two decades. Brazil and Mexico have been important production sites since the late 1960s for vertically integrated exports by TNCs to developed-country markets, especially the USA. This is most notable in certain industries, like motor vehicles, computers, and pharmaceuticals (Newfarmer, 1985; Gereffi and Hempel, 1996). American and Japanese automotive TNCs, for example, have advanced manufacturing plants in Mexico and Brazil for the production of engines, auto parts, and completed vehicles destined for the US, European, and Latin American markets. By the 1970s, component-supply exporting had become an integral part of the regional division of labour in East Asia's electronics industry. In the 1980s, Japanese automotive firms took the lead in creating an elaborate parts supply arrangement with foreign and local capital in Southeast Asia (Henderson, 1989; Doner, 1991; Borrus, 1994). The regional integration scheme for autos that stretches from Japan across East and Southeast Asia entails strategic export-oriented investments similar to those in the North American auto complex, which links component suppliers in Canada and Mexico with a variety of car assemblers in the US market.

An interesting variation on the component-supplier arrangement are the subregional cooperation zones in East and Southeast Asia, known as 'growth triangles'. These subregional divisions of labour typically involve neighboring countries at different levels of development that cooperate in the outsourcing and assembly of various kinds of products, ranging from cars to computers to clothes. The participants each have specific roles. In the Greater South China Economic Region, for example, Hong Kong is the service and finance centre, Taiwan typically provides investment capital and technological expertise, and the Fujian and Guangdong provinces in South China offer land and labour

(Chen, 1994b; Chu, 1994). There are several such triangles operating or planned in Southeast Asia, the best known of which links Singapore, Johor state in Malaysia, and Riau province in Indonesia (the SIJORI triangle). What these subregional integration pacts have in common is a well defined division of labour in which TNCs farm out their parts supply to individual nations; these parts, in turn, are sent to a single destination for final product assembly. While the private sector decides where its investments should go, this arrangement often is facilitated by trade incentives offered by national governments.

**Original Equipment Manufacturing (OEM)**

'Original equipment manufacturing' refers to the production of finished consumer goods by contract manufacturers, who frequently run locally-owned factories in the Third World. The sourcing of inputs and the making of the final product are responsibilities assumed by the contractor, and the output is distributed and marketed abroad by large trading companies, foreign retail chains or branded marketers. Also known as specification contracting, OEM has been the major export niche filled by the East Asian NIEs in the world economy since the 1960s. In 1980, for example, Hong Kong, Taiwan, and South Korea accounted for 72 per cent of all finished consumer goods exported by the Third World to the advanced industrial countries, other Asian nations supplied another 19 per cent, while just 7 per cent came from Latin America and the Caribbean. The USA was the leading market for these consumer products, absorbing 46 per cent of the export total (Keesing, 1983: 338–9). Recently Third World exporters have begun to decrease their reliance on their traditional overseas markets, however, especially the USA. By 1989, the four East Asian NIEs had cut their dependence on the USA to the point where it represented only 25–40 per cent of their total exports. The US market was most important for Taiwan (39 per cent of total exports), followed by South Korea (35 per cent), Singapore (30 per cent) and Hong Kong (27 per cent) (Dicken, 1992: 37).

The OEM role is a potentially profitable, but demanding and unstable, export niche. Unlike the prior two export roles, which are both forms of 'subcontracting' because they involve a linkage with TNCs that take full responsibility for supplying (in export-processing assembly) or buying (in component-supply subcontracting) all component parts for their factory affiliates, OEM producers make finished products that will be sold under another company's brandname. The contract manufacturer must have the capability to interpret designs, source the needed inputs, monitor product quality, meet the buyer's price, and guarantee on-time delivery. The fee charged by the contractor covers all material and production costs, plus a usually modest profit.

The East Asian NIEs have excelled at OEM production, which has been the key to their export growth during the past several decades. There are various reasons for this success. In part, it has to do with East Asia's classic 'pull' rather than 'push' approach to exporting. In the 'push' approach, typical among raw material or standardized product exporters, the manufacturer's philosophy is: 'I will sell what I make'. In the 'pull' approach, the manufacturer's attitude is more market-oriented: 'I will make what you need'. This consumer-driven export mentality has encouraged East Asian entrepreneurs to become full-range 'package suppliers' for foreign buyers. Learning how to piece together all the material and service inputs required to make a wide range of consumer goods gives OEM producers a unique organizational capability for creating and managing elaborate, horizontal networks of suppliers and buyers. Expertise in OEM production increases over time and it can lead to important forms of organizational innovation.

In addition, the pressures exerted by foreign buyers for new products have made industrial upgrading and backward linkages an intrinsic part of the OEM process. The East Asia NIEs are the only Third World nations to establish the diverse array of efficient supporting industries required by a dynamic, embedded model of specification contracting. While their governments have been supportive of this process, the key factor probably lies with an abundant supply of local entrepreneurs. East Asian factories tend to be locally-owned and vary greatly in size. Large, vertically integrated companies, such as South Korea's *chaebol*, have significant advantages in supplying world markets because of their scale economies in mass production and substantial financial support from the state. Established exporters in small firm-dominated economies like Taiwan and Hong Kong have also been successful in their efforts to develop the technology and manufacturing expertise needed for high quality global production, and to adjust their output flexibly to more differentiated export items (see Amsden, 1989; Wade, 1990; Cheng and Gereffi, 1994).

The main advantage of the OEM export role is that it enhances the scope for local entrepreneurs not only to learn how to make internationally competitive finished consumer goods, but also to generate substantial *backward* linkages to the domestic economy. East Asian producers confront intense competition from lower cost exporters in various parts of the Third World. Furthermore, they have discovered that it is very difficult to establish *forward* linkages to their developed-country markets, where the biggest profits are made in buyer-driven commodity chains. East Asian manufacturers have maintained close ties with foreign buyers, which has permitted the former to become middlemen in the triangle of manufacturing networks that shift the production of consumer goods from the NIEs to cheaper export sites. But foreign buyers are frequently driven by cost considerations to set up direct contacts with their main Third World suppliers. Thus, a number of the firms in the East Asian NIEs that pioneered OEM are now pushing beyond it to OBM by integrating their manufacturing expertise with the design and sale of their own-brand merchandise.

**Original Brandname Manufacturing (OBM)**

A final stage in the development of an export economy is to move beyond OEM production to the establishment of proprietary brandnames that give Third World exporters a more visible presence in both local and developed-country retail networks. South Korea is the most advanced of the East Asian countries in this regard, with Korean brands of auto (Hyundai), computers (Leading Edge), and household appliances (Samsung and Goldstar), among other items, being sold in North America, Europe, and Japan. Taiwan also sells its own brands of Acer and Mitac computers, Giant bicycles, Pro-Kennex tennis rackets, and Travel Fox shoes in overseas markets. Mexican beer is one of the only branded products in Latin America that has developed a solid retail niche in the US market.

Hyundai is the most prominent example of a Third World manufacturer that decided to integrate forward to the marketing end of a producer-driven commodity chain. Hyundai entered the North American market for cars in the late 1980s by building an independent marketing network. By contrast, Daewoo and Kia, South Korea's other two major auto companies, relied on their OEM networks with General Motors (GM) and Ford, respectively, to market and sell GM and Ford models made in Korea. This was a risky strategy by Hyundai because it had only 183 dealers in the US market in 1987, compared with 3000 dealers in GM's Pontiac Division and 5700 dealers for Ford. But the strategy was also profitable. Hyundai obtained a 3.7 per cent profit margin from production and a 7 per cent margin from its marketing subsidiary, Hyundai Motor America. Daewoo earned a 3.6 per cent profit for OEM production, while GM appropriated an 8–9 per cent yield from the marketing process. In response to competitive pressures, however, Hyundai changed its marketing system from single-point (or exclusive) dealerships to dual-point dealerships (i.e. dealers could sell other brands), and it launched an export diversification strategy by entering European markets (see Kim and Lee, 1994; Lee and Cason, 1994).

Many Hong Kong apparel manufacturers have embarked on an ambitious program of forward integration into retailing, using their own brandnames and retail chains for the clothing they make. These retail outlets started out selling in the Hong Kong market, but now there are Hong Kong-owned stores throughout East Asia (including China), North America, and Europe. A good example of this is the Fang Brothers, one of the principal Hong Kong suppliers for Liz Claiborne, who now have several different private label retail chains (Episode, Excursion, Jessica and Jean Pierre) in a variety of countries including the United States (Pogoda, 1992; Cawthorne, 1993).

In the personal computer industry, Taiwanese companies are more inclined to export their own brands of computers than their South Korean counterparts. In 1986, exports of personal computers by each country totalled about $400 million. 'Own-brand' computers comprised 28 per cent of Taiwan's overseas sales, but only 16 per cent of the Korean total. Conversely, OEM sales accounted for 44 per cent of Korea's exports of personal computers, but only 22 per cent for the Taiwanese. The remainder, 50 per cent in Taiwan and 40 per cent in South Korea, were personal computer exports by TNC subsidiaries. This contrast in OBM versus OEM orientation reflects the two countries' distinct industrial capabilities: whereas Korea's much larger companies have sought a competitive edge based on price and standardized, mature goods, Taiwan's smaller firms have emphasized flexibility, innovation, and market niches for non-standardized products (Levy, 1988).

The difficulties of OBM should not be underestimated, however, and some East Asian companies are shifting back to OEM work. In 1990 Mitac Corporation, the main competitor to Acer in Taiwan's personal computer market, made 70 per cent of its computers under its own brandname and 30 per cent for OEM clients. By 1993 the OEM ratio was back up to 60 per cent. The reason, according to Mitac's president C.S. Ho, is that the firm was more profitable when it concentrated on its core competencies: 'We asked ourselves: What functions are we best at? Our strengths are in R & D, design and manufacturing' ... 'We are now focusing on designing and supplying products and key components for major OEM customers, whose brands are better-known but which have withdrawn from fully integrated manufacture' (Selwyn,

1993: 24). The OBM option, while still remote even for the relatively advanced Third World nations in Latin America and Southeast Asia, establishes a new benchmark against which the most ambitious export firms will be measured.

## Sequences of Export Roles

There are typical sequences of export roles. Virtually all countries begin their exporting experience with primary commodities (or raw materials), and then turn to staple consumer items such as garments and footwear. At this juncture, countries can go in two directions: They can augment the sophistication and local value added of their production capability by filling the OEM orders of foreign buyers, or they can make components or parts that will be exported for more complex finished goods assembly abroad (component-supply subcontracting). Either of these two export roles can be stepping stones to the export of local brands of finished goods (OBM production), such as Hong Kong clothes, Taiwanese tennis rackets, or Korean cars.

The prominence and sequencing of these export roles varies markedly across Third World regions. This reflects differences in the timing and impact of outward- and inward-oriented development strategies (Gereffi and Wyman, 1990). The East Asian approach was to combine EOI with selective forms of state intervention (export subsidies, import licenses, non-tariff trade barriers (NTBs), preferential credit, privileged access to quotas, etc.), and then to roll back these policies under internal and external pressure after successful export industries had been established. In Latin America and other Third World regions, however, state intervention was used to promote 'import substitute industrialization' ISI, not EOI. When the liberalizing reforms of the 1980s took hold, many nations opened their economies before they were internationally competitive. The resulting import surge has led to widespread plant closures (especially among small and medium-sized firms), job loss, and a worsening of income distribution. At the same time, some of the largest firms have raised their productivity and are increasing exports.

In contrast to those who would argue that EOI by itself can lead to sustained economic growth, the experience of the East Asian NIEs actually shows that a diversified array of backward linkages is essential in moving toward the more complex component-supply, OEM and OBM export roles. The East Asian NIEs have been successful in upgrading their export industries in large measure because of their highly efficient networks of suppliers for intermediate goods (e.g. textiles, plastics, metals) and components (e.g. semiconductors, computer chips, auto parts). These supporting industries allow East Asia's exporters to receive high quality inputs at world market prices. In addition, the East Asian NIEs have developed a full range of local design, financial, transportation, and communication services that give them major advantages over other Third World production sites. The directions the East Asian economies can move in terms of industrial upgrading, however, are constrained by the availability of the natural resources on which these suppliers depend. The importance of raw material-supply networks for successful export industries creates opportunities for resource-rich regions of the Third World. East Asian nations have been forced to adjust to their escalating production costs and labour shortages by gravitating to higher order forms of competitive advantage that are durable, add more value, and lead to constant improvement and industrial upgrading (Porter, 1990).

## THE EMERGENCE OF REGIONAL DIVISIONS OF LABOR IN EAST ASIA: A COMMODITY CHAINS INTERPRETATION[2]

From a commodity chains perspective, there are overlapping, and at times conflicting, networks involved in East Asia's export-oriented development. Producer-driven and buyer-driven chains coexist in each of the tiers of the Asian regional division of labor. While all the nations in the region have pursued strategies of EOI, the timing, products, and linkages involved have varied across the region.

- *Japan* was a significant exporter to the United States in buyer-driven commodity chains (BDCCs) such as apparel and footwear in the 1950s and 1960s, but then switched in the 1970s to producer-driven commodity chains (PDCCs) like autos, electrical machinery and computers. Japan used its large trading companies (*sogo shosha*) to transfer BDCCs to the East Asian NIEs, while Japanese transnationals were the main mechanism employed in setting up and maintaining PDCCs in Southeast Asia.
- The *East Asian NIEs* became successful exporters in the late 1960s and 1970s primarily by mastering the dynamics of BDCCs. Apparel was a leading export sector for each of the four NIEs, toys for all but Singapore, footwear for South Korea and Taiwan, and so on. These countries moved quickly from assembly to OEM production

in BDCCs. Unlike Southeast Asia, however, the East Asian NIEs (with the exception of Singapore) are making the transition to PDCCs on the basis of exports by domestically-owned firms, not transnational companies.

- *Southeast Asia* launched a different form of EOI than that of the East Asian NIEs. Southeast Asia's initial export industries – electronics (semiconductors, disk drives and computers) and autos – were organized in the 1970s and early 1980s as PDCCs. The drivers in these chains were Japanese, US, and European transnationals. In the late 1980s, a second generation of export industries was set up in Southeast Asia: these were the BDCCs (apparel, footwear, toys) that were no longer cost-competitive in the East Asian NIEs because of currency appreciation, rapid wage increases, and the difficulty in hiring workers domestically for labor-intensive production, even at prevailing high wage rates. Instead of core country transnationals (as in PDCCs) or US and European buyers (as in the first-generation BDCCs set up in the NIEs), the main organizing agents in Southeast Asia's buyer-driven chains were investors from the East Asian NIEs who set up 'triangle manufacturing' networks in the region to take advantage of lower labor costs and, in the case of apparel, available quotas.

- The *People's Republic of China* has emerged as the region's dominant player in BDCCs in the 1990s, but it currently has only a minor role in PDCCs. China is the world's biggest volume exporter of a wide range of consumer goods, including clothes, shoes, toys, watches, bicycles, and so on. China's presence as a leading exporter in these global commodity chains is vulnerable to economic and political shifts. These range from economic recession in the North American and European economies that are the major markets for Chinese exports, to the possibility that the US government will fail to renew China's most-favored-nation (MFN) trade status. As a result, Chinese production is likely to be increasingly directed at Asian and other non-quota markets in the latter half of the 1990s.

The interaction of producer-driven and buyer-driven commodity chains within East Asia's regional political economy suggests a hypothesis of *network isomorphism.* These two types of commodity chains give rise to overlapping and competing regional divisions of labor in East Asia that are based on different network structures, as follows:

- PDCCs transfer the hierarchical relations between transnational core firms and their subsidiaries into vertical, investment based networks within East Asia;

- Conversely, the core commercial companies (retailers and designers) in BDCCs convert their specification contracting or OEM relationship with suppliers in Asia into horizontal, trade based networks that establish a distinctive division of labor within and between global regions.

Network isomorphism will be examined in greater detail in the next two sections of this chapter, which focus on the apparel and electronics sectors in East Asia.

In the case of apparel, US buyers initially established direct OEM links with producers in Hong Kong, Taiwan and South Korea. Eventually China and the nations of Southeast and South Asia were incorporated into the chain as lower cost Asian production sites, with Hong Kong and Taiwan employing their cultural ties with the overseas Chinese business communities throughout the region to establish the three-tiered networks used in 'triangle manufacturing'. The intermediary role of the NIEs continued to evolve. In addition to supplying a growing number of regional exporters with apparel orders, fibres, textiles, financing and quota brokerage services, the NIEs moved from OEM to OBM by developing their own brands of clothing for production and sale within Asia. Apparel has now become a leading export sector for nations at lower levels in Asia's regional production hierarchy, such as China, Thailand, Indonesia, Bangladesh, Pakistan and Sri Lanka. As new countries turn to apparel to launch their export-oriented development strategies, the regional hierarchy deepens.

In the electronics commodity chain, Japan and the United States retain central roles through the activities of their TNCs MNEs. Low wages matter less than in buyer-driven chains, and quotas not at all. Compared to apparel, these networks are not very deep (i.e. they have fewer tiers) nor very dense (i.e. there are fewer countries in each tier). This regional division of labor relies on Singapore more than Hong Kong, and transnationals control the necessary capital and technology. Japanese and US transnationals have constructed networks with divergent characteristics (e.g. the former are relatively 'closed' and the latter more 'open'). Company strategies concerning local sourcing are a prime determinant in how these networks are organized. Southeast Asian nations like Malaysia and Thailand have occasionally leapfrogged the East Asian NIEs by making technologically more advanced products, although the backward linkages and product sophistication of the former are still limited.

## THE TRANSFORMATION OF EAST ASIA'S APPAREL COMMODITY CHAIN

The world textile and apparel industry has undergone several major migrations of production during the past four decades, and they all involve Asia. The first migration of the industry took place from North America and Western Europe to Japan in the 1950s and early 1960s, when Western textile and clothing production was displaced by a sharp rise in imports from Japan. Textiles and clothing, which accounted for about one-third of Japan's exports during the first half of the twentieth century, still represented 36 per cent of its total exports and 22 per cent of its manufacturing employment in the 1950s (Park, 1990: 96). The second migration of production was a shift from Japan to the 'Big Three' Asian economies (Hong Kong. Taiwan and South Korea), and allowed the latter group to dominate global textile and clothing exports in the 1970s and 1980s, especially in apparel. During the past ten–fifteen years, however, there has been a third migration of production from the Asian Big Three to a number of other developing economies. In the 1980s, the principal shift was to mainland China, but it also encompassed several Southeast Asian nations and Sri Lanka. In the 1990s, the proliferation of new suppliers included South Asian and Latin American apparel exporters, with new entrants like Vietnam waiting in the wings (Khanna, 1993; Tran, 1995).

There are several perspectives we can use to analyze these shifts: neoclassical economics, the statist perspective, the product-cycle model, and the organization of production (or networks) approach. These theoretical frameworks are complementary and interactive, rather than mutually exclusive. However, it is clear that economic and political models alone are not sufficient to account for the transformation of East Asia's textile and apparel complex.

Neoclassical economics has the simplest prediction: the most labor-intensive segments of the apparel commodity chain should be located in countries with the lowest wages. This theory is supported by the sequential shifts of textile and apparel production from the USA and Western Europe to Japan, the Asian Big Three, and China, since the entrants into each new tier of the production hierarchy had significantly lower wage rates than their predecessors. China, with apparel labor costs of US$0.25 per hour, had become the largest supplier of textiles and clothing to the $34 billion US import market by 1992 (up from fourth place in 1982, when China trailed only the Asian Big Three). China was also the largest volume supplier of textiles and clothing to the European Community in 1992, and in terms of value it ranked second only to Turkey (Khanna, 1993: 16–17). Furthermore, as the NIEs in East Asia were shifting into higher value added production in the 1980s and 1990s, clothing exports became a growth pole for other low wage countries in the region. The Southeast Asian nations of Thailand, Indonesia and Malaysia increased their share of global apparel exports more than five-fold (from 1.3 per cent to 7.2 per cent), while the South Asian economies nearly tripled their portion of the global total (from 2.3 to 6.3 per cent). In Bangladesh, Sri Lanka, and Mauritius, apparel exports climbed to one-half or more of each economy's merchandise exports in 1995 (see Table 2.5).

Textiles and clothing, the pre-eminent export sector in the East Asian NIEs in the 1960s and 1970s, actually shrank as a proportion of these economies' total exports between 1980 and 1995. The share of global apparel exports represented by Hong Kong, South Korea and Taiwan declined from 25 per cent in 1980 to just over 11 per cent in 1995 (Table 2.5). Rising incomes as a consequence of economic development pushed wages in South Korea and Taiwan to the point where the textile and apparel industries were becoming uncompetitive. The labor consequences of these shifts have been quite severe. In South Korea, textile and clothing employment fell from its peak of 784 000 in 1987 to 534 000 in 1991, a loss of 250 000 jobs in just five years. In Taiwan, there was a similar decrease of 150 000 jobs in the textile and apparel sector, from 460 000 workers in 1987 to only 310 000 workers in 1991 (Khanna, 1993: 23, 28). In both countries, the steepest fall in employment was in apparel, followed by textiles and man-made fibres. This job loss occurred despite the fact that wages were rising rapidly for textile and apparel workers. In Taiwan, apparel wages rose from US$420 per month in 1987 to $630 per month in 1991, while the average monthly earnings of textile workers increased from US$540 to $900 during the same period. In South Korea, the wages of apparel workers rose from US$485 per month in 1991 to $550 per month at the beginning of 1992 (Khanna 1993: 24, 28).

Hong Kong represents a special case among the NIEs. While Hong Kong's domestic apparel exports declined from 11.5 to 6 per cent of the global total from 1980 to 1995, Hong Kong's re-exports of textiles and clothing have grown dramatically. In 1980 re-exports accounted for only 6 per cent of Hong Kong's clothing exports, while in 1995 apparel re-exports were 55 per cent of the Hong Kong total (Table 2.5). These re-exports are based primarily on imports from mainland China, which are shipped from Hong Kong to many other sites around the world. If we add the apparel exports from China together with Hong Kong's re-exports, apparel's share of Greater China's export total jumps from 14 to 24 per cent between 1980 and 1995 (Table 2.6). Hong Kong's restoration to mainland China in 1997 will further consolidate China's domination of global textile and clothing exports.

The neoclassical cheap-labor argument does not hold up as well, however, when we get to the proliferation of new Asian suppliers, whose wage rates are often considerably higher than China's. As we can see in Table 2.5, the major apparel exporters have wide variations in their labor costs. Thailand's 1993 clothing exports are greater than Indonesia's, even though the former's labor costs are nearly three times as high. Sri Lanka's exports are about the same as those of Bangladesh, but Sri Lanka's wages are double those of its South Asian neighbor. Furthermore, even though the share of global apparel exports represented by Hong Kong, South Korea and Taiwan declined from 25 to 14 per cent between 1980 and 1993, these NIEs still ranked among Asia's top five apparel exporters in the latter year, despite having the highest apparel labor costs in the region (excluding Japan).

The statist perspective, which argues that government policies will play a major role in shaping the location of apparel export activities, helps to explain these discrepancies. We need to distinguish at least three kinds of government policies: macroeconomic policies that affect the entire economy, industrial policies that target particular sectors, and protectionist policies in the advanced industrial countries that seek to dampen the impact of imports. All three types of government policy have affected the performance of apparel exporters in Asia. As discussed in the first section of this article (p. 000), the East Asian NIEs clearly got their macroeconomic fundamentals right. Since the mid-1960s, they have had relative stability in their exchange and interest rates, they have invested heavily in human capital formation, they have promoted exports, and they have encouraged private investment and domestic competition. The most important factor in the sharp decline of Taiwan's and South Korea's apparel exports in the late 1980s, however, was not their rising wage rates, but the sharp appreciation of their local currencies *vis-à-vis* the US dollar after the Plaza Agreement was signed in 1985. Between 1985 and 1987, the Japanese yen was revalued by close to 40 per cent, the New Taiwan dollar by 28 per cent, and from 1986 to 1988 the Korean won appreciated by 17 per cent (Bernard and Ravenhill 1995: 180).

The East Asian NIEs tended not to use specific industrial policies to promote the booming exports of light manufacturing sectors like

Table 2.5  Shifts in Asian clothing exports, 1980–95

| Countries | Apparel labor costs (US$ per hour)* 1993 | Value (US$ million) 1980 | Value (US$ million) 1995 | Share in world exports (%) 1980 | Share in world exports (%) 1995 | Share in economy's total merchandise exports (%) 1980 | 1990 | 1995 | Δ1980–90 | Δ1990–95 |
|---|---|---|---|---|---|---|---|---|---|---|
| World | | 40 590 | 157,880 | 100.0 | 100.0 | 2.0 | 3.2 | 3.2 | +1.2 | 0.0 |
| Japan | 10.64 | 488 | 530 | 1.2 | 0.3 | 0.4 | 0.2 | 0.1 | −0.2 | −0.1 |
| East Asia | | | | | | | | | | |
| Hong Kong | 3.85 | 4 976 | 21 297 | 11.5 | — | 24.5 | 18.7 | 12.2 | −5.8 | −6.5 |
| domestic exports | | 4 664 | 9 540 | | 6.0 | 34.1 | 31.9 | 31.9 | −2.2 | 0.0 |
| re-exports | | 312 | 11 757 | — | — | 4.7 | 11.5 | 8.2 | +6.8 | −3.3 |
| China[a] | 0.25 | 1 625 | 24 049 | 4.0 | 15.2 | 8.9 | 15.6 | 16.2 | +6.7 | +0.6 |
| South Korea | 2.71 | 2 949 | 4 957 | 7.3 | 3.1 | 16.8 | 12.1 | 4.0 | −4.7 | −8.1 |
| Taiwan | 4.61 | 2 430 | 3 256 | 6.0 | 2.1 | 12.3 | 5.9 | 2.9 | −6.4 | −3.0 |
| Macau | n.a. | 422 | 1 372 | 1.0 | 0.9 | 78.4 | 65.6 | 69.1 | −12.8 | +3.5 |
| *Subtotal (inc. China)* | | *12 402* | *54 931* | *29.8* | *27.3* | | | | | |
| *Subtotal (exc. China)* | | *10 777* | *30 882* | *25.8* | *12.1* | | | | | |
| Southeast Asia | | | | | | | | | | |
| Thailand | 0.71 | 267 | 4 620 | 0.7 | 2.9 | 4.1 | 12.2 | 8.2 | +8.1 | −4.0 |
| Indonesia | 0.28 | 98 | 3 367 | 0.2 | 2.1 | 0.4 | 6.4 | 7.4 | +6.0 | +1.0 |
| Malaysia | 0.77 | 150 | 2 272 | 0.4 | 1.4 | 1.2 | 4.5 | 3.1 | +3.3 | −1.4 |
| Singapore | 3.06 | 427 | 1 464 | | — | 2.2 | 3.0 | 1.2 | +0.8 | −1.8 |
| domestic exports | | 354 | 586 | 0.9 | 0.4 | 2.8 | 2.9 | 0.8 | +0.1 | −2.1 |
| re-exports | | 73 | 878 | | — | 1.1 | 3.3 | 1.8 | +2.2 | −1.5 |

| | | | | | | | | | | |
|---|---|---|---|---|---|---|---|---|---|---|
| Philippines | 0.53 | na | 1 065 | n.a | 0.4 | n.a | 8.4 | 6.1 | n.a. | −2.3 |
| *Subtotal* | | *942* | *12 788* | *2.2* | *7.5* | | | | | |
| **South Asia** | | | | | | | | | | |
| India | 0.27 | 590 | 3 701^c | 1.5 | 2.3 | 6.9 | 14.1 | 14.8 | +7.2 | +0.7 |
| Pakistan | 0.27 | 103 | 1 611 | 0.3 | 1.0 | 3.9 | 18.1 | 20.2 | +14.2 | +2.1 |
| Bangladesh | 0.16 | 2 | 1 244^b | 0.0 | 0.8 | 0.2 | 35.0 | 54.8 | +34.8 | +19.8 |
| Sri Lanka | 0.35 | 109 | 1 474^c | 0.3 | 0.9 | 10.2 | 32.2 | 46.0 | +22.0 | +13.8 |
| Mauritius | 1.04 | 73 | 817 | 0.2 | 0.5 | 17.0 | 51.9 | 55.6 | +34.9 | +13.8 |
| *Subtotal* | | *877* | *8 847* | *2.3* | *5.5* | | | | | |

*Notes:*

^a Includes exports from processing zones.

^b 1993.

^c 1996.

* Including wages and social contributions.

Δ1980–90 and Δ1990–95 refer to the increase or decrease in the percentage share of exports during the selected years.

*Sources:* GATT (1994, p. 81); ILO (1995, pp. 35–6); World Bank (1995, pp. 186–7); WTO (1996).

*Table 2.6*  Relative importance of textiles and clothing in the total exports of East Asia's main economies, 1980–95

| East Asian economies | Segment of Apparel Commodity Chain | Share in economy's total merchandise exports (%) | | | |
|---|---|---|---|---|---|
| | | *1980* | *1995* | *Δ1980–90* | *Δ1990–95* |
| Taiwan | Textiles | 9.0 | 10.7 | +0.1 | +1.6 |
| | Clothing | 12.3 | 2.9 | −6.4 | −3.0 |
| | *T & C* | *21.3* | *13.6* | *−6.3* | *−1.4* |
| South Korea | Textiles | 12.6 | 9.8 | −3.3 | +0.5 |
| | Clothing | 16.8 | 4.0 | −4.7 | −8.1 |
| | *T & C* | *29.4* | *13.8* | *−8.0* | *−7.6* |
| Hong Kong | Textiles | 6.6 | 6.1 | +0.9 | −1.4 |
| (*domestic imports*) | Clothing | 34.1 | 31.9 | −2.2 | 0.0 |
| | *T & C* | *40.7* | *38.0* | *−1.3* | *−1.4* |
| Hong Kong | Textiles | 13.0 | 8.3 | −1.7 | −3.0 |
| (*re-exports*) | Clothing | 4.7 | 8.2 | +6.8 | −3.3 |
| | *T & C* | *17.7* | *16.5* | *+5.1* | *−6.3* |
| China | Textiles | 14.0 | 9.4 | −2.4 | −2.2 |
| | Clothing | 8.9 | 16.2 | +6.7 | +0.6 |
| | *T & C* | *22.9* | *25.6* | *+4.3* | *−1.6* |
| Greater China | Textiles | 27.0 | 17.7 | −4.1 | −5.2 |
| (*China plus Hong* | Clothing | 13.6 | 24.4 | +13.5 | −2.7 |
| *Kong re-exports*) | *T & C* | *40.6* | *42.1* | *+9.4* | *−7.9* |

*Notes*:
Δ1980–90 and Δ1990–95 refer to the increase or decrease in the percentage share of exports during the selected years.
Figures in italic are totals for the segment.
T & C Textiles and clothing combined.

*Sources*: GATT *International Trade* (1994, pp. 81–2); WTO (1996).

apparel, footwear and toys. The government's role was more indirect. In South Korea and Taiwan, a key factor that facilitated clothing exports was the establishment of upstream (petrochemicals, synthetic fibres) and midstream (spinning, weaving, dyeing, finishing and knitting) industries that strengthened the overall textile and apparel complex. In these cases, as well as Hong Kong, the major investors were in the private sector, not state firms. State credit, trade and labor policies were supportive, but not determining. By contrast, in high tech industries like semiconductors and computers, the state in the East Asian NIEs has played a more active role in industrial upgrading through the creation of research centres and science based industrial parks, as well as by designating these sectors as 'strategic industries' that are entitled to a variety of special benefits.

The most important policies that shape apparel exports in East Asia are quotas and preferential tariffs imposed by the importing countries. The impact of quotas is very clear in the textile sector. Prior to 1962, when the Long-Term Arrangement that restricted international trade in cotton textiles was established, Korean and Taiwanese textile firms concentrated almost exclusively (90 per cent or more) on cotton textile production. The Long-Term Arrangement, supplemented by the more comprehensive Multifibre Arrangement (MFA) in the early 1970s, encouraged these firms to switch from cotton to synthetic fibres. By the early 1980s, synthetic textiles accounted for 70 per cent of South Korea's textile output and 78 per cent in Taiwan (Park, 1990: 106). This dramatic increase in synthetic textile capacity also shaped each economy's downstream export niches in apparel. Thus, whereas Hong Kong and China are both very strong global competitors in cotton textiles and cotton apparel items, South Korea and Taiwan have specialized in apparel made from synthetic fibres (polyester, nylon and rayon).

Industrial upgrading in the NIEs was one of the major consequences of import quotas for apparel since they permitted successful Asian exporters to maximize the foreign exchange earnings and the profitability of quantitative restrictions (QRs) on trade. Although the clear intent of these policies was to protect developed-country firms from a flood of low cost imports that threatened to disrupt major domestic industries, the result was exactly the opposite: protectionism heightened the competitive capabilities of Third World manufacturers. Protectionism by core countries had a second consequence as well: the diversification of foreign competition. The imposition of quotas on an ever-widening circle of Third World exporters led producers in Japan and the East Asian NIEs, who had to contend with escalating labor costs and US-mandated currency appreciations, to open up new satellite factories in low wage countries that offered either quota or labor advantages.

The product-cycle model predicts that over time exporters will lose their competitive edge in mature products, and become importers. One way to counter this liability is to move from simple to more sophisticated items within an export niche. Furthermore, we should also expect that high-cost exporters will shift from the labor-intensive segments of the apparel commodity chain (clothing) to the more capital- and technology-intensive segments (textiles and fibres). These expectations are quite well supported in East Asia. In response to rapidly growing demand in the domestic apparel market, clothing imports in South Korea rose by 150 per cent in 1989 and 100 per cent in 1990. Similarly, Taiwan's textile and clothing imports more than doubled from US$1.2 billion in 1986 to $2.6 billion in 1991 (Khanna 1993: 25, 29). One of the reasons the Asian Big Three have continued to be significant apparel exporters despite their relatively elevated wages is that they are able to make better quality apparel items that low wage countries like China and Indonesia cannot yet handle. In addition, the Big Three have gained the confidence of Western buyers for their expertise in OEM production, which leads them to be the logical choices for coordinating offshore production networks.

Generally speaking, the downstream sectors (clothing and accessories) in the apparel commodity chain in the East Asian NIEs have lost international competitiveness relative to midstream (textiles) and upstream (man-made fibre) sectors. There is clear evidence that the NIEs are making the transition from finished apparel exports to becoming textile and fibre suppliers for affiliated downstream producers in China, Southeast Asia and South Asia. Taiwan is a classic example of this process. From 1985 to 1994, Taiwan's exports of clothing declined from 56 to 22 per cent of its textile and apparel total, while the share represented by intermediate goods (textile fibres, yarn and fabrics) rose from 44 to 78 per cent (Gereffi and Pan, 1994: 130, supplemented by more recent data from the Taiwan Textile Federation). The trend in South Korea is the same as in Taiwan: textiles have displaced apparel as the export leader in the apparel commodity chain (see Table 2.6).

What the product-cycle model does not explain is how the East Asian NIEs have moved from OEM to OBM production in apparel. Nor does it identify the reasons why the NIEs have such markedly different geographic profiles in their offshore networks. While low wages, quotas, and product-cycles all play significant roles in accounting for the production migrations among Asia's apparel exporters, by themselves they do not adequately account for either industrial upgrading or patterns of internationalization in the East Asian NIEs. A key element in the NIEs successful transition from short-lived comparative advantage based on low labor costs to sustainable forms of competitive advantage that depend on upgrading and outsourcing are the organizational networks and strategies of the firms that actually do the investing, manufacturing and exporting in East Asia. We thus need to adopt a firm-centred perspective to understand how, when, and where the trade and investment networks in East Asia's apparel commodity chain are changing.

One of the most important mechanisms facilitating the shift to higher value added activities for mature export industries like apparel in East

Asia is the process of 'triangle manufacturing'. The essence of triangle manufacturing, which was initiated by the East Asian NIEs in the 1970s and 1980s, is that US (or other overseas) buyers place their orders with the NIE manufacturers they have sourced from in the past, who in turn shift some or all of the requested production to affiliated off-shore factories in low wage countries (e.g. China, Indonesia, or Guatemala). These offshore factories can be wholly-owned subsidiaries of the NIE manufacturers, joint venture partners, or simply independent overseas contractors. The triangle is completed when the finished goods are shipped directly to the overseas buyer under the US import quotas issued to the exporting nation. Triangle manufacturing thus changes the status of NIE manufacturers from established suppliers for US retailers and designers to 'middlemen' in buyer-driven commodity chains that can include as many as 50 to 60 exporting countries (Gereffi, 1994).

Triangle manufacturing networks are socially embedded. Each of the East Asian NIEs has a different set of preferred countries where they set up their new factories. Hong Kong and Taiwan have been the main investors in China; South Korea has been especially prominent in Indonesia, Guatemala, the Dominican Republic, and North Korea; and Singapore is a leading force in Southeast Asian sites, such as Malaysia and Indonesia. These production networks are explained in part by social and cultural factors (e.g. ethnic or familial ties, common language), as well as by unique features of a country's historical legacy (e.g. Hong Kong's British colonial ties gave it an inside track on investments in Mauritius and Jamaica). However, as the volume of orders expands in new low wage production sites, the pressure grows for the large US buyers to eventually bypass their East Asian intermediaries and deal directly with the factories that fill their orders.

In each of the East Asian NIEs, a combination of domestic supply-side constraints (labor shortages, high wages and high land prices) and external pressures (currency revaluation, tariffs and quotas) led to the internationalization of the textile and apparel complex by the late 1980s and early 1990s. Typically, the internationalization of production was sparked first by quotas, but the process was greatly accelerated as supply-side factors became adverse. Quotas determined *when* the outward shift of production began, while preferential access to overseas markets and social networks determined *where* the firms from the East Asian NIEs went. In this international division of labor, labor-intensive activities are relocated and skill-intensive activities are retained. In the apparel sector, the activities associated with OEM production that tended to remain in the NIEs were jobs such as product design, sample making, quality control, packing, warehousing, transportation, quota transactions, and local financing through letters of credit. These provided relatively high gross margins or profits.

The internationalization of Hong Kong's firms was triggered by textile import restrictions imposed by the UK in 1964, which led Hong Kong manufacturers in the late 1960s to shift production to Singapore, Taiwan and Macau. The Chinese population in these three countries had cultural and linguistic affinities with Hong Kong investors. In addition, Macau benefited from its proximity to Hong Kong, while Singapore qualified for Commonwealth preferences for imports into the UK. In the early 1970s, Hong Kong apparel firms targeted Malaysia, Philippines, and Mauritius. This second round of outward investments again was prompted by quota restrictions, coupled with specific host-country inducements. For example, Mauritius established an EPZ in an effort to lure Hong Kong investors, particularly knitwear manufacturers who directed their exports to European markets that offered preferential access in terms of low tariffs.

The greatest spur to the internationalization of Hong Kong's textile and apparel companies was the opening of the Chinese economy in 1978. At first, production was subcontracted to state-owned factories, but eventually an elaborate outward-processing arrangement with China was set up that relied on a broad assortment of manufacturing, financial and commercial joint ventures. Trading companies have replaced export-oriented factories as the key economic agent in Hong Kong's internationalization. Total manufacturing employment fell in Hong Kong during the late 1980s, due in large part to the relocation of industry to the Chinese mainland. In 1991, 47 000 factories were employing 680 000 workers in Hong Kong, a figure 25 per cent below the peak of 907 000 manufacturing jobs recorded in 1980. While manufacturing declined, trading activities in Hong Kong grew to encompass approximately 70 000 firms and 370 000 jobs in 1991, a five-fold increase in the number of firms and a four-fold increase in the number of workers in the trading sector compared to 1978. The Hong Kong Trade Development Council estimated that in the early 1990s, Hong Kong firms were coordinating the production of 25 000 enterprises employing 3 million workers in the neighboring Chinese province of Guangdong. Hong Kong capital controlled about 6000 of these firms, employing a million workers (Khanna 1993: 19). Thus, Hong Kong manufacturers more than quadrupled their domestic labor force through their outward processing arrangement with China.

As in Hong Kong, the internationalization of South Korea's and Taiwan's apparel producers began as a response to quota restrictions.

Korean garment firms lacking sufficient export quotas initially set up production in quota-free locations like Saipan, a US territory in the Mariana Islands. More recent waves of internationalization have been motivated by the domestic constraints of rising wages and worker shortages. The two low wage regions that have attracted the greatest number of South Korean companies are Latin America, and Southeast and South Asia. The preference of Korean firms for investment in Latin America (Guatemala, Honduras, the Dominican Republic, etc.) is stimulated by its proximity to the US market and easy quota access. The pull of Asian nations such as Indonesia, Sri Lanka and Bangladesh comes mainly from their wage rates, which are among the lowest in the world (see Table 2.5).

When Taiwanese firms moved offshore in the early 1980s, they also confronted binding quotas. While Taiwan's wages in the late 1970s and early 1980s were still relatively low, quota rents were high. Firms had to buy quotas (whose value in secondary markets fluctuated widely) in order to be able to expand exports, thereby causing a decrease in profitability for firms without sufficient quota (Appelbaum and Gereffi, 1994). This led to a growing emphasis on non-quota markets by Taiwan's textile and apparel exporters. Quota markets (the USA, the European Community and Canada) accounted for over 50 per cent of Taiwan's textile and apparel exports in the mid-1980s, but this ratio declined to 43 per cent in 1988 and fell further to 35 per cent in 1991. The USA, which had been Taiwan's largest export market for years, claimed one-quarter of Taiwan's textile and apparel exports in 1991, the European Community 8 per cent, and Canada just 2 per cent. The main non-quota markets, which absorbed nearly two-thirds of Taiwan's textile and apparel exports in the early 1990s, are Hong Kong (30 per cent), Japan (6 per cent), and Singapore (3 per cent) (Khanna, 1993: 29–30). Hong Kong, now Taiwan's leading export market, is mainly a conduit for shipping yarns, fabrics, and clothing to China for further processing and re-export.

Two trends – the shift from OEM to OBM, and the growing importance of non-quota markets for the NIEs – point to an important fact: production and trade networks in the apparel commodity chain are becoming increasingly concentrated in Asia. Table 2.7 indicates a sharp decline in Asian clothing exports to North America (from 27 per cent of the global total in 1984 to 17 per cent in 1995), a levelling off in Asian textile and apparel exports to Western Europe, and a striking increase in intra-Asian trade in apparel (from 4 per cent in 1980 to over 13 per cent in 1995). This rise in intra-Asian trade is even stronger

*Table* 2.7    Regional trade patterns in world exports of textiles and clothing, 1980–95

| | Textiles | | | | |
|---|---|---|---|---|---|
| | *1980* | *1984* | *1987* | *1990* | *1995* |
| World (US$ billion) | $55.6 | $53.9 | $80.2 | $104.8 | $152.6 |
| World (%) | 100.0 | 100.0 | 100.0 | 100.0 | 100.0 |
| Intra-Western Europe | 40.1 | 34.9 | 40.0 | 41.4 | 30.9 |
| Intra-Asia | 13.1 | 17.4 | 18.2 | 20.6 | 28.4 |
| Asia to Western Europe | 1.6 | 4.6 | 5.9 | 5.6 | 5.5 |
| Western Europe to C./E. Europe/Baltic States/CIS | na | na | na | 2.3 | 4.0 |
| Asia to North America | 2.9 | 5.4 | 4.9 | 3.6 | 3.7 |
| Asia to the Middle East | na | na | na | 2.2 | 2.9 |
| Western Europe to Asia | 1.6 | 2.4 | 2.0 | 3.0 | 2.9 |
| Western Europe to North America | 1.6 | 3.2 | 2.9 | 2.4 | 1.9 |
| Other | 39.1 | 32.1 | 26.1 | 21.2 | 19.8 |

| | Clothing | | | | |
|---|---|---|---|---|---|
| | *1980* | *1984* | *1987* | *1990* | *1995* |
| World (US$ billion) | $41.8 | $48.2 | $81.9 | $106.4 | $157.9 |
| World (%) | 100.0 | 100.0 | 100.0 | 100.0 | 100.0 |
| Intra-Western Europe | 36.6 | 29.3 | 33.7 | 35.2 | 27.7 |
| Asia to North America | 14.8 | 26.8 | 22.5 | 19.5 | 16.8 |
| Intra-Asia | 4.3 | 6.2 | 6.0 | 8.8 | 12.8 |
| Asia to Western Europe | 14.4 | 11.0 | 13.2 | 12.9 | 11.7 |
| Latin America to North America | 1.7 | 2.1 | 2.3 | 2.4 | 4.6 |
| C./E. Europe/Baltic States/CIS to Western Europe | na | na | na | na | 3.9 |
| Africa to Western Europe | 1.9 | 1.2 | 2.1 | na | na |
| Other | 26.3 | 23.4 | 20.2 | 21.1 | 22.5 |

*Sources*: GATT, *International Trade* (various years); WTO (1996).

in textiles, where it increases from 13 per cent of the world total in 1980 to 28 per cent in 1995. Asia's growing prominence as a market for its own textile and apparel output, and the continuing migration of production to low cost supply sites around the world, suggest a general movement may be under way toward a regionalization of the apparel commodity chain within Asia, North America, and Europe. The emerging supply relationships that are being fashioned with nearby low cost producers in each area (Vietnam and North Korea in Asia, Central America and the Caribbean *vis-à-vis* North America, and North

Africa and Eastern Europe for the European Union (EU)) are likely to strengthen intra-regional trade and production networks in the apparel commodity chain, thereby giving rise to new forms of economic coordination and competition among local as well as global firms.

## COMPETING US AND JAPANESE PRODUCTION NETWORKS IN THE ASIAN ELECTRONICS COMMODITY CHAIN

There are opposing images of US and Japanese production networks in East Asia's electronics sector. US networks are considered to be relatively open and conducive to local development in host countries, while Japanese networks are perceived as closed and hierarchical with activities confined within affiliates that are tightly controlled by the parent company. Borrus (1994) argues that this contrast in network structures is the main reason why Japanese companies have faltered in industrial electronics in the 1990s and why leadership in the electronics sector has been restored to US firms:

> In Asia today, beneath the superficial similarity engendered by aggregate trade and investment data and macro-analyses, lie distinctly different electronics production networks under the control of U.S. versus Japanese multinationals. The U.S. networks tend to be open to outsiders, fast and flexible in decision-making and implementation, structured through formal, legal relationships and capable of changing contour (and patterns) as needs change – in an image: open, fast, flexible, formal, and disposable. Their activities are centered in the NICs, especially Singapore and Taiwan, but increasingly reach into the rest of Asia and China. By contrast, the Japanese networks tend to be relatively closed to outsiders, slower to make and implement decisions that are generated from Japan, and structured on stable, long-term business and *keiretsu* relationships – that is, closed, slow, rigid, long-term and stable. They are most definitely centered in Japan. (Borrus 1994: 142)

As we will see below, these US and Japanese electronics networks in East Asia utilize distinct supply bases, boast different product mixes and, most significantly, they have established competing divisions of labor within the same geographic space.

The development of Asian production networks in electronics can be traced through three stages. In the first stage (late 1960s–1970s), the investment of most US electronics firms in Asia was motivated by their search for cheap production locations, while Japanese investments in Asia were primarily aimed at supplying nascent local markets behind high tariff walls. Although the assembly-oriented nature of both Japanese and US investments in this first stage may appear similar on the surface, the contrasted export strategies of the core firms led these networks to evolve differently:

> Because their Asian affiliates were integrated into a production operation serving advanced country markets, U.S. firms upgraded their Asian investments in line with the pace of development of the lead market being served, the U.S. market. In essence, they upgraded in line with U.S. rather than local product cycles. By contrast, Japanese firms were led to upgrade the technological capabilities of their Asian investments only at the slower pace necessary to serve lagging local markets. (Borrus, 1994: 134–5)

During the second stage (1980–85), US affiliates in Asia began to source more parts and components domestically. The networks of US transnationals made increasingly sophisticated industrial electronics products like hard disk drives, personal computers, ink-jet printers, and telecom devices. The Japanese networks supplied consumer audiovisual electronics like television sets and videocassette recorders, as well as appliances. As the US industry shifted from consumer to industrial electronics, local producers in places like Taiwan began to follow. A new supply base thus emerged in the East Asian NIEs under the control of US and local, but not Japanese, capital. Meanwhile, Japanese investment created a dual production structure premised on traditional product-cycles: Japanese firms supplied both the domestic and US markets with sophisticated items made in Japan, while local Asian markets received simple low end products made by Japanese subsidiaries in the region.

In the third stage (1985–early 1990s), the division of labor between US affiliates and local producers in East Asia deepened significantly. US electronics transnationals set up Asian networks based on a 'complementary' division of labor: US firms specialized in 'soft' competencies (the definition of standards, designs, and product architecture) and the Asian firms specialized in 'hard' competencies (the provision of components and basic manufacturing stages). The Asian affiliates of US firms developed extensive subcontracting relationships with local manufacturers, who in turn became increasingly skilled suppliers of components, subassemblies and, in some cases, entire electronics systems. By contrast, Japanese networks were characterized by market segmentation and significant production redundancies: electronics firms in Japan made high value, high end products, while their offshore subsidiaries in Asia continued to make low value, low end products (Borrus 1994: 143). While the US networks maximized the contributions from their Asian affiliates, Japanese networks minimized the value added by their regional suppliers.

Apple Computer provides a good illustration of the Asian sourcing networks set up by US firms (Borrus, 1994: 138–9). Apple Computers Singapore (ACS) opened a printed circuit board assembly plant for the Apple II personal computer in 1981. By 1990, ACS was expanded and upgraded to include final assembly of a variety of Apple computer models for the world market. Virtually all components were sourced in Asia (except the US-made microprocessor), and ACS' network of local suppliers grew from nine firms in 1983 to 130 companies by 1990. In 1993, ACS set up a design centre for Macintosh's high volume desk top products (Apple's only hardware design centre outside the USA) and in 1994, ACS became the distribution, logistics, sales and marketing centre for the Asia-Pacific region. Regional sourcing amounted to $2 billion, with Japan accounting for one-half of the total (liquid crystal displays, peripherals, memory, hard disk drives), and Singapore for one-quarter. Taiwan made $250–$500 million worth of merchandise for ACS (OEM supply of low end desktops, printed circuit boards, a Powerbook model and chips), while Korea's Samsung supplied some of the monitors.

The geography of the electronics commodity chain in Asia has changed over time. Henderson (1989) found that Hong Kong was the regional and technological core of East Asia's US-dominated semiconductor industry in the late 1960s. By the mid-1980s, however, Singapore had displaced Hong Kong as the favored location in East Asia for technologically advanced electronics investments, such as wafer fabrication plants, 4- and 16-megabit DRAMs, hard disk drives, and some microprocessors (Lim and Pang, 1991; Henderson, 1994). Furthermore, Southeast Asia has begun to challenge South Korea and Taiwan as the favored Asian production site for new as well as mature electronics products.

Southeast Asia has enjoyed some of the 'advantages of lateness' *vis-à-vis* the East Asian NIEs, but this occurs in distinct ways in Japanese and US production networks. Southeast Asian subsidiaries of Japanese electronics transnationals often are preferred over their Korean and Taiwanese competitors, in part because the Southeast Asian affiliates have access to the latest production technologies used by their

Japanese parent firms. Between 1989 and 1991, for example, Japanese imports of color televisions from Korea and Taiwan fell from 1.6 to 1.3 million units, while Japan's imports of color televisions from Malaysia during this same period soared from 2000 to 385 000 units. By 1991, Malaysia had replaced Taiwan as the second largest supplier of color television imports to Japan, and Malaysia became the largest exporter of radio cassette recorders to the Japanese market (Bernard and Ravenhill, 1995: 198). The advantages for Southeast Asia in this case may be more apparent than real, since the Southeast Asian companies in Japan's production networks are subsidiaries of Japanese transnationals, whose ultimate loyalty is to their home economy, while their Korean and Taiwanese competitors are local manufacturers with more substantial domestic linkages in the NIEs.

Whereas Japanese networks benefited Southeast Asia by displacing Korean and Taiwanese sales of a mature product (color televisions) in Japan, US networks have moved in the opposite direction: they produce more sophisticated exports in Southeast Asia than those available in the East Asian NIEs. In the early 1980s, Malaysia, Singapore, and Philippines were the main manufacturing sites for relatively advanced metal oxide semiconductor (MOS) digital integrated circuits (ICs), while US transnationals in Korea and Taiwan used much simpler technology to export lower value added bipolar digital ICs and linear ICs (UNCTC, 1986: 350–1). The reason these Southeast Asian nations leapfrogged Korea and Taiwan in advanced semiconductor production involves issues of timing and organizational path dependence in US electronics networks. The emergence of MOS as the predominant technology in the 1970s coincided with the rapid expansion of US transnationals into the lower cost assembly locations of Southeast Asia. The new entrants into the offshore assembly business – Malaysia, Singapore, and Philippines – received the largest share of US transnational investments using the MOS technology, while the earlier NIE entrants – Hong Kong, Taiwan, Korea and Mexico – continued to make the mature semiconductor products they began with in the 1960s (Grunwald and Flamm, 1985: 70–1).

Company strategy is a key variable in the evolution of both US and Japanese electronics production networks. Particular companies often are responsible for creating significant export niches for national suppliers. Barbados, for instance, had an unusually high average unit value for its semiconductor exports to the USA in the 1980s. The explanation in this case was straightforward: the overwhelming share of US imports of ICs from Barbados consisted of high value MOS memories and microprocessors assembled within Intel's new subsidiary there (UNCTC, 1986: 353). Thus the 'Barbados effect' was really an 'Intel effect'. Similarly, Dieter Ernst, who believes that Japanese electronics firms are likely to switch to more open regional production networks in Asia, bolsters his argument by reference to the strategies of leading Japanese companies. Hitachi and NEC are taking the initiative in establishing more extensive local procurement networks in East Asia, with NEC's Hong Kong subsidiary in charge of redesigning the motherboard so it can use more of the cheaper, standard components available from Korean, Taiwanese, and perhaps even Chinese suppliers (Ernst, 1994: 43). This trend suggests the possibility of a partial convergence in the production strategies of Japanese and US transnationals.

Product-cycle dynamics vary in apparel and electronics because trade networks operate quite differently in the two sectors. In the 'triangle manufacturing' arrangement that characterizes East Asia's apparel commodity chain, US companies typically supply orders, not inputs; manufacturers in the East Asian NIEs act as intermediaries by passing these orders, and frequently material and service inputs, to contractors in Southeast Asia and China who make the goods on an OEM basis. The exports are then shipped back to the originating country (the USA), utilizing where needed the quotas of the exporting nation. In this fashion, the product-cycle is completed in BDCCs. In the electronics commodity chain, there is a different mechanism known as 'trade triangles' (Bernard and Ravenhill, 1995). Inputs are purchased from Japan (or more recently, South Korea and Taiwan), processed in the NIEs (and increasingly Southeast Asia and China), and exported to third-country markets rather than Japan. The product-cycle in this case fails to go full circle because firms in the originating country (Japan) have not exited from the market. Instead, Japanese companies supply the core technologies and continue to be involved in the production of consumer goods.

## CONCLUSIONS

Prevailing explanations of international competitiveness have been hampered by their inability to move beyond the increasingly sterile debate about the role of states versus markets, and to come to grips with new trends in the organization of production on a world scale. This study argues that the GCCs perspective introduces a critical axis of variation in understanding the evolution of regional divisions of labor in the Third World. PDCCs and BDCCs are based on different types of production and trade networks, they are driven by different types of lead firms, they incorporate different sets of countries into their regional hierarchies, and they have different consequences for industrial upgrading. These trends can be seen most clearly in Asia's various subregions.

The electronics commodity chain in East Asia, which embodies the producer-driven type, is held together in large part by Japanese and US transnationals. These companies have orchestrated regional production hierarchies in which Singapore, South Korea and Taiwan are prominent in the second tier, well below Japan's core status, and Malaysia, Thailand and Philippines are growing third-tier suppliers. While Japanese transnationals have been the leaders in consumer electronics commodity chains, US transnationals are the front-runners in industrial electronics. Furthermore, the dynamics of the trade networks set up by the Japanese and US electronics transnationals are quite distinct. The Japanese networks perpetuate a dualistic system in which electronics production in Japan serves developed-country markets, while the output from Japanese affiliates in Asia serve developing-country markets. By contrast, US electronics transnationals have upgraded the capabilities of their suppliers in the East Asian NIEs and Southeast Asia to meet the sophisticated demand emanating from the US market. This strategy tends to maximize the local value added by Asian contractors in US electronics networks and to promote industrial upgrading in the second and third tiers of the region. In Japan's regional electronics networks, the Asian contribution has been minimized and Japan remains a key supplier of components and new technologies.

The apparel commodity chain, which is buyer-driven, operates very differently. The core companies are not manufacturing transnationals, but US and European buyers that have set up elaborate specification contracting or OEM supply systems encompassing dozens of countries in virtually every corner of the globe. Within Asia, the apparel commodity chain is centred in Hong Kong and China, which together represent over one-fifth of world clothing exports. These two countries play relatively minor roles, however, as exporters in Asia's producer-driven chains. The regional hierarchy for textile and apparel production in Asia has many levels, with Hong Kong, Taiwan and South Korea being the principal intermediaries for US and, to a lesser degree, European retailers and designers. These East Asian NIEs, in turn, subcontract the majority of their orders and provide a wide range of inputs to clothing factories in Southeast Asia, South Asia, Central America, the Caribbean and other parts of the world. The double shift in the role of East Asian NIE suppliers in the apparel commodity chain – from finished to intermediate goods exporters, and from OEM to OBM producers – has led to a substantial rise in the intra-Asian share of global textile and clothing exports, thereby contributing to greater regional closure of the apparel commodity chain within Asia.

The OEM process itself works differently in these producer-driven and buyer-driven chains. In producer-driven chains, transnational manufacturers use numerous subsidiaries and subcontractors to make both components and finished goods, but these core companies also are concerned with safeguarding their proprietary technologies from potential competitors. Japanese electronics transnationals dealt with this problem through 'closed' networks with very little technology transfer to their Southeast Asian affiliates, while US transnationals relied on 'open' networks to tap the relatively advanced technological and manufacturing skills of their subcontractors in the East Asian NIEs. The possibility for an OEM supplier to improve its position in producer-driven chains is enhanced if the technology gap with the lead transnationals is small (rather than large), if it produces unique (rather than standard) components, if it makes sophisticated (rather than simple) finished products, and if the subcontractor complements (rather than duplicates) the capabilities of the core firm. The rapid industrial upgrading experienced by the Korean and Taiwanese firms in the production networks of US electronics transnationals derives from the fact that they made specialized components and high-end finished products for the US market, and these two NIEs had the ability to form local subcontracting networks which the US transnationals could not duplicate. These factors allowed South Korea and Taiwan to reduce (but by no means eliminate) the technological gap with leading Japanese as well as US companies, and thus enhance their production and export options.

In buyer-driven chains, there appears to be more opportunity for learning and entrepreneurship by contractors in the OEM relationship. A number of successful East Asian producers eventually became major brandname competitors to their US clients. Well known cases include the Fang Brothers in Hong Kong, a large apparel manufacturer that now competes at the retail level in Asia and the United States with its main US customer, Liz Claiborne, and the Giant bicycle company in Taiwan that made most of Schwinn's bikes on an OEM basis before coming out with its own nameplate in the late 1980s, a move that eventually helped drive Schwinn into bankruptcy. The opportunity for producers in other regions, like Latin America, to move from OEM to OBM is extremely limited because the lower tier contractors there are only entrusted with recruiting workers and assembling finished goods using imported inputs. Therefore these manufacturers do not develop the skills nor can they count on the diversified array of local collaborators utilized by East Asia's full-package suppliers (Gereffi and Hempel, 1996).

Commodity chains in Asia encompass coherent trade and investment networks that lie below the aggregate picture for the entire region but 'above' the interactions between states. Nonetheless, these production systems must be grounded in local contexts. In this regard, the shared understandings embodied in institutionalized conventions are extremely important. When we look closely at the multiplicity of industrial, commercial, and financial networks that make up East Asia's highly successful form of OEM production, it is evident that numerous conventions underpin the functioning of both the micro and macro institutions and routines that allow this system to operate. The importance of conventions grows in direct proportion to the spatial and cultural distances implied by globalization. Understanding East Asian development requires far more than a 'market friendly' environment, export promotion, and selective state interventions. International competitiveness by East Asian firms has been spurred by organizational learning through networks and it is anchored in conventions that are an amalgam of Western and Asian institutions, norms, and practices. New and potential entrants into the apparel and electronics commodity chains that link East Asia with the rest of the world are likely to find that the unwritten conventions of these product worlds are every bit as important as modern technologies and regulatory frameworks in accounting for economic success.

**Notes**

1. The subsequent discussion of these roles draws substantially from Gereffi (1995).
2. This section of the chapter, including the analysis of the apparel and the electronics industries, is taken from Gereffi (1996).

# References

Amsden, A.H. (1989), *Asia's Next Giant: South Korea and Late Industrialization* (New York: Oxford University Press).

Appelbaum, R.P. and G. Gereffi. 1994. 'Power and Profits in the Apparel Commodity Chain', in E. Bonacich, L. Cheng, N. Chinchilla, N. Hamilton and P. Ong (eds), *Global Production: The Apparel Industry in the Pacific Rim* (Philadelphia: Temple University Press: 42–62).

Bernard, M. and J. Ravenhill (1995), 'Beyond Product Cycles and Flying Geese: Regionalization, Hierarchy, and the Industrialization of East Asia', *World Politics*, 47(2) (January): 171–209.

Borrus, M. (1994), 'Left for Dead: Asian Production Networks and the Revival of U.S. Electronics', in E.M. Doherty (ed.), *Japanese Investment in Asia: International Production Strategies in a Rapidly Changing World* (San Francisco: The Asia Foundation and the University of California's Berkeley Roundtable on the International Economy (BRIE)): 125–46.

Cawthorne, Z. (1993), 'Paris Chapter for Episode', *South China Morning Post*, (24 July).

Chen, X. (1994a), 'The Changing Roles of Free Economic Zones in Development: A Comparative Analysis of Capitalist and Socialist Cases in East Asia', *Studies in Comparative International Development*, 29(3) (Fall): 3–25.

Chen, X. (1994b), 'The New Spatial Division of Labor and Commodity Chains in the Greater South China Economic Region', in G. Gereffi and M. Korzeniewicz (eds), *Commodity Chains and Global Capitalism* (Westport: Praeger).

Cheng, L.-L. and G. Gereffi (1994), 'The Informal Economy in East Asian Development', *International Journal of Urban and Regional Research* 18(2) (June): 194–219.

Chu, Y. (1994), 'The East Asian NICs: A State-led Path to the Developed World', in B. Stallings (ed.), *Global Change, Regional Response: The New International Context of Development* (New York: Cambridge University Press).

Deyo, F.C. (1989), *Beneath the Miracle: Labor Subordination in the New Asian Industrialism* (Berkeley and Los Angeles: University of California Press).

Dicken, P. (1992), *Global Shift: The Internationalization of Economic Activity* (New York: Guilford), 2nd edn.

Doner, R.F. (1991), *Driving a Bargain: Automobile Industrialization and Japanese Firms in Southeast Asia* (Berkeley: University of California Press).

Ernst, D. (1994) 'Carriers of Regionalization: The East Asian Production Networks of Japanese Electronics Firms', *BRIE Working Paper*, 73 (November) (Berkeley: University of California's Berkeley Roundtable on the International Economy (BRIE)).

Florida, R. and M. Kenney (1991), 'Transplanted Organizations: The Transfer of Japanese Industrial Organization to the United States', *American Sociological Review*, 61(3) (June): 381–98.

Fowdar, N. (1991), 'Textiles and Clothing in Mauritius', *Textile Outlook International*, 38 (November): 68–86.

General Agreement on Tariffs and Trade (GATT) (1994), *International Trade: Trends and Statistics 1994* (Geneva: GATT).

Gereffi, G. (1994), 'The Organization of Buyer-Driven Global Commodity Chains: How US Retailers Shape Overseas Production Networks', in G. Gereffi and M. Korzeniewicz (eds), *Commodity Chains and Global Capitalism* edited by (Westport: Praeger), 98–122.

Gereffi, G. (1995), 'Global Production Systems and Third World Development', in B. Stallings (ed.), *Global Change, Regional Response: The New International Context of Development* (New York: Cambridge University Press).

Gereffi, G. (1996), 'Commodity Chains and Regional Divisions of Labor in East Asia', *Journal of Asian Business* 12(1): 75–112.

Gereffi, G. and L. Hempel (1996), 'Latin America in the Global Economy: Running Faster to Stay in Place', *NACLA Report on the Americas*, 29(4) (January/February): 18–27.

Gereffi, G. and M. Korzeniewicz (1990), 'Commodity Chains and Footwear Exports in the Semiperiphery', in W. Martin (ed.), *Semiperipheral States in the World-Economy*, (Westport: Greenwood Press), 45–68.

Gereffi, G. and M.-L. Pan (1994), 'The Globalization of Taiwan's Garment Industry', in E. Bonacich, L. Cheng, N. Chinchilla, N. Hamilton and P. Ong (eds) *Global Production: The Apparel Industry in the Pacific Rim* (Philadelphia: Temple University Press): 126–46.

Gereffi, G. and D.L. Wyman (eds) (1990), *Manufacturing Miracles: Paths of Industrialization in Latin America and East Asia* (Princeton: Princeton University Press).

Grunwald, J. and K. Flamm (1985), *The Global Factory: Foreign Assembly in International Trade* (Washington, DC: Brookings Institution).

Henderson, J. (1989), *The Globalisation of High Technology Production: Society, Space and Semiconductors in the Restructuring of the Modern World* (London and New York: Routledge).

Henderson, J. (1994), 'Electronics Industries and the Developing World: Uneven Contributions and Uncertain Prospects', in L. Sklair (ed.), *Capitalism and Development* (London: Routledge): 258–88.

Hill, R.C. (1989), 'Comparing Transnational Production Systems: The Automobile Industry in the USA and Japan', *International Journal of Urban and Regional Research*, 13(3) (September): 462–80.

Hong Kong Government Industry Department (1992), *Techno-Economic and Market Research Study of Hong Kong's Textile and Clothing Industries, 1991–1992* (Hong Kong: Government Printing Office).

International Labor Organization (ILO) (1995), *Recent Developments in the Clothing Industry*, Report I (Geneva: ILO).

Keesing, D.B. (1983), 'Linking Up to Distant Markets: South to North Exports of Manufactured Consumer Goods'. *American Economic Review*, 73: 338–42.

Khanna, S.R. (1993), 'Structural Changes in Asian Textiles and Clothing Industries: The Second Migration of Production', *Textile Outlook International*, 49 (September): 11–32.

Kim, H.K. and S.-H. Lee (1994), 'Commodity Chains and the Korean Automobile Industry', in G. Gereffi and M. Korzeniewicz (eds), *Commodity Chains and Global Capitalism* (Westport: Praeger): 281–96.

Lee, N. and J. Cason (1994), 'Automobile Commodity Chains in the NICs: A Comparison of South Korea, Mexico, and Brazil', in G. Gereffi and M.

Korzeniewicz (eds), *Commodity Chains and Global Capitalism* (Westport: Praeger).

Levy, B. (1988), 'Korean and Taiwanese Firms as International Competitors: The Challenges Ahead', *Columbia Journal of World Business* (Spring): 43–51.

Lim, L.Y.C. and P.E. Fong (1991), *Foreign Direct Investment and Industrialization in Malaysia, Singapore, Taiwan and Thailand* (Paris: OECD Development Centre).

Newfarmer, R. (ed.) (1985), *Profits, Progress and Poverty: Case Studies of International Industries in Latin America* (Notre Dame: University of Notre Dame Press).

Organization for Economic Co-operation and Development (OECD) (1988), *The Newly Industrializing Countries: Challenge and Opportunity for OECD Industries* (Paris: OECD).

O'Rourke, M.T. (1992), 'Labor Costs – From Pakistan to Portugal', *Bobbin* 34 (1) (September): 116–122.

Park, Y. (1990), 'A Sequential Development of the Textile and Clothing Industries in Northeast Asia and China's Effect on World Markets', *Pacific Focus* 5(2) (Fall): 91–113.

Pogoda, D.M. (1992), 'Two Foreign Retailers Find Niche in U.S.', *Women's Wear Daily* (7 July).

Porter, M. (1990), *The Competitive Advantage of Nations* (New York: Free Press).

Republic of China (1991), Council for Economic Planning and Development *Taiwan Statistical Yearbook* (Taiwan).

Republic of China (1994) Council for Economic Planning and Development, *Taiwan Statistical Data Book* (Taiwan).

Selwyn, M. (1993), 'Radical Departures', *Asian Business* (August): 22–25.

Sklair, L. (1993), *Assembling for Development: The Maquila Industry in Mexico and the United States* (La Jolla, CA: Center for U.S.–Mexican Studies, University of California, San Diego).

Tran, A.N. (1995), 'Can the Vietnamese State Play a Developmental Role? Integrating the Vietnamese Textile and Garment Industries into the Global Economy' (unpublished manuscript).

United Nations Centre on Transnational Corporations (UNCTC) (1986), *Transnational Corporations in the International Semiconductor Industry* (New York: UNCTC).

Wade, R. (1990), *Governing the Market: Economic Theory and the Role of Government in East Asian Industrialization* (Princeton: Princeton University Press).

World Bank (1982) *World Development Report 1982* (New York: Oxford University Press).

World Bank (1983) *World Development Report 1983* (New York: Oxford University Press).

World Bank (1992), *World Development Report 1992* (New York: Oxford University Press).

World Bank (1993), *The East Asian Miracle: Economic Growth and Public Policy* (New York: Oxford University Press).

World Bank (1994), *World Development Report 1994* (New York: Oxford University Press).

World Bank (1995), *World Development Report 1995* (New York: Oxford University Press).

World Trade Organisation (WTO) (1996) *Annual Report* (Geneva: WTO).

# 3 Changing International Division of Labour in the Electronics Industry[1]

Jeffrey Henderson

## INTRODUCTION

This chapter is concerned with the implications for labour forces of the emergence and transformation of a number of related international divisions of labour in the electronics industry. It describes the locational and technical features of these divisions of labour and outlines their causal dynamics. Throughout, however, the report emphasizes that issues of employment, wages, working conditions, etc. should be seen as only part of our concern. Equally as important as these are the questions of whether investment by multinational enterprises or domestic companies, in addition to the generation of jobs, leads over time to more technology-intensive production processes and products, a proliferation of human capabilities through linkages to domestic suppliers, and thus to the creation of higher value added in the economy. Only in this way can demands for higher skill, higher wage forms of employment be realized and general prosperity, together with low levels of income inequality, begin to be delivered.

In what follows it will be argued that achievement of these goals cannot be left to the market-driven operations of companies themselves. Left to their own devices companies will produce divisions of labour consistent with their own strategic requirements and these are not necessarily conducive to the economic health of workers or nations. Drawing on examples from East Asia it will be shown that in many cases government intervention in various forms has been necessary to deliver the economic package out of which skilled employment, rising wages and the rest arises.

We begin by outlining some of the general issues associated with electronics industries. Concentrating largely on the developing economies of East Asia, we then proceed to identify two related international divisions of labour that have emerged in recent years and already outlined in Chapter 2 of this book: one organized and driven by the strategic interests of multinational enterprises (MNEs); the other driven by major buyers in the USA, European Union and Japan, but organized in 'commodity chains' via a dense network of subcontracting firms. In this discussion, we shall focus on the causal dynamics of these evolving divisions of labour and on their implications for the nature of the electronics industries and their labour forces in particular locations. We then outline some of the explanatory issues connected with these divisions of labour and their impact, before moving, finally, to discuss the implications of the analysis for labour forces at various nodes of the global electronics production system.

## GENERAL FEATURES OF THE ELECTRONICS INDUSTRY

The electronics industry probably employs more people globally than any other manufacturing industry with the exception of textiles and garments. As can be seen from Table 3.1, for a selection of electronics producing economies, employment in the electronics industry ranges from around 6–7 per cent of total paid manufacturing employment in Brazil, China, India and Canada to 9 per cent in the USA, 15–17 per cent in the Republic of Korea and Japan, 22 per cent in Malaysia and 41 per cent in Singapore. Like textiles and garments, but unlike engineering and chemicals, for instance, electronics industries tend to employ large proportions of women. Thus, in most electronics producing economies, close to half the work force tends to be women – overwhelmingly employed in lower skill assembly jobs although in Hong Kong and Singapore the proportions approach, or are in excess of, two-thirds (Table 3.1).

Electronics industries are significant for the global economy for reasons other than merely the employment they provide. They are significant additionally in ways that far outstrip textiles and garments and a number of other manufacturing industries in terms of their importance for national and regional economic and social development. This is the case, first, because the higher technology content of their products and production processes provides the capability of delivering higher productivity and value added, and hence rapid economic growth coupled with faster increases in general prosperity. Secondly, because they tend to be capital- and knowledge-intensive industries, they stimulate domestic demands for engineers and technicians and thus exert pressure on governments to upgrade their education systems. Thirdly, as with

*Table* 3.1   Paid employment in electronics industries (1000s), selected countries*, selected years

| | Total manufacturing | Total electronics | % electronics | Men | Women | % women |
|---|---|---|---|---|---|---|
| USA [1991] | 18 426 | 1 591 | 8.6 | 918 | 673 | 42.3 |
| Japan [1989] | 10 776 | 1 798 | 16.7 | | | |
| Germany [1989] | 8 364 | 173 | 2.1 | n.a. | n.a. | |
| Italy [1989] | 4 054 | 264 | 6.5 | n.a. | n.a. | |
| UK [1989] | 5 405 | 530 | 9.8 | | | |
| France [1989] | 4 338 | 218 | 5.0 | n.a. | n.a. | |
| Canada [1989] | 1 878 | 128 | 6.8 | n.a. | n.a. | |
| Korea [1990] | 3 038 | 456 | 15.0 | 234 | 222 | 48.7 |
| Singapore [1990] | 352 | 145 | 41.2 | 42 | 103 | 71.0 |
| Hong Kong [1990] | 716 | 85 | 11.8 | 34 | 51 | 60.0 |
| Malaysia [1988] | 596 | 132 | 22.1 | n.a. | n.a. | |
| Indonesia [1986] | 1 691 | 39 | 2.3 | n.a. | n.a. | |
| Philippines [1987] | 671 | 43 | 6.4 | n.a. | n.a. | |
| India [1988] | 6 261 | 410 | 6.5 | 375 | 36 | 8.8 |
| China [1991] | 54 428 | 3 641 | 6.7 | 1 899 | 1 742 | 47.8 |
| Brazil [1988] | 5 736 | 330 | 5.8 | n.a. | n.a. | |
| Mexico [1991] | 953 | 84 | 8.8 | n.a. | n.a. | |

*Notes*:
[a] Data is for 383 category of ISIC – 1968.
   n.a. = Not available.

*Sources*: Derived ILO (1992, Table 5B:501–64). For Germany, Italy, the UK and France, data for employment in the electronics industry are derived from the UNIDO database.

automobile industries, they generate substantial demands for specialized supplies, components and services and hence provide opportunities for the development of production linkages with myriad other companies. In other words, electronics industries offer the possibility of substantial add-on effects in terms of further employment, skill upgrading and increasing capital and knowledge intensity in related industries. Finally electronics industries have an image of being relatively non-polluting, providing pleasant working environments, and being capable of delivering high incomes relative, for instance, to the 'sweatshops' of the garment industry.

   The problem with all this is that while the potential for electronics industries to make major contributions to skill-upgrading, economic growth and prosperity is clearly there, its realization has been very uneven. This uneven contribution has been evident in the geographic spread of the industries; in their levels of technological intensity; in their capacity to generate higher skill, higher wage employment; and in their ability to provide a major pay-off in terms of genuine development.

When we speak of global electronics production in terms of output and exports, we are speaking in effect of only seventeen national economies (see Table 3.2). These are: the technological and productive giants – the USA and Japan; the European industrial economies – Germany, France, Britain, Italy, Netherlands and Switzerland; Canada; the East Asian NIEs – the Republic of Korea (hereafter Korea), Taiwan (POC), Singapore and Hong Kong; the Southeast Asian near-NIEs; the Latin American NIEs – principally Brazil; and China. Four things are of additional note here; India, Thailand and Mexico may develop significant electronics industries as we approach the twenty-first century; the Philippines, though previously significant as a labour-intensive assembly base, is now much less so; Vietnam could become an important location for electronics production, now that the problem of the US trade embargo has been resolved; and in comparison with the output of developed industrial economies, the electronics industries of the developing world, with the exceptions of those in Korea, Taiwan (POC) and Singapore and (to some extent) China, remain minor players.

Within these economic and spatial concentrations of electronics production there exist substantial variations. In the industrial economies these vary from the global dominance of Japanese consumer electronics companies to the twin domination of Japanese and US companies in semiconductors; from the domination of US companies in computers, communications and industrial electronics, to the persistent structural weakness of the EU industries, with the exception of telecommunications, relative to Japan and the USA (Table 3.2; Hobday, 1992a).

Within the developing world's electronics industries there are even greater variations. The East Asian NIEs – particularly Korea and Taiwan (POC) – have the largest and most technologically sophisticated industries which in some product areas (semiconductors and consumer electronics in Korea, microcomputers in Taiwan (POC)) are beginning to compete directly with the dominant Japanese, US and European producers. There and only there at present is there any possibility of firms moving to the innovation-led forms of competition necessary to become major players in the world electronics industry. Singapore is probably at a higher level technologically, though its industry is overwhelmingly foreign-owned and its domestic firms, with a few exceptions, remain underdeveloped. Malaysia and, increasingly, Thailand have significant industries but, like Singapore, these are largely foreign-owned and in spite of some recent upgrading (particularly in Malaysia) generally do not contain the most capital- and knowledge-intensive parts of the production system which are capable of delivering the higher

Table 3.2 Electronics production and exports ($m), principal producer economies, 1990

| | Office automation equipment | | Industrial controls | | Communications equipment | | Consumer electronics | | Electronic components | | Totals | |
|---|---|---|---|---|---|---|---|---|---|---|---|---|
| | $P^a$ | E | P | E | P | E | P | E | P | E | P | E |
| USA | 54 050 | 22 711 | 34 374 | 9 255 | 66 107 | 9 255 | 6 518 | 1 263 | 41 376 | 11 172 | 202 425 | 50 216 |
| Japan | 58 373 | 22 206 | 11 747 | 4 820 | 23 779 | 7 359 | 32 069 | 20 200 | 58 641 | 21 614 | 184 628 | 76 200 |
| Germany | 11 623 | 8 740 | 12 692 | 6 527 | 8 644 | 2 620 | 4 510 | 3 643 | 11 015 | 4 297 | 48 484 | 30 672 |
| France | 8 269 | 5 155 | 3 704 | 1 911 | 12 155 | 3 166 | 1 841 | 1 552 | 4 944 | 4 944 | 30 914 | 16 882 |
| Britain | 9 393 | 10 319[b] | 5 148 | 2 681 | 7 182 | 2 468 | 2 127 | 1 807 | 4 895 | 5 324[b] | 28 745 | 22 670 |
| Italy | 6 928 | 4 275 | 3 532 | 1 379 | 7 646 | 871 | 1 128 | 644 | 2 640 | 2 256 | 21 874 | 9 425 |
| Netherlands | 3 568 | 6 690[b] | 1 945 | 1 321 | 1 693 | 688 | 160 | 995[b] | 1 792 | 2 927[b] | 9 159 | 12 620[b] |
| Switzerland | 644 | 501 | 2 411 | 1 713 | 932 | 478 | 2 489 | 2 620[b] | 868 | 963[b] | 7 345 | 6 276 |
| Spain | 1 795 | 1 075 | 461 | 202 | 3 521 | 199 | 1 003 | 393 | 871 | 641 | 7 650 | 2 509 |
| Canada | 2 749 | 2 425 | 1 308 | 540 | 2 418 | 1 414 | 429 | 152 | 653 | 2 609[b] | 8 556 | 7 139 |
| Korea | 3 446 | 2 560 | 368 | 259 | 2 453 | 948 | 6 305 | 4 491 | 10 539 | 7 424 | 23 111 | 15 682 |
| Singapore | 7 177 | 9 029[b] | 256 | 433 | 498 | 662[b] | 2 117 | 3 659[b] | 4 777 | 5 991[b] | 14 885 | 19 773[b] |
| Taiwan | 5 247 | 5 796[b] | 273 | 259 | 1 907 | 1 260 | 1 824 | 1 554 | 4 948 | 4 593 | 14 199 | 13 462 |
| Hong Kong | 2 142 | 3 437 | 208 | 405[1] | 1 032 | 1 772[b] | 2 485 | 6 576[b] | 2 253 | 5 396[b] | 8 121 | 17 586 |
| Malaysia | 484 | 672[b] | 139 | 79 | 930 | 618 | 1 947 | 1 914 | 4 056 | 5 010[b] | 7 557 | 8 294[b] |
| Brazil | 4 949 | 120 | 810 | 45 | 2 196 | 77 | 2 170 | 347 | 2 082 | 136 | 12 207 | 725 |
| China | 1 223 | 531 | 460 | 120 | 1 327 | 626 | 6 207 | 3 227 | 2 446 | 1 050 | 12 663 | 5 554 |

Notes:
[a] P = production; E = exports.
[b] Excess of exports over production reflects the re-export of products originally imported as semi-finished manufactures. In the case of Hong Kong and Taiwan (POC), these largely originated in China.

Source: Yearbook of World Electronics Data, 1992 (Vols 1, 2, 3) (Oxford: Elsevier Advanced Technology, 1992).

levels of value added, and encouraging the skill upgrading that is essential to innovative, dynamic companies. The others still have limited capacity, or operate overwhelmingly at the labour-intensive, low value added end of the spectrum. The partial exception here is Brazil which has a significant presence in computers, communications equipment, certain consumer products and components (though not semiconductors) (see Table 3.2).

Among other things, this brief overview of the current state of the global electronics industry has served to highlight the fact that whatever the potential benefits of the industry, they have largely by-passed the vast majority of the world's population. While the coming years may see the emergence and strengthening of (civilian) electronics industries in various parts of Central and Eastern Europe, the prospects for most developing countries are bleak. Given that they do not have the pools of engineering and technical personnel required even for assembly operations, because of foreign indebtedness do not have the huge sums now necessary to induce production (as East Asian governments on occasion have done in the past), have underdeveloped telecommunications and transport infrastructures, do not themselves possess significant market potential, and that the increasing focus of foreign manufacturing investment is on those economies identified above, suggests that the potential benefits of electronics industries for much of the developing world are likely to remain elusive for a very long time to come.

Before proceeding further it is necessary to identify the types of electronics industries on which our discussion will focus. The generic term covers a vast array of processes, technologies and products: from components such as semiconductors to consumer electronics, computers of various sizes and capacities, industrial control systems, office automation and telecommunications equipment. In addition to the hardware, the production of software such as computer programmes is beginning to become important in a number of economies, as is the emergence of certain design functions such as electronic circuitry. From Table 3.2 it can be seen that the principal concentrations of electronics activity – as far as the developing world is concerned – are in three broad product areas: components, principally semiconductors; consumer electronics; and office automation equipment, principally microcomputers. Consequently these are the industries that will provide the empirical focus of our discussion. While software engineering is beginning to develop a strong presence in countries such as Singapore, India and Taiwan (POC), there is as yet insufficient information available on this phenomenon to ground an argument about its likely consequences for labour forces and economies (Ernst and O'Connor, 1992).

## MULTINATIONAL ENTERPRISES, FOREIGN DIRECT INVESTMENT AND THE INTERNATIONAL DIVISION OF LABOUR

### Origins

Semiconductor production was the vehicle for the first major – and still significant – wave of electronics foreign direct investment (FDI) in the developing world. Originating in Hong Kong in 1961 with the establishment of an assembly plant by the US producer, Fairchild, semiconductor FDI spread throughout the following two decades to six other locations in East Asia and to a number in Latin America and the Caribbean also. In its wake, the largely US and more recently Japanese companies responsible for the FDI developed a global production system which, until the late 1970s, was perhaps the supreme example of an industry organized according to the principles of the 'new international division of labour' thesis (Fröbel *et al.*, 1980; Henderson, 1989). Specifically, global managerial control and the knowledge-intensive parts of the system such as Research & Development, which were largely responsible for the companies' competitive advantage, remained firmly locked into the home country locations. While much of the more capital- and technology-intensive parts of the production process such as maskmaking and wafer fabrication also remained inside of the home base, some of it had been dispersed to other industrial economies such as the European Union and (for US companies) Japan where it was necessary to supply major, but protected, markets by investment in production facilities rather than through exports. Additionally, some circuit design functions had also been established in these economies. Developing economies, on the other hand, were recipients largely of low value added, low skill and labour-intensive assembly operations (Henderson, 1987, 1989).

### A Regional Division of Labour

By the mid-to late 1980s, the international division of labour as represented by semiconductor production had already been transformed.[2] Specifically in two East Asian locations – Hong Kong and Singapore

– US, Japanese and European MNEs had invested in more technology and skill-intensive processes such as computer controlled testing operations, circuit design, and in Singapore, wafer fabrication (see Table 3.3 for the case of US MNEs). Investment in these higher value added processes was contingent on the ability of these locations to supply high quality engineering and technical labour at costs far below those available in the core economies (Henderson, 1989; Lim and Pang, 1991: pp. 123–34). In the context of Singapore it was also a response to the government's strategy of forcing up labour costs, thus encouraging MNEs to restructure their operations to emphasize technology rather than labour intensive operations (Castells *et al.*, 1990: 155–208). For many of the MNEs involved, these developments also were associated with the emergence of Asian regional headquarter operations in Hong Kong and Singapore consistent with the growing significance of East Asian semiconductor markets.

These transformations in the global operations of MNEs pointed to a distinct regional division of labour within their East Asian operations. The peripheries of the division of labour such as Malaysia, Thailand, the Philippines and Indonesia had begun to become subjected to new and specifically regional forms of dependency. In addition to the decisionmaking controls and technological dependency which emanated from the core economy bases of the respective transnationals, the peripheries were now subject to a secondary layer of managerial and technical control which originated in Hong Kong and Singapore (Henderson, 1989; see also Henderson and Scott, 1987; Scott, 1987).

This regional division of labour and its implications has been supplemented and strengthened from two quarters: massive intra-regional flows of investment by Japanese semiconductor and consumer electronics companies (now by far the largest source of electronics FDI in the region); and an increasing integration of the peripheral economies into the production systems of electronics companies from the East Asian NIEs themselves. This latter development is part of the buyer-driven, commodity chain based, international division of labour which was mentioned above and to which we shall return later.

In the former case, the period since the late 1970s has seen the location in East Asia of about 70 per cent of Japanese offshore production facilities for semiconductors and other components. The favoured locations have been Taiwan (POC), Korea, Singapore, Malaysia and, more recently, Thailand. While most of this investment has gone into assembly and test operations, wafer fabrication plants have emerged in Singapore and Malaysia (Lim and Pang, 1991). Though the drive to

*Table 3.3* International division of labour in US semiconductor production, selected companies and locations, c. 1985-8

| Company | USA | Scotland | England and Wales | Germany | France | Ireland | Switzerland | Japan |
|---|---|---|---|---|---|---|---|---|
| Motorola | c, rd, w, a, t, ms, m | w, a, t | | w, t | w, t | | d, r, m | w, d |
| National Semiconductor | c, rd, w, a, t, ms, m | d, w | r, m | | | | | |
| Fairchild | c, rd, w, a, t, ms, m | | d, r, m | | w, t, m | | | w, d, a, t |
| Texas Instruments | c, rd, w, t, ms, m | | | | w, t, r | | | w, d |
| General Instrument | c, rd, w, t, ms, m | w | d, m, r | | m | | | |
| Hughes | c, rd, w, a, t, ms, m | w, a, t, (ms) | d, r, m | | | | | |
| Siliconix | c, rd, w, t, ms, m | | a, t, m | | | | | |
| Teledyne | c, rd, w, t, ms, m | | | | | | | |

| | | | | |
|---|---|---|---|---|
| Advanced Micro Devices | c, rd, w, t, ms, m | | w | |
| Silicon Systems | c, rd, w, t, ms, m | | | |
| Sprague | c, rd, w, t, ms, m | | | |
| Zilog | c, rd, w, t, ms, m | | w | |
| Burr-Brown | c, rd, w, t, ms, m, a | w, a, t, d | | a, t |

*continued on p. 102*

Table 3.3  continued

| Company | Rep. of Korea | Taiwan | Hong Kong | Singapore | Malaysia | Philippines | Thailand | Indonesia |
|---|---|---|---|---|---|---|---|---|
| Motorola | a | a | d, t, r, m | | a | a | | |
| National Semiconductor | | | a, t, m | t, d, m, r | w, a, t | a | a, t | a |
| Fairchild | a, t, | d | t,m | a, t, m | | a | | a |
| Texas Instruments | | a | | a, t, m | | a | | a |
| General Instrument | | a, t | | | a | | | |
| Hughes | | | (a) | | | (a) | | |
| Siliconix | | a | a, t, d | | | | | |
| Teledyne | | | a,t | | | | | |
| Advanced Micro Devices | | | m | t, m | a | a | a | |
| Silicon Systems | | | | d, a, t | | | | |
| Sprague | | a | r, t, m | | | a | | |
| Zilog | | | d, r, m | | | a, t | | |
| Burr-Brown | | | | | | | | |

*Key:* c Corporate control; rd Research & Development; d Design centre; ms Maskmaking; w Wafer fabrication; a Assembly; t Final testing; r Regional headquarters; m Marketing centre; ( ) Operation under subcontracting arrangement.

*Source:* Henderson (1989, Figure 4.2:56–67).

reduce labour costs (including on engineering and technical labour) has been partly responsible for this development, it has been associated also with the demands created by the subsidiaries of Japanese consumer electronics companies that have emerged in various parts of the region (Dicken, 1992: 333–4). As some of these subsidiaries have the same parent companies as the semiconductor plants (Hitachi and Matsushita, for instance), it is likely that their just-in-time (JIT) manufacturing systems have contributed to increasing investments in localized component production.

The growth of Japanese consumer electronics subsidiaries in the developing world has been more widespread than with semiconductor production, with plants emerging in Latin America (particularly Brazil and Mexico), as well as in East Asia. In the East Asian context where the investment has been in televisions, VCRs, air-conditioners and microwave ovens, Taiwan (POC), Malaysia, Singapore and Thailand have been the principal recipients of investment, with Taiwan (POC) receiving the dragon's share in both semiconductors and consumer products.[3] While one of the reasons for this internationalization of consumer electronics assembly has been the drive for lower manual labour costs, an equally important reason has been the need to circumvent import quota restrictions in the US market (Dicken, 1992: 339).

Consistent with rapidly rising labour costs at home, Korean and Taiwanese consumer electronics and computer manufacturers have developed assembly operations on a subsidiary or joint venture basis in a number of ASEAN countries and, increasingly, in China. Since 1988 Taiwan (POC), for instance, has been the second most important source of new manufacturing FDI in Malaysia. Some of this has been in electronics and has included an investment in PC assembly by the principal Taiwanese computer manufacturer, Acer.[4] Similarly, the major Korean electronics producers, Samsung and Goldstar, now have manufacturing operations in Thailand, Indonesia, the Philippines and China as well as Mexico (Bloom, 1992, Table 12: 109–12). While much of the electronics assembly by Hong Kong companies has shifted to China in recent years, some of it has relocated to parts of Southeast Asia where there are well developed business networks among the local Chinese populations (Redding, 1990).

The emergence of these flows of FDI and managerial controls and decisionmaking associated with them are but part of a more general process of economic integration taking place within East Asia. In addition to the regionalization of NIE electronics industries, considerable investment by other NIE manufacturing industries is taking place, particularly in garments, footwear and certain forms of engineering. Central to these developments, as well as some of those in electronics are production systems organized in the form of 'commodity chains' (see Chapter 2 in this volume; Gereffi and Korzeniewicz, 1994). As this second international division of labour is overwhelmingly associated with domestically-owned companies, it is to those which we now turn.

## HOME-GROWN INDUSTRIES AND COMMODITY CHAINS

While investment by MNEs has been the primary factor responsible for the emergence of electronics production in most industrializing societies, including Singapore, Malaysia and Thailand, this has not been true to the same extent in Hong Kong, Taiwan (POC) and Korea. Though FDI has certainly been significant in semiconductor production in all three economies since the 1960s, a notable feature of these economies is that they have developed substantial domestically-owned industries. Since the 1970s, for instance, the Korean *chaebols* (conglomerates), Goldstar, Samsung, Hyundai and Daewoo, began to move into the production of TVs and audio products and in the 1980s, VCRs, microwave ovens, microcomputers, compact disk players and semiconductors. The share of electronics in Korea's total manufacturing output rose from 6 per cent in 1980 to nearly 18 per cent in 1988. By that year electronics production accounted for nearly 15 per cent of GNP and exports had reached around 25 per cent of the total, overtaking textiles and garments as the largest contributor to manufactured exports. Korea now ranks sixth in the world in terms of total electronics production and third (after Japan and the USA) in consumer electronics.

Product sophistication had also increased in some areas, with Samsung, for instance, capable of fabricating 4 and 16 megabit DRAM semiconductors, and Korea becoming the second largest producer of memory devices in the world (Hobday, 1992b). By the late 1980s, domestic companies had become the dominant force in the Korean electronics industry. In 1987, for instance, domestic companies were responsible for 65 per cent of total Korean electronics output, with joint venture companies responsible for another 24 per cent and wholly foreign-owned companies only 11 per cent, of which the bulk were semiconductors. Similarly, with regard to employment provision, domestic companies in 1987 were responsible for 72 per cent of total employment, or about 271 000 jobs (Bloom, 1992: 72).

As with other NIE electronics industries, those of Taiwan (POC) began with foreign (overwhelmingly US) investment in semiconductor assembly in the mid-1960s which diversified in the 1970s into investment in TV and other consumer products by companies such as RCA, Philips and Matsushita. Taiwanese companies emerged initially to supply the MNEs with simple components such as capacitors, resistors and transformers, but soon began to assemble radios and TVs of their own. By the 1980s firms began to move into the production of semiconductors, VCRs, colour TV monitors and particularly microcomputers. By 1988, for instance, Taiwanese firms were exporting more than 2 million personal computers which accounted for about 10 per cent of world PC production (Bello and Rosenfeld, 1992: 266]. By 1987 electronics industries were contributing over 5 per cent of Taiwan's GNP and about 20 per cent of its exports, becoming the largest export sector (Hobday, 1992b). Consistent with the growth of consumer electronics and microcomputer production, Taiwan (POC) has evolved its own semiconductor production capacity.

Hong Kong's electronics industry began with the assembly of transistor radios for Japanese producers in the late 1950s and expanded by the attraction of US and other foreign investment in semiconductor production. Since then, Hong Kong's electronics industries have come to be dominated by local producers. Although even the biggest Hong Kong firms such as Video Technology, Semi Tech, Wong Industrial, Tomei and Conic are very small by Taiwanese and particularly Korean standards, they have helped to contribute to the 23 per cent share of manufactured exports which electronics held in 1987 (Henderson, 1989, Table 5.3: 85). These firms and their smaller counterparts produce such things as personal computers, electronic games, TVs, audio products and watches. Although electronics industries contributed a high of over 135 000 jobs in 1984, since then employment in this as in other manufacturing industries has declined drastically. By 1990 employment in electronics was down to 85 000 and in manufacturing generally to 716 000. In 1992, manufacturing employment has fallen further to around 560 000, down more than a third since 1987. The reasons for this decline are not hard to discern. Rather than invest in more capital- and technology-intensive processes as labour costs in the colony have risen, Hong Kong's manufacturers have sought to relocate much of their productive capacity to China's neighbouring Guangdong Province where Hong Kong-invested factories now employ over 3 million people (see Skeldon, Chapter 5 in this volume).

Two issues that have been central to the growth of indigenous electronics capacities in these economies need to be highlighted. The first of these is the organizational arrangements under which much of their electronics production continues to take place. The second concerns the interventionist role of their national states.

### Subcontracting and Buyer-driven Commodity Chains

From the beginning of their emergence as electronics producers through to the present day, the indigenous firms of the East Asian NIEs have continued to operate substantially under original equipment manufacturer (OEM) arrangements with foreign companies. Under such an arrangement the purchaser supplies the designs, some of the components, monitors production quality and markets under its own brandname. The OEM tends merely to assemble the final product. The benefits to the purchaser lie largely in the cost reductions (both labour costs and overheads) while for the OEM they lie in the relatively easy and cheap access to overseas markets and in theory represent a useful conduit for technology transfer. Hong Kong's electronics firms are the ones that remain most thoroughly absorbed into OEM arrangements. There is hardly a single electronics manufacturer there that does not produce the vast majority of output under an OEM arrangement with a Japanese, US or EU firm.

Even with the more technologically sophisticated producers of Taiwan (POC) and Korea, the incidence of OEM arrangements remains high. In the case of Taiwanese computers and related goods, for instance, OEM accounted for around 43 per cent of production in 1989 with the principal buyers being IBM, Philips, NEC, EPSON, Hewlett Packard and NCR. Taiwan's largest electronics manufacturer, Tatung, for instance, exports about half its PCs and colour TVs under OEM arrangements, and TECO sells about 65 per cent of its TV monitors on the same basis. The leading computer manufacturer, Acer, continues to produce a substantial proportion of its PC output for AT&T, Unisys and Siemens (Hobday, 1992b). The situation of Korean firms is much like their Taiwanese counterparts if not more so. In 1988, for instance, OEM arrangements still accounted for 60 to 70 per cent of local firm output (and 30 per cent of all manufactured exports). That same year nearly all the sales of 256K DRAM ICs by Hyundai Semiconductor to Texas Instruments were on an OEM basis. In 1987 OEM sales constituted 50 per cent of the exports of TVs by the main Korean manufacturers (Samsung, Goldstar and Daewoo), while half of Samsung's sales of VCRs to the USA were on an OEM basis and for Goldstar the proportion was considerably higher (Hobday, 1992b; Bloom,

1992: 32). It is necessary to temper the discussion at this point, however, by adding that sales of own-brandname microcomputers by Taiwanese producers such as Acer, Tatung and Mitac, have risen in recent years. In 1988 the share of Taiwan's own-brandname PCs stood at 28 per cent of the total but by 1989 had reached 40 per cent (Ernst and O'Connor, 1992: 153). The significance of own-brandname sales lies in the fact that the higher their proportion of the total, the higher the value added that is likely to be retained by the manufacturer and hence the domestic economy.

There are two other issues that bear on the significance of OEM arrangements for East Asian NIE electronics manufacturers. First, much of the production in Taiwan (POC) and Hong Kong – though not to the same extent in the other NIEs – arises out of dense, socially embedded networks of small and medium-sized enterprises but also including some of the larger firms. Many of these small and medium-sized enterprises operate within the informal economy and hence largely beyond state control (Cheng and Gereffi, 1994). Secondly, and more importantly for our current purposes, many of these OEM arrangements reflect international production systems organized on the basis of buyer-driven commodity chains (BDCCs). For electronic products, these chains, depending on the product in question, now link many manufacturing operations in Korea, Taiwan (POC) and Hong Kong not only to the US, Japanese and EU manufacturers and buyers but, in the case of a growing number of Taiwanese and Hong Kong firms, to downstream producers and subcontractors in China and, increasingly, Vietnam. Given that this is a production system in which value accrues according to the particular nodes in the commodity chain one controls (and the bulk of the value accrues to the buyers and distributors in the major industrial economies), it has important implications for technological and skill upgrading and more generally for development prospects. This is the case particularly for China, Vietnam and other peripheral economies that are, or are likely to be, incorporated into the world economy partly on the basis of this version of an international division of labour.

## State Policy

The second substantive issue that arises here is the fact that many of the electronics industries in the East Asian NIEs owe their origins, technological trajectories and (in the latter cases) competitive advantage in some measure to state industrial policy. Although these economies have benefited from vigorously functioning markets, state orchestration of their development projects has been central to their success (Amsden, 1989; Wade, 1990; Appelbaum and Henderson, 1992; Henderson, 1993a, 1993b). Even in the supposed free market paradise of Hong Kong, state ownership of land and housing and welfare provision have been decisive features of economic growth and redistribution (Castells *et al.*, 1990; Schiffer, 1991). As part of their general attempts to induce and upgrade their industrial bases and labour force composition, the governments of the East Asian NIEs have at various moments acquired foreign technology under licence for dissemination to favoured companies, encouraged joint venture arrangements with foreign partners, protected the domestic market from foreign competition, delivered subsidized credit through nationalized or heavily regulated banking systems (Korea and Taiwan (POC)) for approved projects and invested in their own Research & Development facilities to help boost the technological capabilities of the private sector manufacturers.[5] Beginning in 1979 with the 'Basic Plan for Electronics Industry Promotion' the Korean government has been particularly active in encouraging the development of the electronics sector. Identified as a strategic industry (in both commercial and military senses) the government has invested heavily in research institutes and in engineering and technical skills to help ensure that the competitive edge of companies such as Samsung and Goldstar is enhanced through product competition (i.e. more technology-intensive) and not merely price competition associated with low costs. The Korean Institute of Electronics Technology (KIET), for instance, was set up in 1976 to ensure that research into IC design and wafer fabrication was undertaken. In other electronics industries, such as telecommunications, the Electronics and Telecommunications Research Institute (ETRI) partly formed from KIET in 1985, has operated to ensure that foreign technologies, sometimes by means of 'reverse engineering'[6] are more rapidly absorbed by local companies than would have been the case had they been left to their own devices (Bloom, 1992: 28–58).

The story of the Taiwan government's relation with the country's electronics companies is much the same as in the Korean case. Arguably in Taiwan (POC), however, state initiatives have been even more important owing to the relatively small size of the companies, and hence their lack of capital compared with their Korean counterparts. Additionally in Taiwan (POC), as in Hong Kong, there has probably been an over-riding interest in quick profits among manufacturers and therefore a tendency to boost productivity by squeezing the labour process rather than by investing in more technology-intensive (and higher value added) processes and products. In this context, state Research & Development expenditures have been particularly important. Central here has been the way in which state research institutes have acquired foreign technologies, adapted them and encouraged their absorption by Taiwanese companies. With wages rising by 20 per cent per annum in the late 1970s it became clear to state economic planners that companies had to be encouraged to technologically upgrade their operations. It was in this context that the state instituted the Electronics Research and Service Organization (ERSO) which, via a technology transfer arrangement with the US producer, RCA, became Taiwan's first designer and fabricator of ICs and effectively laid the foundations for the country's electronics industry. In 1979 ERSO developed a state-owned semiconductor industry when it 'spun-off' United Microelectronics, subsequently privatizing the company in 1985. More recently ERSO has played a central role in the acquisition and subsequent transfer of 16 bit microcomputer technology to what are now leading producers such as Acer and TECO (Chen, 1993).

The experience of state involvement with electronics production in Hong Kong and Singapore has differed significantly from that of the other East Asian NIEs. In the case of Hong Kong the colonial government's commitment to free market ideology has resulted in its woeful neglect of manufacturing industry. Companies have been allowed to exploit the abundant opportunities for cutting labour costs that exist across the border in Southern China, and hence have disinvested in the colony rather than having been encouraged – or pressured – to invest in more technology-intensive processes and higher value added products. In addition, the government's own contribution to Research & Development compared with other East Asian NIEs, has been derisory. The consequence has been that value added by electronics companies in Hong Kong remains low and there must now be some doubt as to whether Hong Kong will retain much of a presence in electronics manufacturing beyond the 1990s (Whitla, 1991; Henderson, 1991: 177–8).

Though Singapore's electronics industry, in common with the rest of its manufacturing base, has been far from 'home grown', state policies have been fundamental to its technological trajectory. Singapore has the most corporatist of Asian governments in that it has successfully engineered a triadic relation between organized labour (which has been absorbed into the ruling People's Action Party since the mid-1960s) and multinational firms. On the one hand it has neutralized labour and legitimated its rule by delivering Asia's most advanced welfare state, and on the other it has encouraged the upgrading of MNE investments which are responsible for over 70 per cent of manufacturing output by value (Mirza, 1986). Recognizing that cheap labour was a declining competitive advantage and having invested heavily in education and skill enhancement in previous years – including software training institutions such as the IBM-assisted Institute of Systems Analysis (Ernst, 1983) – state planners began to force up labour costs in order to squeeze low skill assembly work out of the economy and encourage the MNEs to invest in more technology-intensive processes and products. The means to this end, beginning in 1979, was to increase the compulsory employer contributions to the Central Provident Fund so as to double labour costs by the late 1980s. The government's gamble was that, rather than disinvest, the MNEs would convert Singapore into their principal Asian location for high technology processes and products. The gamble seems to have paid off (Castells *et al.*, 1990, Part II). As part of this strategy, the government is now trying to compensate for high labour costs in Singapore by giving local firms (Teal, 1995) access to cheap labour in Malaysia and Indonesia via its promotion of the 'Growth Triangle'. The export of capital to cheap labour sites is seen by the government as preferable to importing non-Chinese labour into Singapore (Parsonage, 1992).

In these various ways, then, state intervention has been central to the growth of the developing world's most successful electronics industries. This is perhaps particularly relevant for those economies such as Malaysia and Thailand which, while having a strong presence in the sector, have so far failed to develop a significant locally-owned capacity or (with a number of Malaysian exceptions) to move into the more technologically advanced processes and products.


THE CONTEXT OF LABOUR FORCE UPGRADING

In the Introduction to this chapter, it was suggested that, where the foreign sector becomes embedded in production linkages with local firms, a positive implication for the quantity of employment in the manufacturing sector is likely to result. In this section we turn to look in more detail at the significance of production linkages and technological transfer and upgrading as a centrally important context for skill development.

## Linkages

Whether an MNE subsidiary becomes embedded in a host economy by virtue of its linkages with local firms depends on a number of factors. One is the global strategy and production system of the MNE concerned. Major Japanese companies, for instance, because of their systems of relational subcontracting with firms from their respective *keiretsu* (enterprise groups) often tend to continue those arrangements when they internationalize their operations. Even where local companies are capable of supplying components in required quantities and qualities, then, production linkages are not developed to the extent that could have been expected. This is the case for economies such as those of Thailand, but particularly for Malaysia and Singapore whose FDI-driven electronics industries are their largest manufacturing sectors. Other factors that can inhibit linkage formation include the nature of the product itself and whether the MNE is deliberately segregated from the domestic economy by virtue of its location in an export processing zone (EPZ). Semiconductors, for instance, because of the proprietary nature of their embodied technology, tend not to be good candidates for linkage formation. Similarly, where MNEs as a result of government policy are located in EPZs, local firms in search of linkages must themselves locate in the EPZs. Consequently they must be prepared to relinquish an interest in the domestic market and weld their fortunes to a small number of firms and export markets only. Countries such as Malaysia whose electronics industry remains dominated by semiconductor production organized in EPZs (although with growing investment in consumer electronics) seem particularly exposed.

Among the developing countries with FDI-driven electronics industries, it is indeed Malaysia that presents the greatest paradox when it comes to linkage formation. Not only does the economy suffer from the sort of problems indicated above, but the development of a local electronics industry capable to linking with the MNEs seems to have been stillborn. In spite of over two decades of foreign investment in electronics, linkage formation is still very limited when compared, for instance, with Taiwan (POC), Hong Kong and, recently, Singapore. Part of the problem is associated with the regional division of labour, or at least the Southeast Asian subregion (Henderson, 1989: 49–76; Parsonage, 1992). Specifically, the emergence of Singapore as the high tech fulcrum of the subregion has meant that MNEs have preferred to link with their affiliates or local firms there, rather than in Malaysia. This having been said, however, there is still a Malaysian domestic problem and its roots lie in the fact that, on the one hand, the Malay-dominated state has systematically discriminated against Malaysian–Chinese business, when the fastest route to an indigenous manufacturing industry in the short to medium term is Chinese entrepreneurship. On the other hand, state policies have encouraged the growth of a rentier capitalism among Malays and Chinese and hence diverted investment and energies into unproductive activities that otherwise could have been channelled into manufacturing (Salih, 1988; Jesudason, 1989; Lubeck, 1992).

In spite of these structural problems, the most recent research suggests that linkage formation is beginning to emerge. Ismail (1993a), for instance, reports that for a selection of US and Japanese electronics companies, many of them now source a wide variety of machinery, components, cables, etc. from locally-owned companies. The US producer, Harris Semiconductor, for instance, sources its entire requirement for basic tools and machinery from Malaysian companies. Additionally, some US MNEs have worked with local companies to upgrade the quality and add value to their supplies and components. This has been particularly true of Intel and National Semiconductor who have worked with local firms such as Eng Hardware and Loh Kim Teow Engineering for some years. Furthermore at least four Malaysian manufacturers are now producing PCs for the domestic market, one of them, Techtrans, on the basis of a technology transfer arrangement with a Taiwanese firm (Lim and Pang, 1991: 116). Although these are hopeful signs, the continued weakness of the local manufacturing sector in Malaysia is a problem that could seriously limit the benefits to the labour force and the economy generally that could otherwise accrue from that country's industrialization process.

With regard to linkage formation with electronics MNEs in other Southeast Asian countries, with the sole exception of Singapore, the situation is more problematic than in Malaysia. In Thailand, although a number of joint ventures have been formed – including with Korean companies Goldstar and Samsung – the local electronics manufacturing base is still very underdeveloped (Lim and Pang, 1991: 18–123). As the bulk of FDI in electronics dates only from 1987, however, it would be premature to draw conclusions about the possibilities for linkage formation. In Philippines and Indonesia the prospects for higher value added linkage formation look particularly bleak, though there is some evidence that local firms capable of performing certain specialized functions, including circuit design, have arisen in the former in recent years (Scott, 1987).

The Southeast Asian 'star' when it comes to linkage formation, as with so much to do with electronics production, is Singapore. After an inauspicious start in the 1970s when state policy worked against manufacturing SMEs and hence linkages with MNEs (Lim and Pang, 1982), the 1980s witnessed a re-think of state priorities and a consequent upsurge in SME activity. In recent years local firms have moved into such areas as circuit boards and other subassemblies; membrane switches to replace keyboards on computers, calculators, microwave ovens, etc.; computer software and circuit design; microcomputers; and electronic health-care products such as equipment for monitoring blood pressure and diagnosing AIDS (Lim and Pang, 1991: 130–2).

For the other East Asian producers, the earlier significance of linkages with MNEs has given way to domestically-owned producers which for some time have been the dominant force in their respective electronics sectors. While OEM arrangements with foreign companies remain important for these producers, in the case of Taiwan (POC) and Hong Kong the linkage issue has been transformed into one of linkages between domestic companies in the context of dense inter-firm networks. Korean companies are the exception when it comes to linkage formation with other local firms. As Korean electronics production is heavily concentrated, with Samsung and Goldstar alone responsible for over 46 per cent of sales in 1988 (Bloom, 1992, Table 3: 41), the opportunities for linkages with SMEs tend to be limited. The *chaebols* so far have preferred to produce in-house, or source their components from overseas.

## Technology Transfer and Upgrading

The extent of genuine technology transfer by MNEs and upgrading by indigenous companies themselves is again very uneven. With regard to the transfer of more advanced semiconductor technologies I have discussed already the situation which pertained by the mid-to late 1980s. Since then this situation, if anything, has been compounded. The peripheries continue to be the principal recipients of investments in assembly facilities, though test facilities are becoming more prevalent. While some technology-intensive investments have been made in Malaysia, these remain fairly limited and in any case are designed to produce less technologically sophisticated products. Investment in the most advanced processes has continued to flow to the 'hubs', but with Singapore now becoming the favoured location rather than Hong Kong. Thus the nineteen semiconductor MNEs that produce in Singapore (e.g. AT&T, Texas Instruments, National Semiconductor, Philips, Matsushita,

NEC) tend to focus on the more advanced products (14 and 16 mega-bit DRAMs and some microprocessors). While most of these companies still concentrate on assembly and test, their plants tend to be highly automated.

In other electronics industries, the picture is much the same. The bulk of investment in assembly processes continues to flow into the more peripheral economies, which in the case of consumer products now includes China. Again only in Malaysia is there evidence of some investment in higher value added and skill-intensive processes. The Japanese producer, Sharp, for instance, is currently developing a training centre intended in part to transfer certain design skills (Ismail, 1993b). Singapore, however, is once again the primary focus for investment in the higher value added processes and products. In addition to the examples cited previously, Singapore since the early 1980s has become a major centre for disk drive production, which now accounts for almost 10 per cent of domestic exports. In recent years most of the principal producers with plants in Singapore (Seagate, Control Data, Unisys etc.), in response to government-induced labour cost increases, have pushed their lower end products to other Southeast Asian locations, while upgrading their Singapore plants in terms of processes and products. There disk drive production is highly automated and concentrates on the more technology-intensive 3.5 inch drives. At least two of the companies – Seagate and Maxtor – have developed Research & Development facilities in Singapore (Lim and Pang, 1991: 123–4).

As I have already suggested, Taiwan (POC) and Korea have the most technologically advanced semiconductor, consumer electronics and probably microcomputer industries in the developing world. The fact that a number of their leading companies now possess high quality production facilities and technical personnel is reflected in the technological alliances and OEM arrangements they are able to forge with leading-edge foreign producers. In the Korean case, for instance, Samsung currently has 61 'technology transfer' agreements with North American, Japanese and European producers; Goldstar has 79, Hyundai 33 and Daewoo 20 (Bloom, 1992: 127–33). While there are problems in many of these arrangements for the future development and continued upgrading of the Korean and Taiwanese industries,[7] it is unquestionably the case that on this and most of the other criteria, electronics production in these societies has made an enormous contribution to technological and skill upgrading, rising wages and more generally to prosperity and economic development.

Much the same can be said for Singapore. There, technological up-grading in the electronics industries can be clearly seen in value added data. Between 1980 and 1987, for instance, value added per worker increased by over 150 per cent, approaching in some instances US levels.[8] In Hong Kong, however, its earlier prominence in electronics technologies and products seems to be in decline. For the reasons ident-ified above it seems that, though value added has continued to in-crease in the industry, this is occurring more slowly than in its NIE competitors (Whitla, 1991).

## WORKING CONDITIONS

Considerable attention has been paid to working conditions in the elec-tronics industry, largely, though not exclusively, in the developing world.[9] With regard to assembly operations where the vast majority of the work is done by women, the research consensus is that these generally have been particularly oppressive. In terms of wage rates, hours of work, compulsory overtime, supervisory control, health hazards, sexual harassment, limited paid holidays, dismissal without redundancy pay-ments and hostility to trade unions, the record has often been one of unremitting exploitation (Grossman, 1979; Elson and Pearson, 1981; Arrigo, 1984; Heyzer, 1986; Ong, 1987; Women Working Worldwide, 1991). Against this general background, however, distinctions which roughly correlate with the two international divisions of labour ident-ified in this report need to be drawn. First, subsidiaries of electronics MNEs tend to have a better record than their locally-owned equiva-lents, particularly where the latter are relatively small enterprises (Chiang, 1984). There is evidence of semi-militaristic factory discipline in the Korean *chaebols* (Deyo, 1989) and long working weeks (an average of 56 hours in Hong Kong, for instance), continue to be the norm. Where locally-owned or overseas Chinese-invested factories, absorbed into the BDCC form of the international division of labour are concerned, work-ing conditions are probably even more harsh. In their search for pro-ductivity with minimum investment in technology, the new Hong Kong-and Taiwanese-invested factories in China, for instance, seem to have developed particularly problematic working conditions. While I know of no systematic research on the phenomenon, the growing number of informal reports from Guangdong Province, adjacent to Hong Kong, points to the extensive use of child labour and forced overtime for the largely female work force extending, on occasion, to 72 hour shifts![10]

EXPLANATORY ISSUES

Having outlined the changing divisions of labour in the international electronics industry and highlighted the asymmetrical nature of their impact on particular producer countries, it is now time to turn to a discussion of the explanations for these phenomena.

The first thing to emphasize is that the principal driving force producing these divisions of labour is increasing competition between producers on the one hand and among buyers on the other, in the context of a recession in world markets for manufactured commodities. In this economic environment corporate concerns to reduce costs have been heightened, but under circumstances in which acceptable levels of productivity can be delivered.

But competition in electronics markets is no longer merely about price; it is also about the quality of the product and its technological sophistication. Electronics companies, then, confront two additional requirements which influence the location of their investments: the need to guarantee high quality production processes and products; and the need to systematically innovate on product technology. As production systems for electronic products tend to be technically disarticulated, they do not require as a technical necessity production of the entire product in a single location (Henderson, 1989). Given that world markets for labour of various skills and qualities are now almost as flexible as those for capital, the more skill-intensive elements of the final product in principle can be moved wherever the requisite labour is located. While this is a general feature of the global operation of MNEs and has been given popular credence by the work of Robert Reich (1991), a number of provisos need to be registered.

### Labour Costs, Productivity and Product Quality

First, while labour costs were never as significant a driving force of the world factory phenomenon as some scholars had argued (cf. Fröbel *et al.*, 1980; Henderson, 1989; Elson, 1988) they remain an important feature of corporate calculation. The concern, however, is not especially with the cost of unskilled or semi-skilled labour but more with that of engineering and technical personnel. As a consequence, certain types of technology-intensive production processes (such as wafer fabrication for semiconductors) and design functions have emerged in those locations where significant supplies of skilled personnel are available at relatively low cost. A number of Asian economies – Singapore, Taiwan

(POC), Hong Kong, for instance – have benefited from foreign investment seeking to tap their supplies of low cost technical and engineering labour, as have EU locations such as Scotland (Henderson, 1987, 1989). But investment of this sort does not arise merely because of the existence of such labour supplies. As I have already mentioned, the host economy must be capable of delivering the social arrangements and managerial competence necessary for high productivity and the production of high quality products. This fact is of equal significance for investment in assembly processes.

Issues of low and skilled labour costs in the context of socio-economic regimes which allow quality production at acceptable levels of productivity are as important for the BDCC forms of the division of labour as they are for the form associated with direct investment by MNEs. The development of business organization in Korea and Taiwan (POC) capable of delivering both of these has allowed consumer electronics and micro computer firms to reduce costs drastically by utilizing the subcontracting networks associated with OEM arrangements. In the most extreme cases – such as with the British firm, Amstrad – the commodity chain system allows core economy firms to dispense with the need for direct investment in production facilities. The logic of this arrangement – already evident in garment and footwear production, for instance – is that it points to a situation in which even major electronics companies could become 'manufacturers without factories' (Henderson, 1992).

## Market Size and Protection

While we can take for granted the fact that efficient communications – particularly telecommunications – systems are an essential condition of electronics investment of almost any sort, the market significance of the host economy is the second important proviso. This is true for both investment in technology-intensive, higher skill production processes as well as for assembly operations. Consequently, while investment to tap supplies of technical and engineering labour in, say, Singapore and Hong Kong continues to be associated with supplying world markets, this investment – by US, EU and Japanese companies alike – is becoming increasingly conditioned by the growing market for electronic products in the East Asian region itself. This is even more the case where major markets are protected by high tariff and other barriers, such as with the European Union and the North American Free Trade Area (NAFTA).

With regard to assembly operations – particularly by Japanese and, increasingly, Korean consumer electronics companies – costs of market protection in the European Union and North America clearly have over-ridden labour cost considerations for some time. Protection of these major markets has rendered direct investment in final assembly operations there essential to capturing and expanding market share, in spite of the fact that this has necessitated higher production costs (assuming equivalent productivity levels) than would have been the case had the markets been able to be supplied entirely from developing-country locations.

## Innovation

The switch away from price competition in electronics commodities markets to a situation in which product competition has become equally important has highlighted the relation of technological innovation to corporate success. This raises the question of whether companies are now able to generate the core of their technological dynamics – basic Research & Development – internationally, or whether this remains confined to the home bases of the companies concerned. While it is clear that some design, software and product development functions have been dispersed by the MNEs to locations other than their home base and for the reasons discussed above, it is not clear that basic Research & Development has been dispersed. Reich's arguments notwithstanding,[11] the available evidence suggests that, with a few exceptions (US semiconductors in Israel, Korean and Taiwanese companies in the US), the bulk of Research & Development by major electronics companies continues to be performed within their home economies. While the reasons for this appear to be associated with questions of proprietary control over the technologies and with social, economic and technical synergies necessary for building economies of scope (Porter, 1990), it raises the question of how the supplies of highly creative scientists and engineers necessary for basic Research & Development are to be replenished. While Korea, Taiwan (POC), Brazil, India and China probably will be capable of meeting their demands themselves, this may not be true of the USA, Japan and the European Union. If it is not, then the implications of the international divisions of labour in electronics may be that rather than invest in basic Research & Development elsewhere, Research & Development engineers will have to be bought from the developing world, thus compounding the political problems triggered by the presence of migrant/immigrant workers.

## IMPLICATIONS FOR LABOUR

In this final section, I extract and highlight from the general discussion what appear to be the principal implications of the evolving international divisions of labour for electronics industry labour forces. Before reaching that point, however, it is necessary to reconsider an earlier comment on the prospects for economies – and hence their labour forces – which are currently outside of both the electronics divisions of labour.

Direct investment by MNEs was responsible for initiating the international division of labour in electronics production and has continued to be the principal driving force of all developing-country electronics industries with the exception of Korea, Taiwan (POC), Hong Kong and, to a lesser extent, Brazil and India. In the light of my earlier comments, the only way that potential newcomers could break into electronics production would be through FDI. Despite the FDI recession in the early 1990s, flows into developing countries have continued to boom. However, the vast majority of this has been destined for countries in Asia. China, in particular, has emerged as the largest host country in the developing world, accounting for well over half of the increase in FDI into developing countries in 1992 and 1993 (UNCTAD, 1994). On this basis, the possibility of other developing countries creating viable electronics industries in the foreseeable future seems remote. The only exception here, as I have already indicated, is Vietnam which, in addition to investment from Taiwan (POC) and Hong Kong, received over $1 billion of Japanese investment in 1991 (Mitter, 1992).

What, then, of the economies and labour forces that are already component parts of the divisions of labour? There are a number of points to be made, but the first is perhaps the most important from the perspective of the further development of the industry in each location.

1.  Whether the economies in question are the technological-, knowledge- and skill-intensive cores of the global production system, or locations where intermediate processes, or labour-intensive assembly processes still predominate, the fundamental implication of our analysis remains the same. The expansion of employment, skill upgrading, rising wages and the promise (or continuation) of general prosperity can best be achieved if they are conceived as part of national and regional development strategies for electronics industries, which while orchestrated by governments or inter-governmental agencies, arise out of systematic relations between labour, business (domestic and foreign) and the governments themselves. The future

of electronics industries and their workforces are simply too important to a range of national and regional economies to be left to the
vicissitudes of relatively free markets. The experience of Japan, Korea,
Taiwan (POC) and Singapore has shown that state guidance of the
industry (though achieved in different ways) by competent economic
bureaucracies is probably the best route to dynamic industries capable of moving into more technology-intensive, higher value added
operations, thus creating more demands for skilled labour. The experiences of Hong Kong (where the industry has declined) and
Malaysia (where technological upgrading is more limited than might
have been expected after 20 years of electronics production), both
of which have had limited government involvement with their electronics industries, should be taken as lessons in how not to develop
electronics production.

2. Cheap, unskilled or semi-skilled labour is at best a temporary comparative advantage in relation to both forms of the international
   division of labour outlined above. Diversifying into higher value
   added products, fostering an engineering and technical labour force
   and, in the case of firms locked into OEM commodity chains, moving to own-brand products, are prerequisites for the sustainability
   of the industries.

3. Investment in training – neither directly by governments, by levies
   on firms, or by international agencies – is essential to attracting
   foreign and domestic investment and thus sustaining the industries.
   In the process of technological and skill upgrading, women workers
   are likely to be the losers in terms of declining employment opportunities. To avoid this, investment in the multiskilling and technical
   advancement of low skilled workers is essential.

4. Where electronics production is driven by FDI, the greatest benefits in terms of increasing employment – particularly for women –
   technology transfer and thus skill upgrading, rising wages and the
   rest, are likely to be achieved where there are strong production
   based linkages between the MNE subsidiaries and locally-owned
   supplier and subcontracting companies. Central to formation of linkages are: (a) the existence of local companies capable of delivering
   the quality products necessary for linkages to develop; (b) government policies that stimulate locally-owned manufacturing companies;
   and (c) tough bargaining by host governments to ensure that MNEs
   subcontract locally, and not merely with subsidiaries of other MNEs
   or, in the case of Japanese firms, other companies within their *keiretsu*
   (enterprise group). In the latter case it is possible that joint venture

companies where the local partner is active (rather than merely an investor) have a higher propensity to form local production linkages.

5. With the development of regional economic blocs, it may be that much electronics production, including assembly, may yet emerge within major protected markets. While this would be a disaster for developing economies which rely on productive, but cheap low skilled labour, those that invest heavily in technical and engineering skills probably would continue to receive significant FDI flows. The Japanese Ministry of International Trade and Industry (MITI), has estimated that, by the turn of the century, Japanese companies will experience a shortfall of about 1 million in their demand for software engineers (quoted by Mitter, 1992). In the context of opposition to migrant/immigrant labour in Japan and other major economies, companies will continue to access technical labour wherever it may be located.

6. The ownership of electronics companies still matters. With the exception of Singapore, which is an unusual case (Castells *et al*, 1990; Part II), domestically-owned firms, supported and encouraged by their respective governments, have been central to technological and skill upgrading and to the proliferation of human capabilities throughout their economies. Where a national electronics industry has been dominated by MNE subsidiaries, such as in Malaysia, Thailand, Philippines, Mexico and the consumer electronics industry in Brazil (Hewitt, 1992), these benefits have not accrued to anywhere near the same extent.

7. While unionization among electronics workers continues to be important internationally for the usual reasons (employment, wage bargaining, health and safety, etc.), it is also important as a mechanism to lobby governments to develop and apply industrial strategies for their electronics industries. It is in this sense – the improvement of national technological capabilities – that the development of sound industrial relations systems may be able to help labour forces in the international electronics industry.

**Notes**

1. This chapter is an updated version of a paper presented at the Third Meeting of the Forum Series on Labour in a Changing World Economy, organized by the International Institute for Labour Studies (16–17 September 1993) (Geneva).

2. For critiques of the new international division of labour thesis see Jenkins (1984), Cohen (1987: 220–53), Schoenberger (1988) and Henderson (1989: 16–24, 156–62).
3. The relative under-investment by Japanese consumer electronics firms in Korea may be a reflection partly of the Korean government's attempts to protect the domestic market from foreign competition, and partly a concern by the companies to leak technology to their Korean competitors.
4. Author's interviews in Malaysia (July 1992). See also Ernst and O'Connor (1992: 190).
5. The 'governed market' or 'plan rational' model for Korean and Taiwanese industrialization was Japan. On the Japanese experience see Johnson (1982), Okimoto (1989) and Sheridan (1993). For surveys of the arguments see Wade (1992, 1993), Castells (1992) and Henderson (1993b).
6. 'Reverse engineering' is a process of technology acquisition that involves taking apart the product, its components and embodied processes and tracing them to their basic elements. It is a laborious and time-consuming process that often can result in mistakes, leading to poor quality products.
7. This issue is discussed in Henderson (1993c).
8. Calculated from data presented by Lim and Pang (1991, Table 18: 133).
9. On 'first world' working conditions and associated environmental issues see Siegel and Markoff (1985).
10. Author's interviews with members of the Hong Kong Christian Industrial Committee and the Asia Monitor Resources Centre, Hong Kong (Autumn 1991). In the absence of systematic research on labour conditions in the new Chinese factories, Leung's (1988) work is indispensable. On the situation in Korea and Taiwan (POC), as well as the trade union response, see respectively, Asia Monitor Resources Center (1988), Ho (1990), and a number of the essays in Women Working Worldwide (1991). Deyo's book (1989) is the most important academic work to date on labour and industrialization in the East Asian NIEs.
11. Reich's (1991) argument that there is now a world market for all labour skills – including basic Research & Development seems overdrawn. For instance, his claim that Honda performs Research & Development in the USA seems to be untrue. Only market research and some product development takes place (personal communication from Martin Carnoy, Stanford University). For a critique of Reich's 'globalization' thesis that deals, *inter alia*, with the issue of the location of Research & Development by TNCs, see Hu (1992).

## References

Amsden, A.H. (1989), *Asia's Next Giant: South Korea and Late Industrialization* (New York: Oxford University Press).
Appelbaum, R.P. and J. Henderson (eds) (1992), *States and Development in the Asian Pacific Rim* (Newbury Park, Sage Publications).

Arrigo, L.G. (1984), 'Taiwan electronics workers', in M. Sheridan and J.W. Salaff (eds), *Lives: Chinese Working Women* (Bloomington: Indiana University Press): 123–45.

Asia Monitor Resources Center (1988), *Min-Ju No-Jo: South Korea's New Trade Unions* (Hong Kong: Asia Monitor Resources Center).

Bello, W. and S. Rosenfeld (1992), *Dragons in Distress: Asia's Miracle Economies in Crisis* (London: Penguin Books).

Bloom, M. (1992), *Technological Change in the Korean Electronics Industry* (Paris: Organisation for Economic Co-operation and Development).

Castells, M. (1992), 'Four Asian Tigers with a Dragon Head: A Comparative Analysis of the State, Economy and Society in the Asian Pacific Rim', in R.P. Appelbaum and J. Henderson (eds), *States and Development in the Asian Pacific Rim* (Newbury Park: Sage Publications): 33–70.

Castells, M. *et al.* (1990), *The Shek Kip Mei Syndrome: Economic Development and Public Housing in Hong Kong and Singapore* (London: Pion).

Chen, E.K.Y. (1971), 'The Electronics Industry of Hong Kong: An Analysis of its Growth', (University of Hong Kong) (unpublished M Soc Sc thesis).

Chen, S.Y. (199), 'The Historical Development of Technology Transfer in Taiwan' (Manchester Business School) (unpublished MBA dissertation).

Cheng, L.L. and G. Gereffi (1994), 'The Informal Economy in East Asian development', *International Journal of Urban and Regional Research*, 18: 194–219.

Chiang, S.N.C. (1984), 'Women and Work: Case Studies of two Hong Kong Factories', (University of Hong Kong) (unpublished M Phil thesis).

Cohen, R. (1987), *The New Helots: Migrants in the International Division of Labour* (Aldershot: Gower).

Deyo, F.C. (1989), *Beneath the Miracle: Labor Subordination in the New Asian Industrialism* (Berkeley and Los Angeles: University of California Press).

Dicken, P. (1992), *Global Shift: The Internationalisation of Economic Activity* (London and New York: Paul Chapman and Guilford).

Elson, D. (1988), 'Transnational Corporations in the New International Division of Labour: A Critique of "Cheap Labour" Hypotheses', *Manchester Papers in Development*, 4 (3): 352–76.

Elson, D. and R. Pearson (1981), 'Nimble Fingers make Cheap Workers: An Analysis of Women's Employment in Third World Export Manufacturing', *Feminist Review*, 7: 87–107.

Ernst, D. (1983), *The Global Race in Microelectronics* (Frankfurt: Campus Verlag).

Ernst, D. and D. O'Connor (1990), 'New Technology, Latecomer Industrialisation and Development Today', in *Background Report for the Technology/Economy Programme* (Paris: OECD Development Centre).

Ernst, D. and D. O'Connor (1992), *Competing in the Electronics Industry: The Experience of Newly Industrialising Economies* (Paris: OECD Development Centre).

Evans, P. (1986), 'State, Capital and the Transformation of Dependence: The Brazilian Computer Case', *World Development*, 14(7): 791–808.

Fong, M.Y. (1989), 'Hong Kong Manufacturing Investment in China: Social and Spatial Implications' (University of Hong Kong) (unpublished MSoc. Sc. dissertation).

Fröbel, F. *et al.* (1980), *The New International Division of Labour* (Cambridge: Cambridge University Press).

Gereffi, G. (1994), 'The Organisation of Buyer-driven Global Commodity Chains: How US Retailers Shape Overseas Production Networks', in G. Gereffi and M. Korzeniewicz (eds), *Commodity Chains and Global Capitalism* (Westport: Greenwood Press).

Gereffi, G. and M. Korzeniewicz (eds) (1994), *Commodity Chains and Global Capitalism* (Westport, Greenwood Press).

Grossman, R. (1979), 'Women's Place in the Integrated Circuit', *South-East Asia Chronicle* 66: 2–17.

Henderson, J. (1987), 'Semiconductors, Scotland and the International Division of Labour', *Urban Studies* 24: (5): 389–408.

Henderson, J. (1989), *The Globalisation of High Technology Production: Society, Space and Semiconductors in the Restructuring of the Modern World* (London and New York: Routledge).

Henderson, J. (1991), 'Urbanisation in the Hong Kong-South China Region: An Introduction to Dynamics and Dilemmas', *International Journal of Urban and Regional Research*, 15(2): 169–79.

Henderson, J. (1992), 'Global Economic Integration, Business Systems and States in East Asian and European Development', paper given to the First European Conference of Sociology (26–29 August) (Vienna).

Henderson, J. (1993a), 'The Role of the State in the Economic Transformation of East Asia', in C. Dixon and D. Drakakis-Smith (eds), *Economic and Social Development in Pacific Asia* (London: Routledge): 85–114.

Henderson, J. (1993b), 'Against the Economic Orthodoxy: On the Making of the East Asian Miracle', *Economy and Society*, 22 (2): 200–17.

Henderson, J. (1993c), 'Electronics Industries and the Developing World: Uneven Contributions and Uncertain Prospects', *Working Paper*, 247 (Manchester: Manchester Business School).

Henderson, J. and A.J. Scott (1987), 'The Growth and Internationalisation of the American Semiconductor Industry: Labour Processes and the Changing Spatial Organisation of Production', in M. Breheny and R. McQuaid (eds), *The Development of High Technology Industries: An International Survey* (London: Croom Helm): 37–79.

Hewitt, T. (1992), 'Employment and Skills in the Brazilian Electronics Industry', in H. Schmitz and J. Cassiolato (eds), *Hi-tech for Industrial Development: Lessons from the Brazilian Experience in Electronics and Automation* (London: Routledge): 180–205.

Heyzer, N. (1986), *Working Women in Southeast Asia* (Milton Keynes: Open University Press).

Ho, S.Y. (1990), *Taiwan – After a Long Silence* (Hong Kong: Asia Monitor Resources Center).

Hobday, M. (1992a) 'The European Electronics Industry: Technology and Structural Change', *Technovation*, 12 (2): 75–97.

Hobday, M. (1992b), 'Foreign Investment, Exports and Technology Development in the Four Dragons', paper given to the conference on 'Global Trends in Foreign Direct Investment and Strategies of Transnational Corporations in Brazil' (3–6 November) (University of Campinas, Brazil).

Hu, Y.S. (1992), 'Global or Stateless Corporations are National Firms with

International Operations', *California Management Review*, 34 (2): 107–26.

International Labour Organization (ILO) (1992), *Yearbook of Labour Statistics* (Genea: International Labour Organization).

Ismail, M.N. (1993a), 'Linkages Between Foreign Electronics Multinationals and Local Firms in Malaysia' (Manchester Business School) (unpublished paper).

Ismail M.N. (1993b), 'Manpower Upgrading and Integration in Malaysia', (Manchester Business School) (unpublished paper).

Jenkins, R. (1984), 'Divisions over the International Division of Labour', *Capital and Class*, 22: 28–57.

Jesudason, J. (1989), *Ethnicity and the Economy: The State, Chinese Business and Multinationals in Malaysia* (Singapore: Oxford University Press).

Johnson, C. (1982), *MITI and the Japanese Miracle: The Growth of Industrial Policy 1925–1975* (Stanford: Stanford University Press).

Leung, W.Y. (1988), *Smashing the Iron Rice Pot: Workers and Unions in China's Market Socialism* (Hong Kong: Asia Monitor Resources Center).

Lim, L.Y.C. and P.E. Fong (1982), 'Vertical Linkages and Multinational Enterprises in Developing Countries', *World Development* 10 (6): 585–95.

Lim, L.Y.C. and P.E. Fong (1991), *Foreign Direct Investment and Industrialisation in Malaysia, Singapore, Taiwan and Thailand* (Paris: OECD Development Centre).

Lubeck, P. (1992), 'Malaysian Industrialisation, Ethnic Divisions and the NIC Model: The Limits to Replication' in R.P. Appelbaum and J. Henderson (eds), *States and Development in the Asian Pacific Rim* (Newbury Park: Sage Publications): 176–98.

Milkman, R. (1991), *Japan's California Factories: Labour Relations and Economic Globalisation* (Los Angeles: UCLA Institute of Industrial Relations).

Mitter, S. (1992), 'New Skill Requirements and Appropriate Programmes for the Enhancement of Participation of the Female Labour Force in Industry in Selected Economies of the Asia-Pacific Region', paper given to the Economic and Social Commission for Asia and the Pacific Regional Workshop on 'Promoting Diversified Skill Development for Women in Industry', (23–27 March) (Chiang Mai, Thailand).

Mirza, H. (1986) *Multinationals and the Growth of the Singapore Economy* (New York: St Martin's Press).

Okimoto, D.I. (1989), *Between MITI and the Market: Japanese Industrial Policy for High Technology* (Stanford: Stanford University Press).

Ong, A. (1987), *Spirits of Resistance and Capitalist Discipline: Factory Women in Malaysia* (Albany: State University of New York Press).

Parsonage, J. (1992), 'Southeast Asia's "Growth Triangle": A Subregional Response to Global Transformation', *International Journal of Urban and Regional Research*, 16 (2): 307–17.

Porter, M.E. (1990), *The Competitive Advantage of Nations* (London: Macmillan).

Redding, S.G. (1990), *The Spirit of Chinese Capitalism* (Berlin: De Gruyter).

Reich, R. (1991), *The Work of Nations: Preparing Ourselves for the Twenty First Century* (New York: Vintage Books).

Salih, K. (1988), 'The new economic policy after 1990', *MIER Discussion Paper*, 21 (Kuala Lumpur: Malaysian Institute of Economic Research).

Schiffer, J. (1991), 'State Policy and Economic Growth: A Note on the Hong

Kong Model', *International Journal of Urban and Regional Research*, 15 (2): 180–96.

Schoenberger, E. (1988), 'Multinational Corporations and the New International Division of Labour', *International Regional Science Review*, 11 (2): 105–19.

Scott, A.J. (1987), 'The Semiconductor Industry in Southeast Asia: Organisation, Location and the International Division of Labour', *Regional Studies*, 21 (2): 143–60.

Sheridan, K. (1993), *Governing the Japanese Economy* (Cambridge: Polity Press).

Siegel, L. and J. Markoff (1985), *The High Cost of High Tech: The Dark Side of the Chip* (New York: Harper & Row).

Teal, G. (1995), 'The JSR (Johor-Singapore-Riau) Growth Triangle' Paper presented at a conference organised by the International Institute for Labour Studies and the ILO Regional Office for Asia and the Pacific, 23–26 January, Bangkok, Thailand.

UNCTAD (1994), *World Investment Report 1994: Transnational Corporations, Employment and the Workplace* (Geneva: UNCTAD).

Wade, R. (1990), *Governing the Market: Economic Theory and the Role of Government in East Asian Industrialisation* (Princeton: Princeton University Press).

Wade, R. (1992), 'East Asia's Economic Success: Conflicting Perspectives, Partial Insights, Shaky Evidence', *World Politics*, 44 (2): 270–320.

Wade, R. (1993), 'Managing Trade: Taiwan and South Korea as Challenges to Economics and Political Science', *Comparative Politics*, 25 (2): 147–67.

Whitla, P. (1991) 'The Competitive Position of Hong Kong' (Manchester Business School) unpublished MBA dissertation).

Women Working Worldwide (1991), *Common Interests: Women Organising in Global Electronics* (London: Women Working Worldwide).

# Part III

# Regional and Subregional Integration

# 4 Regional Integration of East and Southeast Asian Economies: The Role of Japan

Susumu Watanabe

Stimulated by rapidly expanding market potentials within the region, by persisting labour shortages at home and by the continuing appreciation of the yen, Japanese firms are now concentrating their foreign direct investment (FDI) more heavily in East and Southeast Asia (ESEA). The current surge of Japanese FDI differs from the earlier wave in the 1970s in that it is aimed at promoting an intra-regional horizontal division of labour, particularly in the metal engineering industries, as opposed to a vertical division of labour between basic material and light consumer goods producers in the region (textiles in particular) and Japanese producer goods manufacturers, as was the case in the previous period. In consequence, it is causing not only the growth of, but also significant structural changes in, Japan's intra-regional trade. This naturally has important implications for employment in host economies. At the same time, an increasing shift of manufacturing facilities to outside the country has sparked concern over the 'hollowing-out' of the Japanese industrial base and consequent decline in employment opportunities for Japanese workers.

Unlike the 'regionalization' of European economies and that of North American economies which have been systematically planned on largely defensive grounds, the integration of ESEA economies has been advancing spontaneously on the basis of independent corporate decisions. Until now, this has been a rational choice for Japan and for its regional partners: any collectively defensive move within the region would inevitably be countered on North American and European markets, and yet these markets are still too important for them to take such a risk. However, a more systematic, collaborative strategy is now called for. For one thing, in order to move ahead with regional integration, ASEAN

countries will have to reduce supply constraints with respect to infrastructure and technical manpower, while Japan (and increasingly the
Republic of Korea and the Taiwan Province of China as well) need to
minimize the potential for a 'hollowing-out' effect.

This chapter discusses the above points in turn, beginning with a
recent statistical overview of Japan's role in ESEA regionalization.


JAPANESE INVESTMENT IN ASIA

After phenomenal growth during the second half of the 1980s, Japanese FDI declined just as dramatically during the next four years, back
to the 'pre-bubble' level of 3–4 billion dollars a year. The enormous
capital flow during the late 1980s was directed almost exclusively to
the industrialized regions and to Asia. North America, Europe and Oceania
received 75 per cent of total Japanese FDI and 77 of Japanese investment in the primary and secondary sectors, while Asia hosted 12.4
and 19.5 per cent, respectively (cf. Watanabe, 1993a). The average
annual rate of FDI flows during FY 1991–3 was 22 per cent lower
than in the previous five years, although the trend reversed in FY 1993.
The decline took place mainly in the industrialized regions. In Asia,
Japanese FDI continued to increase, particularly in the manufacturing
sector and in China (Tables 4.1 and 4.3). Consequently, Asia's share
of Japanese FDI has started to recover and this trend will almost certainly persist for years to come, as attractive investment opportunities
are now growing rapidly in Asia, notably in China and Vietnam.

Asia's share in the overall flow of Japanese FDI fell from 27.6 per
cent in the 1970s to 12.4 per cent in the second half of the 1980s
before recovering to 17 per cent in FY 1991–3 (Table 4.2). During the
1970s, Japanese firms, particularly textile manufacturers, invested actively in this region in order to cope with the first round of the 'high
yen'. Increasing trade frictions with industrialized countries and the
prospect of regional integration of European markets, however, diverted
Japanese capital to North America and Europe during the following
decade. Under the 'bubble' economic conditions of 1986–9, Japanese
firms also invested heavily in tax havens in Latin America and Africa.
Within the manufacturing sector, Asia's share has been higher than in
the total: 37 per cent during the 1970s, 20 per cent during the second
half of the 1980s and 29 per cent in FY 1991–3.

The current wave of investment in the region is partly motivated by
the further appreciation of the yen, but is different from the earlier one

in that it is more concentrated in metal engineering industries (Table 4.1) and more oriented towards regional markets. As will be shown below, Japanese industries are now becoming more closely integrated with their counterparts in the region either on the basis of product-wise specialization and division of labour or through international sub-contracting of parts and component manufacturing.

Within Asia, 98 per cent of the cumulative total of Japanese FDI since 1951 is located to the east of Malaysia in the newly-industrializing economies (NIEs–Hong Kong, Korea, Singapore and Taiwan), the ASEAN-4 (Indonesia, Malaysia, Philippines and Thailand) and China (Table 4.3). The bulk of recent investment in Hong Kong is in fact related to operations in Southern China (cf. JETRO, 1993, Chapter III]. Although the share of the NIEs in the region's cumulative total is larger (49 per cent) than the ASEAN-4's (44 per cent), the latter group has received more of Japan's manufacturing FDI than the former since 1988. It is not difficult to explain why. ASEAN markets are growing rapidly, and the governments in this subregion have added to incentives for foreign investors and reduced restrictions. In Korea and Taiwan, on the other hand, labour costs and industrial disputes have increased considerably, as have trade frictions with western countries, so much so that Korean and Taiwanese firms are now investing elsewhere in the region.

According to MITI's *4th Basic Survey* on Japanese firms' overseas business activities, as of spring 1990 (MITI, 1991) access to labour supply was the most common motive of Japanese FDI in ASEAN manufacturing industries (67.6 per cent of the respondents), followed by 'access to local market' (58.9 per cent) and 'official incentives for foreign investors' (42.4 per cent). This conforms to the well established motivation for foreign investment in developing countries. In contrast, 65 per cent of Japanese investors in the NIEs mentioned 'access to local market' as at least one of their motives, while labour supply and investment incentives were quoted by 62 and 23 per cent, respectively. As nearly 20 per cent of the respondents in both groups quoted 'export to Japan', however, the relative importance of labour supply was somewhat greater than the above figures suggest. 'Access to third markets' was mentioned by 31 per cent in the NIEs and 21 per cent in the ASEAN-4, which broadly indicates the degrees of involvement of the two groups of economies in Japanese firms' regional or global operations.

Even among the NIEs and among the ASEAN-4, however, there are significant inter-country differences (Table 4.4). Among the NIEs, labour supply is a more important motive of investment in Korea than

Table 4.1 Japanese overseas direct investment as approved by or reported to the Ministry of Finance, FY1951-93 (US$ million)

| Sector/industry | All regions | | | | | | Asia | | | | | |
|---|---|---|---|---|---|---|---|---|---|---|---|---|
| | 1951–93 | 1951–70 | 1971–80 | 1981–85 | 1986–90 | 1991–93 | 1951–93 | 1951–70 | 1971–80 | 1981–85 | 1986–90 | 1991–93 |
| I. Primary sector | 22 561 | 886 | 7 094 | 4 995 | 5 659 | 3 925 | 8 945 | 315 | 2 993 | 3 239 | 1 335 | 1 063 |
| | (5.3) | (24.8) | (21.5) | (10.6) | (2.5) | (3.5) | (13.4) | (41.9) | (32.9) | (33.6) | (4.8) | (5.6) |
| Agriculture & fishery | 2 803 | 82 | 827 | 312 | 876 | 706 | 700 | 47 | 239 | 61 | 178 | 175 |
| Mining | 19 758 | 804 | 6 267 | 4 683 | 4 783 | 3 219 | 8 245 | 268 | 2 754 | 3 178 | 1 157 | 888 |
| II. Secondary sector | 115 112 | 928 | 11 645 | 11 826 | 57 213 | 33 500 | 28 356 | 320 | 4 258 | 2 946 | 11 141 | 9 691 |
| | (27.2) | (25.9) | (35.4) | (25.1) | (25.2) | (30.0) | (42.6) | (42.6) | (46.9) | (30.6) | (39.7) | (51.0) |
| Food | 6 123 | 51 | 535 | 505 | 2 994 | 2 037 | 1 536 | 23 | 125 | 108 | 912 | 368 |
| Textiles | 5 540 | 189 | 1 448 | 445 | 1 915 | 1 542 | 2 610 | 107 | 813 | 261 | 685 | 744 |
| Timber, paper, pulp | 4 057 | 212 | 546 | 362 | 1 847 | 1 089 | 695 | 15 | 127 | 49 | 335 | 169 |
| Chemicals | 16 300 | 50 | 2 576 | 1 356 | 6 958 | 5 359 | 4 690 | 19 | 702 | 570 | 1 350 | 2 049 |
| Metals | 12 794 | 138 | 2 481 | 2 571 | 5 119 | 2 485 | 3 650 | 34 | 997 | 666 | 1 108 | 845 |
| General machinery | 11 491 | 68 | 826 | 1 077 | 5 961 | 3 559 | 2 551 | 15 | 258 | 307 | 1 069 | 902 |
| Electrical & electronic machinery | 27 235 | 73 | 1 506 | 2 166 | 16 613 | 6 875 | 6 469 | 45 | 498 | 289 | 3 342 | 2 295 |
| Transport equipment | 15 007 | 87 | 892 | 2 395 | 7 507 | 4 126 | 2 207 | 14 | 252 | 307 | 1 006 | 628 |
| Other | 16 565 | 61 | 833 | 947 | 8 297 | 6 427 | 3 819 | 48 | 476 | 272 | 1 335 | 1 688 |
| III. Tertiary sector | 284 882 | 1 763 | 14 181 | 30 331 | 164 284 | 74 320 | 29 225 | 116 | 1 837 | 3 449 | 15 579 | 8 244 |
| | (65.7) | (49.3) | (43.1) | (64.3) | (72.3) | (66.5) | (43.9) | (15.5) | (20.2) | (35.8) | (55.5) | (43.4) |
| Construction | 3 627 | 36 | 360 | 401 | 1 592 | 1 237 | 1 043 | 4 | 72 | 149 | 516 | 302 |
| Commerce | 45 364 | 381 | 5 028 | 7 269 | 18 638 | 14 048 | 5 964 | 17 | 384 | 658 | 2 734 | 2 171 |
| Financing & insurance | 81 271 | 318 | 2 108 | 8 433 | 54 459 | 15 952 | 6 387 | 65 | 201 | 515 | 3 450 | 2 156 |
| Services | 50 152 | 49 | 1 344 | 3 293 | 29 980 | 15 486 | 7 224 | 5 | 624 | 1 271 | 3 802 | 1 522 |
| Transport | 23 809 | – | – | 5 900 | 11 538 | 6 371 | 1 808 | – | – | 249 | 847 | 712 |
| Real assets trade | 65 966 | – | – | 2 533 | 43 316 | 20 116 | 3 966 | – | – | 307 | 2 683 | 976 |
| Other | 14 693 | 978 | 5 342 | 2 500 | 4 764 | 1 110 | 2 834 | 25 | 556 | 300 | 1 547 | 406 |

| | | | | | | | | | | | |
|---|---|---|---|---|---|---|---|---|---|---|---|
| Total | 422 555 | 3 577 | 32 920 | 47 152 | 227 157 | 111 747 | 66 517 [15.7] | 751 [21.0] | 9 078 [27.6] | 9 634 [20.4] | 28 056 [12.4] | 18 998 [17.0] |
| Average total per year | 9 827 | 179 | – | 3 292 | 9 430 | 45 431 | 1 547 | 38 | 908 | 1 927 | 5 611 | 6 333 |
| Growth index relative to the previous period | – | – | 1 839 | 286 | 482 | –22 | – | 2 389 | 216 | 291 | 113 | |

*Notes*:

1. All ODI projects were subject to official approval until December 1980, since which date only those exceeding certain amounts have been required to be reported in advance. The cutting point for reporting was 3 million yen until March 1984 and 10 million yen between April 1984 and June 1989. It has remained at 30 million yen since July 1989. Neither reinvestment of overseas affiliates' profits nor locally financed investment is included in the data. 2. '–' stands for a negligible amount. Due to these entries and rounding-up the sum does not always equal the total or sub-total. 3. The figures in parentheses stand for shares in the regional totals, and those in brackets for shares in the world totals. 4. 'Commerce' includes manufacturers' sales offices. 'Transport' is largely related to ship registry in tax havens. 'Other' in the tertiary sector includes 'branch offices' in the original source, as well as 'real assets' up to 1980, after which date purchase of real assets was excluded from the ODI data.

*Source*: Compiled using annually published data from the Ministry of Finance, the Government of Japan *Kaigai Chokesetu Tōshi (Todokeide Bēsu)* (overseas direct investment statistics on the reporting basis).

*Table* 4.2   Changes in the geographical distribution of Japanese ODI, FY1951–93 (per cent)

| Year | North America | Europe | Oceania | Asia | Latin America | Africa | Middle East |
|---|---|---|---|---|---|---|---|
| 1951–93 | 43.8 | 19.8 | 6.1 | 15.7 | 11.8 | 1.7 | 1.1 |
| 1951–70 | 25.5 | 17.9 | 7.9 | 21.0 | 15.9 | 2.6 | 9.3 |
| 1971–80 | 27.0 | 11.6 | 6.8 | 27.6 | 17.0 | 4.1 | 5.8 |
| 1981–5 | 36.4 | 13.9 | 3.6 | 20.4 | 20.1 | 4.1 | 1.5 |
| 1986–90 | 48.1 | 21.2 | 6.1 | 12.4 | 10.9 | 1.2 | 0.2 |
| 1991–3 | 43.6 | 21.8 | 6.9 | 17.0 | 8.4 | 1.4 | 0.9 |

*Note*:
Over 70 per cent of investment in Latin America and in Africa was absorbed by tax havens in the Caribbean and in Liberia.

*Source*: See Table 4.1.

*Table* 4.3   Japanese direct investment in Asia, FY1951–93 (US$ million)

| Country | 1951–93 | 1951–70 | 1971–80 | 1981–5 | 1986–90 | 1991–3 |
|---|---|---|---|---|---|---|
| Indonesia | 15 222 | 242 | 4 182 | 3 999 | 3 117 | 3 682 |
| Hong Kong | 12 748 | 29 | 1 067 | 1 836 | 6 918 | 2 898 |
| Singapore | 8 481 | 33 | 904 | 1 333 | 4 285 | 1 927 |
| Thailand | 6 465 | 91 | 305 | 363 | 3 663 | 2 042 |
| China | 6 163 | – | 26 | 262 | 2 535 | 3 340 |
| Malaysia | 5 615 | 50 | 600 | 480 | 2 105 | 2 384 |
| Korea | 4 868 | 32 | 1 104 | 545 | 2 456 | 730 |
| Taiwan | 3 719 | 85 | 284 | 391 | 1 970 | 989 |
| Philippines | 2 150 | 74 | 541 | 278 | 687 | 570 |
| Other | 1 085 | 115 | 65 | 147 | 320 | 436 |
| All Asia | 66 517 | 751 | 9 078 | 9 634 | 28 056 | 18 998 |

*Source*: See Table 4.1.

in Singapore. The latter has become Japanese firms' component supply base and service centre for the ASEAN subregion. In other words, some Japanese firms in Singapore are there to support other Japanese firms' operations in neighbouring countries, as is testified by the high frequency of reply 'Japanese clients' request' in Table 4.4. Among the ASEAN-4, Indonesia attracts Japanese manufacturers mainly with its huge market potentials, whereas Philippines, Malaysia and Thailand function more as offshore production bases. It should be noted that 'local market' in the latter two countries is related, more often than not, to supply of parts and components to other Japanese firms operating

*Table* 4.4   Motivation of Japanese manufacturing FDI in Asia (per cent)

|  | Korea (107) | Singapore (112) | Indonesia (126) | Malaysia (208) | Philippines (50) | Thailand (261) |
|---|---|---|---|---|---|---|
| Local market | 48.6 | 51.8 | 59.5 | 30.8 | 28.0 | 37.5 |
| Labour supply | 20.6 | 5.4 | 10.3 | 23.6 | 38.0 | 23.8 |
| Third-country market | 15.9 | 11.6 | 11.9 | 20.2 | 24.0 | 14.2 |
| Japanese clients' request | 1.9 | 30.4 | 9.5 | 20.2 | 6.0 | 19.2 |
| Other | 23.4 | 26.8 | 29.3 | 33.1 | 26.0 | 24.9 |

*Note*:
The figures in parentheses represent the number of respondents, who were allowed to give more than one reply.

*Source*: JETRO (1993, various pages).

in these countries, i.e. at 'Japanese clients' request'. For these two countries, however, the meaning of this 'request' in Table 4.4 – i.e. vertical supply linkages – is different between these two countries and Singapore.

## JAPANESE TRADE WITH ASIA

Just as its FDI, Japan's exports and imports have been growing much faster within Asia than elsewhere, and the ESEA is now the country's largest trade partner (Table 4.5). In 1993, the NIEs accounted for 69 and 45 per cent of the country's intra-regional exports and imports, respectively. The corresponding figures for the ASEAN-4 were 28 and 50 per cent. A major import item from this subregion is Indonesia's petroleum.

What is even more striking are structural changes in Japanese imports. While the total amount of imports from the region doubled between 1985 and 1993, fuel imports declined by nearly 20 per cent and manufactured imports more than quadrupled. In particular, machinery imports expanded more than eight times, including electronics components such as semiconductors (Table 4.6). Exports to Asian countries increased by 3.5 times over the same period, but their product composition remained relatively stable, although the share of machinery rose by 10 points to offset the declines in light industry goods and in metals. One may say, therefore, that Japanese industries' integration with their Asian counterparts is advancing primarily through the restructuring

*Table* 4.5   Changes in the geographical structure of Japanese trade, 1960–93

|  | 1960 | 1970 | 1980 | 1990 | 1993 |
|---|---|---|---|---|---|
| *Exports* (US$ million) | 4055 | 19 318 | 129 807 | 286 948 | 360 911 |
| Asia | 32.2 | 28.5 | 28.1 | 31.1 | 37.5 |
| North America | 29.7 | 33.7 | 26.0 | 33.8 | 31.0 |
| Latin America | 7.5 | 6.1 | 6.9 | 3.6 | 4.7 |
| Western Europe | 11.7 | 15.0 | 16.5 | 21.9 | 17.7 |
| Eastern Europe | 1.6 | 2.3 | 2.8 | 1.2 | 0.6 |
| Oceania | 4.9 | 4.2 | 3.4 | 3.1 | 2.7 |
| Middle East | 3.5 | 2.8 | 10.1 | 3.4 | 3.7 |
| Other | 22.7 | 20.0 | 19.3 | 9.9 | 10.1 |
| *Imports* (US$ million) | 4491 | 18 881 | 140 528 | 234 799 | 240 670 |
| Asia | 2.1 | 17.6 | 25.8 | 28.8 | 34.3 |
| North America | 39.1 | 34.4 | 20.7 | 25.9 | 26.4 |
| Latin America | 6.9 | 7.3 | 4.1 | 4.2 | 3.5 |
| Western Europe | 8.8 | 10.2 | 7.4 | 18.0 | 15.2 |
| Eastern Europe | 2.1 | 3.1 | 1.5 | 1.7 | 1.4 |
| Oceania | 9.0 | 9.6 | 6.0 | 6.3 | 6.3 |
| Middle East | 9.4 | 12.0 | 31.3 | 13.4 | 11.3 |
| Africa | 3.6 | 5.8 | 3.2 | 1.7 | 1.6 |

*Source*: MITI, *Tsûshó Hakusho (White Paper on External Trade 1994)*, volume on individual products and countries: 786.

of their imports rather than exports. Obviously, it is Japanese firms' direct investment in this region which has induced growth and structural changes in their intra-regional trade.

The pursuit of economies of scale and the appreciation of the yen encourage the growth of exports from overseas plants back to the home markets. On the basis of its *22nd Survey* on Japanese firms' overseas business activities (MITI, 1993) MITI estimates that Japan's 'reversed imports' from overseas manufacturing plants in FY 1991 amounted to 2124 billion yen (US$16 billion), which corresponded to 13.2 per cent of the country's total manufactured imports and to 8.4 per cent of the aggregate turnover of the overseas Japanese firms cooperating in the survey. Asia accounted for 60 per cent of the total. Affiliates in this region exported 16 per cent of their annual turnover to Japan, of which 60 per cent represented electrical and electronic products. The share of transport equipment remained at about 10 per cent of total 'reversed imports', but the Japanese automakers' share grew from below 5 per cent of total car imports in 1990 to 19 per cent in 1993. In this industry, the ratio of overseas to domestic production rose from 26 to 31 per

*Table* 4.6 Structural changes in Japan's trade within Asia, 1985 and 1993
(US$ million)

| | 1985 Amount | % | 1993 Amount | % | Growth index (1985 = 100) |
|---|---|---|---|---|---|
| *Imports* | 30 264 | (100.0) | 60 592 | (100.0) | 200 |
| Food | 3714 | (12.3) | 9833 | (16.2) | 265 |
| Raw materials | 4028 | (13.3) | 6261 | (10.3) | 155 |
| Mineral fuels | 14 863 | (49.1) | 11 994 | (19.8) | 81 |
| Manufactured imports | 7147 | (23.6) | 31 264 | (51.6) | 437 |
|   Machinery | 1429 | (4.7) | 11 476 | (18.9) | 803 |
|   General | 295 | (1.0) | 3524 | (5.8) | 1194 |
|   Electrical and electronic | 872 | (2.9) | 6436 | (10.6) | 738 |
|   Electronics parts | 295 | (1.0) | 2120 | (3.5) | 719 |
| *Exports* | 33 248 | (100.0) | 117 425 | (100.0) | 353 |
| Food | 437 | (1.3) | 1164 | (1.0) | 266 |
| Raw materials | 541 | (1.6) | 2079 | (1.8) | 384 |
| Light industry goods | 4961 | (14.9) | 12 251 | (10.4) | 247 |
| Chemicals | 3161 | (9.5) | 10 103 | (8.6) | 320 |
| Metals | 4876 | (14.7) | 11 336 | (9.7) | 232 |
| Machinery | 18 799 | (56.5) | 78 471 | (66.8) | 417 |

*Source*: See Table 4.5.

cent between 1992 and 1994, while it jumped from 12 to 41 per cent
in the case of VTR (video tape recorders) (*NKS*, 6 March 1995: 7).
Such ratios will no doubt continue to rise in various industries; in the
JETRO survey in October 1993, 35 per cent of a total of 189 responding firms reported that they had already been importing their products
from abroad and 75 per cent of 177 responding to a separate question
anticipated that they would be doing so in five years' time (JETRO
1994: 56–60).

In the same JETRO survey, just about half of the respondents anticipated that their overseas production would continue to grow while
domestic production would remain at its current level or decline during the next five years. Moreover, their factories abroad, in whatever
region, would become more integrated in regional or global operations. In Asia, the proportions of factories primarily catering to host
country (Japanese) markets would decline from 39 (21) per cent in
1993 to 26 (17) per cent while those working primarily for the Asian
market (other regions) would rise from 21 (18) per cent to 31 (22) per
cent over the same period (JETRO, 1994: 64–70).

## THE IMPACT ON HOST ECONOMIES

### Japan's Share in FDI and External Trade

Japan has become the first or second investor in the NIEs and the ASEAN-4 in terms of the cumulative total or the annual amount. In the cumulative total it accounted for 40.6 per cent of the total stock of FDI received by Korea and for between 20 and 30 per cent in Indonesia, Thailand and Taiwan (including FDI by overseas Chinese). In 1991–3, its share was 25–35 per cent in Hong Kong, Thailand, Taiwan and Philippines, just below 20 per cent in Malaysia and Korea and 12 per cent in Indonesia. A striking exception is China. Here, Japan had invested US\$4.5 billion by the end of FY 1992, which corresponds to no more than 4 per cent of the FDI the country received between 1979 and 1992 (on the contract basis).[1]

With respect to trade, Japan remains a predominant export market for Indonesia with its petroleum and other minerals. For most countries, Japan's share in their total exports has broadly tended to decline over the last 10 or 15 years. This is no doubt attributable, in part, to the increasing diversification and globalization of these economies. In the case of Korea and Taiwan, their industrial structures are becoming more competitive with, rather than complementary to, Japanese industries. Japan is still a primary supplier of machinery and processed industrial materials to the region, and its shares in individual economies' total imports appear to increase when their industrial growth accelerates as has been the case in Malaysia, Philippines and Thailand (Table 4.7). Regarding China, it is important to note that its trade pattern changed significantly during the second half of the 1980s: between 1985 and 1990, the share of exports through Hong Kong grew from 26 to 43 per cent of the total, and that of imports through Hong Kong from 11 to 27 per cent. Japanese trade with China may thus be understated in Table 4.7. But, even allowing for this factor, there is no denying that Japan's involvement in this economy is still at an initial stage, with respect not only to direct investment but also to trade.

### Direct Employment

According to MITI's *22nd Survey Report,* in Spring 1992, Japanese firms abroad employed 1.62 million workers, 78 per cent in the manufacturing sector and 20 per cent in the tertiary sector. Asia accounted for 46 per cent of the total employment and 52 per cent of the industrial

*Table* 4.7    Japan's shares in external trade of Asian economies, 1965–93
(per cent)

| Country | Exports/imports | 1965 | 1970 | 1975 | 1980 | 1985 | 1990 | 1993 |
|---------|-----------------|------|------|------|------|------|------|------|
| Korea | E | 25.1 | 28.1 | 25.4 | 17.4 | 15.0 | 19.4 | 13.8 |
| | I | 36.0 | 40.8 | 33.5 | 26.6 | 24.3 | 26.6 | 24.0 |
| Taiwan | E | 31.1 | 15.1 | 13.1 | 11.0 | 11.3 | 12.4 | 10.6 |
| | I | 37.1 | 38.1 | 30.4 | 27.1 | 27.6 | 29.3 | 30.1 |
| Hong Kong | E | 5.9 | 7.1 | n.a. | 4.7 | 7.1 | 5.7 | 4.3 |
| | I | 16.1 | 23.8 | 20.9 | 23.0 | 23.1 | 16.1 | 16.6 |
| Singapore | E | n.a. | 7.6 | 8.7 | 8.1 | 9.4 | 8.7 | 7.6 |
| | I | n.a. | 19.4 | 16.9 | 17.8 | 17.1 | 20.2 | 21.9 |
| Indonesia | E | 18.9 | 40.8 | 44.1 | 49.3 | 46.2 | 42.5 | 30.3 |
| | I | 32.3 | 29.4 | 31.0 | 31.5 | 25.8 | 24.8 | 22.1 |
| Malaysia | E | n.a. | n.a. | n.a. | 22.8 | 24.6 | 15.3 | 13.0 |
| | I | n.a. | n.a. | n.a. | 22.8 | 23.0 | 24.2 | 27.5 |
| Philippines | E | 28.2 | 39.6 | 37.7 | 26.6 | 19.0 | 19.9 | 16.3 |
| | I | 24.2 | 31.6 | 27.9 | 19.9 | 14.0 | 18.4 | 22.8 |
| Thailand | E | n.a. | 25.5 | 27.6 | 15.1 | 13.4 | 17.1 | 17.0 |
| | I | n.a. | 37.4 | 31.5 | 21.2 | 26.5 | 30.4 | 30.3 |
| China | E | n.a. | 13.9 | 24.1 | 22.2 | 22.3 | 14.6 | 17.2 |
| | I | n.a. | 33.0 | 37.8 | 26.5 | 35.7 | 14.1 | 22.4 |

*Notes*:
Hong Kong's export figures do not include re-exports, and its 1980 figures relate to 1981.

*Source*: Bank of Japan, *Gaikoku Keizai Tôkei Nempô* (Statistical Yearbook on Foreign Economies), various issues.

employment (744 000 and 656 000 workers, respectively). This implies that Japanese investment in this region has been much more labour-intensive than in other regions, since Asia received no more than 15.7 per cent of the global total of postwar Japanese FDI in all sectors and 24.6 per cent in the manufacturing sector (Table 4.1).

Employment at Japanese firms' affiliates as ascertained by this survey exceeded 1 per cent of total employment in four Asian economies: Singapore (4.2 per cent), Malaysia (1.8 per cent), Hong Kong (1.2 per cent) and Taiwan (1.1 per cent). In the manufacturing sector alone, the share was over 1 per cent in all the countries except China and Indonesia (Table 4.8). As noted above, Indonesia received the lion's share of the Japanese FDI in the past, but the bulk of the investment received was absorbed in low labour-intensity projects such as aluminium and petro-chemicals production.

*Table* 4.8　Employment at Japanese manufacturing affiliates in Asia, Spring 1992

| Country | Total manufacturing employment in 1992 (1) | Employment at Japanese affiliates | |
|---|---|---|---|
| | | No. of workers (2) | % in total (3) |
| NIEs | | | |
| Hong Kong | 565 600 | 15 582 | 2.8 |
| Singapore | 434 100 | 53 187 | 12.3 |
| Rep. of Korea | 4 768 000 | 83 318 | 1.7 |
| Taiwan | 2 620 000 | 85 465 | 3.3 |
| ASEAN-4 | | | |
| Indonesia | 7 847 600 | 71 413 | 0.9 |
| Thailand | 3 132 500[a] | 141 431 | 4.5 |
| Malaysia | 1 332 800[a] | 109 874 | 8.2 |
| Philippines | 2 546 000 | 30 263 | 1.2 |
| China | (99 490 000)[b] | 35 919 | – |
| Other | n.a. | 29 940 | n.a. |
| All Asia | n.a. | 656 392 (6922)[c] | n.a. |

*Notes*:
[a]　1990 figure.
[b]　1991 figure including mining and utilities.
[c]　The number of Japanese employees includes in the total.

*Sources*: Column (2) is from ILO, *Yearbook of Labour Statistics* (1993) and *Industry of Free China* (February 1993) for Taiwan. Column (3) from MITT's *22nd Survey Report* (1993): 127–8.

It must be noted, however, that the above estimates are subject to a number of qualifications. First, the response ratio in the survey was 78.5 per cent of the total number of Japanese firms' overseas affiliates on the MITI list (8505 out of 10 835 firms) and the direct employment effects are thus understated.

Second, not all the affiliates are wholly owned by Japanese. Therefore, employment at these firms is not entirely attributable to Japanese FDI. Nor can one simply apply their equity shares to assess their contribution because at least some of the firms partially owned by Japanese could not have come into existence or survived competition without their participation.

Third, the data in Table 4.8 ignore the quality of employment. Official employment figures in the Third World include under-employed workers in agriculture and in urban 'informal sectors'. If we use the number of 'unpaid family workers' and 'employers and own-account workers' as a proxy of under-employment, these categories accounted, around 1990, for 72 per cent of the economically active population in Indonesia, 70 per cent in Thailand, 50 per cent in the Philippines and 38 per cent in Malaysia (ILO, *Yearbook of Labour Statistics*, 1993 and earlier issues). Clearly, the employment effect of Japanese investment ought to be assessed in relation to formal-sector employment only. If so, it must have been much more significant than the percentage figures in Table 4.8 suggest. For example, according to Charoenloet (Chapter 7 in this volume), formal-sector employees accounted for 13.3 per cent of total industrial employment in Thailand in 1986. If this percentage is applied to the industrial employment figure for the country in Table 4.8, the Japanese firm's share will be increased to 33.9 per cent.

Finally, one also needs to take account of indirect employment effects accruing from the Keynesian multiplier effect and from backward and forward linkage effects. It is beyond the scope of the present study to assess these effects. It may simply be noted that, using input–output analysis, Yamashita (1989, p. 19) argues that the total employment effect of Japanese investment in the ASEAN economies may be about three times as large as its direct effect. This is broadly consistent with Yokota (1987, quoted in Sibunruang and Brimble, 1988: 18) who estimates the ratio of total indirect to direct employment generated by foreign manufacturing firms in Thailand at 2.23 using the 1980 input–output table of the country. However, the ratio is bound to vary from one country to another, depending on the structures of Japanese investment and of the host economy. Existing estimates will also become dated quickly due to rapid changes in these factors.

MITI's *4th Basic Survey* shows that the import dependence of Japanese firms operating in developing countries tends to rise with the degree of sophistication of their products. In the ASEAN region, the local content ratio was the lowest in the precision, electrical and electronic, and transport machinery industries, being 39, 55 and 62 per cent, respectively. As most local parts and component suppliers are also owned by Japanese firms, a significant portion of the indirect employment effect accruing from linkage effects is in fact included in the direct effect of the Japanese FDI.

*Table* 4.9   Training methods used by Japanese firms, selected countries, 1992 (no. of replies)

| Training method | Korea (111) | Singapore (121) | Thailand (264) | Indonesia (126) | Malaysia (219) | Philippines (54) |
|---|---|---|---|---|---|---|
| *Managerial staff* | | | | | | |
| OJT | 69 | 84 | 201 | 101 | 173 | 41 |
| Training in Japan | 73 | 57 | 157 | 74 | 125 | 35 |
| External seminars/ lectures | 40 | 56 | 175 | 89 | 146 | 34 |
| Overseas study | 6 | 3 | 18 | 9 | 7 | 1 |
| *Line staff* | | | | | | |
| OJT | 75 | 92 | 222 | 110 | 188 | 44 |
| Training in Japan | 83 | 59 | 187 | 93 | 153 | 36 |
| Training by Japanese instructors | 45 | 54 | 176 | 80 | 133 | 32 |
| Training at related firms outside Japan | 7 | 10 | 21 | 17 | 39 | 11 |
| QC circle | 34 | 24 | 97 | 55 | 80 | 22 |
| Suggestion scheme | 46 | 34 | 104 | 53 | 82 | 27 |

*Source*: JETRO (1993, various pages).

## Training Effects

With a view to achieving 'no defect production' or 'total quality control (TQC)' and eliminating waste in their production processes, Japanese firms devote considerable resources to the training of their employees – much more so than their Western counterparts, because the Japanese production system relies more heavily on human factors for its smooth operation:

> While the American firms try to develop a 'structure' which functions sufficiently well irrespective of the personalities and attitudes of the workforce, the Japanese approach is to create the right people, who can work effectively irrespective of structure (Takamiya, 1985: 193)

On the basis of his survey of Japanese firms operating in Indonesia, Malaysia and Thailand Sato (1985: 19, 24) argues similarly and shows that the most common training methods are OJT (on-the-job training) and training in Japan. This is consistent with findings of the 1993 JETRO Survey (Table 4.9). While the survey data presumably relate to regular training methods, workers are usually trained at home plants when a new plant or new production line is set up. Local employees are also sent to Japan for the purposes of familiarizing them with corporate culture, improving intra-firm communications through developing a 'human network' and/or simply providing them with incentives.

Training in Japan is supported partly by official and semi-official bodies for international technical cooperation such as the Japan International Cooperation Agency (JICA) and the Association for Overseas Technical Scholarship (AOTS). While the official JICA programme is more focused on the training of policy makers and scholars, the AOTS programme is heavily concentrated both geographically and industry-wise: over the period 1959–93, 80 per cent of the cumulative total number of its trainees (43 588 out of 54 662) came from Asia and nearly 60 per cent (32,380) from metal engineering industries.

Of course, many more workers have been sent to Japan on individual companies' own account. A recent Malaysian study reports that

> Although some companies send their employees in conjunction with AOTS training programmes, most send on a private basis . . . The large multinationals which are well established in Malaysia send significant numbers of their Malaysian employees to their parent or associated companies regularly. (Chew *et al.*, 1993: 45)

Because of the rising costs of training in Japan and of improving technical standards of their Asian affiliates, Japanese firms have started to organize training programmes on a regional or subregional basis. The cost of training in Japan has further increased as a result of job-hopping or poaching of trainees after they return home. Companies such as Matsushita and Toyota, which are known for their thorough training methods, seem to suffer particularly from this problem.[2]

The training method within individual factories varies, depending on local conditions. For example, in Malaysia and Singapore where western influence is stronger, Japanese firms rely more on manuals and manuals are more detailed than elsewhere. In contrast, in Thailand and Indonesia, training is given mainly on the job (Yamashita *et al.*, 1989).

## Development of Local Suppliers

FDI's linkage effects on local industries, in terms of both output and employment, grow with the age and scale of the factory (cf. Watanabe, 1993a: 138–9). In FY1991 Japanese manufacturers' affiliates in Asia procured 45 per cent of their material inputs locally and imported 39 per cent from Japan and 11 per cent from other Asian countries. By and large, the proportion of imports from Japan increases with the degree of sophistication of the product, amounting to 68 per cent in precision machinery and 50 per cent in transport equipment (MITI's *22nd Survey Report*: 92–3).

Japanese firms have been endeavouring to raise local content ratios of their affiliates' products, partly because of the appreciation of the yen. They do this through the in-house production of hitherto imported parts and components and by encouraging their home suppliers' FDI and fostering local subcontractors [MITI's *4th Basic Survey Report*: 33–4). In order to improve local suppliers' capabilities, their personnel visit these firms and provide technical advice as a matter of routine as in any other part of the world.[3] Touring consultancy service, workshops, secondment of technical personnel, and provision of manufacturing and/or testing equipment are not rare. Sometimes, a training programme in Japan is arranged for local suppliers' workers (JETRO, 1993).

One of the basic difficulties in developing subcontractors in the Third World is the small size of local market, which also discourages FDI for import substitution of parts and components. To overcome this constraint, Japanese firms have started networking their affiliates, especially those in the ASEAN subregion, for the purpose of mutual supply of parts and components. For this, they benefit from the Brand-to-Brand Complementation (BBC) Programme, whereby reduced import tariffs are applied to parts and components produced within the subregion. Nearly two decades after it was officially announced, in the late 1980s (January 1995 in the case of Indonesia), the Programme came on-stream, albeit hesitantly, under the leadership of Japanese car manufacturers.[4] Table 4.10 shows main items they have selected for BBC operations. Toyota seems to have an advantage in utilizing the Programme, because it produces its Corolla and Corona models in all four countries. With the implementation of its 'Asian car' programme in 1997, this company intends to expand its regional parts complementation scheme from the current 12 to about 100 items (*NKS*, 23 January 1995).

## EFFECTS ON JAPANESE INDUSTRIES AND LABOUR

### Personnel Management Practices

Integration with industries in the region (as well as in any other part of the world) implies frequent movement of personnel within the regional

*Table* 4.10   Japanese car manufacturers' BBC Programme applications

| Manufacturer | Thailand | Philippines | Malaysia | Indonesia[a] |
|---|---|---|---|---|
| Toyota | 2400cc diesel engine<br>Floor panel | Transmission | Steering ring<br>Steering gear | 1800cc<br>gasoline<br>engine |
| Nissan | Large panel<br>Inner trim | Middle-sized<br>panel | Steering gear | – |
| Honda | Stamped parts | Intake manifold | Bumper | Engine block |
| Mitsubishi | Bumper<br>Intake manifold | Transmission | 1300, 1500<br>and 1600cc<br>engines<br>Door steering | – |

*Note*:
[a] In Indonesia the programme became operational in January 1995.

*Source*: *NKS* 30 December 1994, morning.

(global) corporate network and employment of non-Japanese even at offices in Japan. In consequence, adjustments to conventional personnel and management practices become necessary. An increasing number of major companies in Japan are introducing a contract work or annual salary system as an alternative to their conventional lifetime-employment cum seniority-pay system. Some companies now offer their employees a choice between different retirement ages and correspondingly varied pay–promotion paths with a view to making their employment and pay systems more flexible. Of course, these adjustments are only partly motivated by the needs of regionalization and globalization: they are also aimed at coping with rapidly-changing manpower requirements in high tech industries and also with more diverse work attitudes of younger Japanese workers (Watanabe, 1993b).

All these changes constitute just another step in the evolutionary process of the employment and pay systems, which proceeds continuously as a matter of routine adjustment to changing domestic and external business and economic conditions. What is potentially a far more serious problem is the 'hollowing-out effect' of FDI – the deindustrialization and consequent loss of job opportunities caused by shifts of factories outside the country.

**The 'Hollowing-out' Effect**

The prolonged stagnation of the Japanese economy after the collapse of the bubble economy in 1990, which has been aggravated by diminished exports due to the appreciation of the yen, makes it difficult to determine the current scale of the 'hollowing-out effect'. Also, to many observers the problem is still potential, rather than real. Nevertheless, a quarter of the respondents in the 1993 JETRO Survey (55 out of a total of 213) felt that it was quite possible for the expansion of overseas production to cause deindustrialization of the Japanese economy, while two-thirds (139 firms) believed that the problem could be overcome by means of suitable countermeasures (JETRO, 1994: 74). In the Export and Import Bank's survey in late 1994, a quarter of 382 responding firms felt it difficult to strengthen their international competitiveness while maintaining employment at home. The remaining companies were struggling to reconcile the two objectives, mostly by developing new high value added products (*NKS*, 18 March 1995: 24).

In the large survey which was conducted in autumn 1994 involving 833 machinery and plastic product manufacturers in different parts of the country (Nikkei RIM, June 1995), 47 per cent of the respondents (391 firms) reported that their main clients had newly-established or expanded production facilities in the ESEA region since 1991, and 61 per cent of them (29 per cent of the total) had experienced a decline in the amount of work received. 101 firms out of the 391 (26 per cent) had slashed their workforce, regular and/or part-time. The smaller the firm, the more serious the situation tended to be. Industry-wise, producers of parts and components of precision machinery and home appliances had been hit hardest. So were the localities of their concentration such as Suwa, Hitachi and Kadoma Cities.

68 per cent of 238 firms reporting countermeasures stated that they were exploring new outlets often in other industries, and 48 per cent were endeavouring to improve productivity through restructuring. 28 per cent were developing new products or re-examining their products. On the other hand, 42 per cent were reducing their regular or part-time employees and 41 per cent were internalizing work hitherto subcontracted to other firms.

JETRO (1994: 85–7) suggests the following as solutions to the problem:

1. prevention of excessive appreciation of the yen through a further opening up of the domestic market to imports,

2. shift of the domestic industrial structure towards higher value added products,
3. helping smaller subcontractors in acquiring specialized technological capabilities, diversifying clients, or developing unique products to become independent manufacturers as opposed to subcontractors,
4. deregulation of business activities for the purpose of stimulating new entrepreneurship and improving labour productivity through greater competition in non-manufacturing sectors which will reduce labour shortage in manufacturing industries.

While the central government is still in the process of formulating a concrete programme to cope with the problem, local governments have already started acting with a view to discouraging departure of industries and encouraging new investments, e.g. by reversing their policy from restriction to promotion of factory construction and expansion, by leasing expensive Research & Development equipment to smaller enterprises at low fees, and by encouraging collaboration among enterprises of different cities across varied industries so that they can develop new businesses and outgrow the status of subcontractors.

Given the vulnerability of the yen to unpredictable non-economic influences, it seems clear that rationalization efforts aimed at cost reduction offer only a partial and temporary solution to the problem. Japanese industries' main area of effort should shift from process to product innovation and from improvement of existing technologies to creation of basic technologies, so that they can be less worried about price fluctuations.

## CONCLUSION

ESEA economies are now becoming closely integrated, largely as a result of Japanese FDI and related trade. An impetus is also coming from Korea and Taiwan, as well as overseas Chinese businesses. As should be clear from the analysis in the first two sections of this chapter, the ongoing integration of economies in this part of the world is quite different from the 'regionalization' of Western European economies and that of North American economies. These are essentially defensive and they are something planned. In the Asian case, in contrast, there is nothing to defend since virtually all the economies in this region are still at the threshold or in the middle of 'take-off' and therefore their markets are potential rather than actual. Japan is the only mature economy, but until recently its industrialists and policymakers were preoccupied, understandably, with North American and European markets. The situation appears to have been similar in the NIEs, as well. The legacy of the Pacific War, reflected as recently as in the 1970s in anti-Japanese movements in ASEAN countries, continues to inhibit the Japanese from taking the political initiative in economic regionalization. Thus, there has been no planning element either, despite the urge for a more consolidated and aggressive approach by some politicians such as Prime Minister Mahathir of Malaysia.

The situation is changing rapidly, however. For one thing, in the view of Asian firms, promising investment frontiers for East Asian capital have been more or less exhausted in North America and Europe, at least for the time being,[5] while Southeast Asian markets are growing rapidly and investment opportunities are also emerging quickly in China and in Vietnam. Intra-regional FDI and trade based on a horizontal division of labour are bound to grow fast. In order to avoid or minimize their negative 'hollowing-out' effects, major investing economies such as Japan, Korea and Taiwan need to formulate long-term national strategies and medium-term investment and trade policies. At the same time, it will be necessary to organize adequate training programmes for involved workers, both in these economies and in their host countries. Advancement in the regional integration of industries through horizontal division of labour necessitates, increasingly, regional cooperation and division of labour in the domain of education and training as well. In other words, these countries ought now to formulate their medium- and long-term manpower development plans in a regional perspective, instead of on the basis of their national manpower forecasts only as has been the case up to now. In the same vein, for the purpose of encouraging a further inflow of FDI, the host countries would need to improve their physical and institutional infrastructure at sufficient speeds.

Formulation of workable strategies and action programmes at industrial and corporate levels would require close consultation and collaboration at regional and subregional levels. Policymakers of Japanese localities threatened by the 'hollowing-out' effect of FDI are fully aware of this fact and some have already started to act accordingly. One example is the government of Ohta District, Tokyo, which organized an 'APEC–Ohta International Forum on Small and Medium-sized Enterprises' in December 1995 in search of a clearer image of their enterprises' role in the regional division of labour (*NKS*, 28 August 1995). A more systematic approach to 'regionalization' for ESEA economies would certainly make local planners and individual entrepreneurs' efforts easier and reduce the overall cost of regional economic integration. Half a century after the end of the Pacific War, it seems high time for the Japanese to take up a more active role in the formation of a systematically integrated regional economy.

**Notes**

1. JETRO (1994, various pages based on national sources); *Taiwan Statistical Data Book* (1992: 246–7); and *Statistical Yearbook of China* (1993: 647).
2. Information confided by a number of interviewees during field work in the ASEAN (1993 and 1994).
3. See, for example, Dunning (1986); Oliver and Wilkinson, (1988: 131); Sibunruang and Brimble (1988); Lawrence (1990).
4. This pattern of development of the Industrial Complementation Programme in the ASEAN auto industry is exactly what the present author anticipated in the late 1970s (cf. Watanabe, 1980).
5. 'Japanese Firms' Automobile Production in North America will not Grow after 1997' (*NKS*, 5 December 1994, morning).

**References**

Charoenloet, V. (1995), 'Thailand in the Regional Division of Labour', Chapter 7 in this volume.
Chew, Chilly, Leay Chan Henry, Kuzue Sugiyama and Stephen Leay (1993), *Human Resource Development in Malaysia – Japan's Contribution since 1980* (Malaysia: Institute of Strategic and International Studies (ISIS).
Dunning, J.H. (1986), 'Decision-making Structures in US and Japanese Manufacturing Affiliates in the UK: Some Similarities and Contrasts', *Multinational Enterprises Programme Working Paper*, 41 (Geneva: International Labour Office).
JETRO: (various years), *Sekai to Nihon no Kaigai Chokesetsu Tôshi* (JETRO White Paper on World and Japanese Foreign Direct Investment) (Tokyo).
JETRO (1993), *NIEs oyobi ASEAN no Nikkei Seizôgyô Katsudô Jittai Chôsa* (Survey on Japanese Manufacturing Firms in NIEs and ASEAN-4) (October) (Tokyo).
JETRO (1994), *White Paper* (Tokyo).
Lawrence, R.Z. (1990), *Foreign-affiliated Automakers in the United States: An Appraisal* (Washington, DC: Brookings Institution) (March).
Ministry of Finance (annual), *Taigai Chokusetsu Tôshi Tôkei (Todokeide-bêsû)* (Statistics on Japanese Overseas Direct Investment as declared by Investors) (Tokyo).
MITI (Ministry of International Trade and Industry) (various years), *Tsûshô Hakusho* (White Paper on External Trade) (Tokyo).

MITI (1991), *Daiyonkai Kaigai Jigyô Katsudô Kihon Chôsa: Kaigai Tôshi Tôkei Sôran* (The 4th Basic Survey on Japanese Firms' Overseas Business Activities: Comprehensive Statistics on Overseas Investment) (Tokyo: Keibun Shuppan).

MITI (1993), *Dai-22-kai Waga Kuni Kigyô no Kaigai Jigyô Katsudô* (The 22nd Survey on Overseas Business Activities by Japanese firms) (Tokyo: Ministry of Finance, Print Office).

Nikkei RIM (Nikkei Sangyô Shôhi Kenkyûjo, Nihon Keizai Shimbun-sha) (1995), *Seizôgyô no Ajia Shinshutsu to Sangyô Kûdôka* (Japanese Manufacturers' FDI to Asia and its Hollowing-out Effect) (June) (Tokyo).

*NKS (Nihon Keizai Shimbun)* (daily economic newspaper, various issues).

Oliver, N. and B. Wilkinson (1988), *The Japanisation of British Industry* (Oxford, Basil Blackwell).

Rôdô Kenkyû Center (1985), *Kaigai Nihon Kigyô no Koyô to Keiei ni kansuru Chôsa Kenkyû* (A study on employment and managerial practices at overseas Japanese firms) (Tokyo).

Sato, H. (1985), 'Nikkei Kigyô no Performance to Jinteki Shigen Kanri System' (Business Performance and Human Resources Management Systems at Japanese-owned Firms Abroad), in Kokusai Sangyô (International Research Institute for Labour and Industry) (Tokyo).

Sibunruang, A. and P. Brimble (1988), 'The Employment Effects of Manufacturing Multinational Enterprises in Thailand', *Multinational Enterprises Programme Working Paper*, 54 (Geneva: International Labour Office).

Takamiya, M. (1985), 'Conclusions and Policy Implications', in S. Takamiya and K. Thurley (eds), *Japan's Emerging Multinationals* (Tokyo: University of Tokyo Press).

Watanabe, S. (1980), 'International Sub-contracting and Regional Economic Integration of the ASEAN Countries: The Role of Multinationals', in D. Germidis (ed.), *International Subcontracting* (Paris: OECD Development Centre).

Watanabe, S. (1993a), 'Growth and Structural Changes of Japanese Overseas Direct Investment: Implications for Labour and Management in Host Economies', in P. Bailey, *et al.* (eds), *Multinationals and Employment* (Geneva: International Labour Office).

Watanabe, S. (1993b), 'Searching for a Global Management Model: The Case of Japanese Multinationals', in M. Humbert (ed.), *The Impact of Globalisation on Europe's Firms and Industries* (London: Pinter).

Yamashita, S. (1989), 'Economic Development of ASEAN and the Role of Japanese Direct Invesment', paper presented at the Hiroshima Conference, 'Beyond Japanese-style Management in ASEAN Countries: Assessments and Adaptations' (12–13 October).

Yamashita, S. *et al.* (1989), 'ASEAN Shokoku ni okeru Nihon-gata Keiei to Gijutsu Iten ni kansuru Keieisha no Ishiki Chôsa (A Survey of ASEAN Managers' Attitudes Towards Japanese-style Management and Technology Transfer)', in *Nempô Keizaigaku* (Economic Annals of the Faculty of Econonomics, Hiroshima University) (March).

Yokota, K. (1987), 'Trade Policies and Employment in Thailand' (MA programme, Thammasat University) (unpublished term paper).

# 5 Hong Kong and Coastal China Growth Linkages

## Ronald Skeldon

This chapter attempts to do two things: first, to review the main changes that have occurred in the economies of Hong Kong and southern China over the fifteen years from 1979 to 1994 and, second, to assess the development of the linkages between these two economies. The period since the Third Plenum of the XI Party Central Committee meeting in Beijing in December 1978 has seen a complete transformation of the economies of both Hong Kong and southern China. This meeting set in motion the internal reforms in China that have come to be known as 'the open door' policies and that have wrought the transformation of China's and Hong Kong's economies.

In 1978, Hong Kong's economy was still based primarily upon manufacturing, with some 816 683 employed in that sector. This represented 47.6 per cent of the employed population in 1978 and manufacturing accounted for around 25 per cent of GDP at that time. Numbers engaged in manufacturing continued to increase after 1978, with some fluctuations, until 1984 when they began to decline. By 1992, the numbers employed in manufacturing had dropped to 565 137, representing 23 per cent of the employed population and generating only about 15 per cent of GDP. The changing patterns of employment and unemployment since 1976 are shown in Figure 5.1. The area immediately contiguous to Hong Kong in China was designated the Special Economic Zone (SEZ) of Shenzhen in 1979, to be managed by a Hong Kong based company controlled by the Chinese Ministry of Communication (Sung, 1991: 11–12). In 1980, industry only accounted for just over one-quarter of the local GDP of Shenzhen, whereas by 1991 its contribution had risen to over 60 per cent.[1]

## The Pre-1978 Background

The economy of Hong Kong has always been linked with that of southern China. The British colony of Hong Kong was established as a base for traders to gain access to the perceived vast market of China's population,

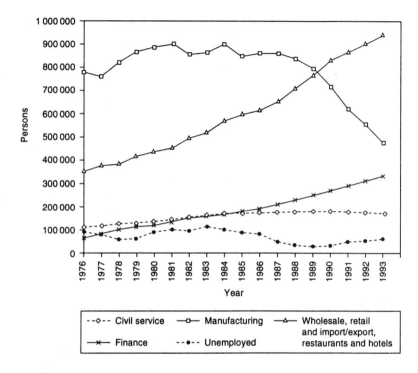

*Figure* 5.1   Employment and unemployment in Hong Kong, 1976–93

*Source*: *Hong Kong Annual Digest of Statistics*, Census and Statistics Department, Hong Kong.

which at that time was for opium. Until the Second World War, there was an intimate relationship between the colonial enclave and its hinterland in China. The population in the urban areas came primarily from that hinterland, and it was essentially male. Men came from villages in the Pearl River delta region to work in the city, leaving their families behind. For example, in 1901, there were 237 males for every 100 females among the Chinese population of Hong Kong and this ratio had declined to only 135:100 by 1931. An intense system of human circulation existed linking Hong Kong with its hinterland, with remittances being channelled back into the home areas as part of the sojourner migration that had characterized much of southern China from the mid-nineteenth century (see Skeldon, 1986; Sinn, 1995).

Hong Kong acted as an entrepôt for China trade until 1949 when the newly established People's Republic of China (PRC) attempted to isolate itself from the international community. With the loss of its trading hinterland in China but the gain in entrepreneurs fleeing the victorious communist armies, Hong Kong commenced a transition towards an industrial economy. This historical progression has been well described elsewhere (for example, Hopkins, 1971; Vogel, 1991) and Hong Kong essentially reoriented itself towards the international community as its export-led industrialization took off to provide it with the foundation for prosperity. The growth in *per capita* GDP per annum averaged 10 per cent throughout the 1960s, 9.2 per cent through the 1970s and 6.7 per cent through the 1980s – a remarkable achievement for any economy.

Although the key to Hong Kong's emergence as a Newly Industrial-ized Economy (NIE) lay in overseas markets, its relations with China were not entirely severed. There was still some movement of people across the border even if this was, with the exception of one or two years, tightly controlled by both China and Hong Kong. There was, nevertheless, trade between the two economies, primarily in a one-way direction, with primary commodities, mainly food, coming from China and flows of hard currency from Hong Kong (and overseas) to China. The balance of trade was heavily in China's favour (Hsueh and Woo, 1994: 691). Informal linkages between Chinese overseas and their home communities in coastal Guangdong and Fujian were important conduits for remittances right through the Maoist period. The state recognized the legitimacy of overseas remittances as a source of in-come for 'emigrant-dependent' households from 1955. The amounts of money remitted could be substantial, consisting of almost $US70 mil-lion in the 1950s and $US90 million in the decade of the 1960s for Taishan County in the western Pearl River delta region alone (Chan, 1990). These moneys were used mainly for basic needs such as the purchase of grain for emigrant-dependent households but also for the construction of infrastructure in the home areas such as schools, col-leges, roads and so on. Much of the money was channelled through Hong Kong into southern China although it may have originated fur-ther afield. Hence, Hong Kong has always played a key role in the development of southern China, and its more recent, post-1978, inte-gration into its hinterland should not be seen as anything new even if the nature of the linkages is indeed new.

**The Post-1978 Situation**

Even before the reforms were introduced in China one important change was beginning to occur: the increasing movement of labour. During the latter stages of the Maoist period, population movements were tightly controlled through the household registration system. By the second half of the 1970s, this control was beginning to erode. Very large numbers of people came in to Hong Kong from China during 1979 and 1980 in particular, although numbers of illegal immigrants had been increasing from 1977 (Skeldon, 1986). The net addition of some 400 000 people between 1976 and 1981 effectively expanded the labour force providing a 'reserve army' on which manufacturers could draw. It was even whispered that this massive immigration was not unrelated to Hong Kong's growing need for labour (Turner, 1980: 55). During this period, there was no significant increase in unemployment, which shows that the majority of the new migrants were productively absorbed into Hong Kong's economy. Their addition to the labour force almost certainly caused the persistence of the particular labour market conditions of the time, allowing labour-intensive manufacturing to continue even though the economy had already been experiencing a labour deficit for over a decade.

After October 1980, British and Chinese officials agreed to control immigration and, since then, there has been no unregulated flow of one of the principal factors of production into Hong Kong: labour. Nominal wages virtually tripled for male and female labourers between 1981 and 1990. In the manufacturing sector as a whole, nominal wages again almost tripled over the same period, with real wages increasing by 47 per cent. While other sectors showed more marked increases (Table 5.1), it has been the labour-intensive manufacturing sector which has been squeezed out of Hong Kong's economy because of comparative advantages in China. There, labour costs are estimated to be 70 per cent lower than in Hong Kong, while other factor costs, such as rent and payment for materials, are also 70 per cent lower (Hsueh and Woo, 1994: 708). Maruya estimated the difference in wage rates between Hong Kong and Shenzhen in the late 1980s for an unskilled worker at 5.5 to 1, with the average monthly wage in Hong Kong at the time at $US412 compared with $US75 in Shenzhen (Maruya, 1992: 136). The monthly wage in Shenzhen was lower than in any other ASEAN country except Indonesia, where it was $US60. The monthly industrial rental at the time was $HK8 per square foot in Hong Kong versus between $HK0.8 and 1.5 per square foot in Shenzhen.

There are other incentives to investing in or transferring production to China than these simple income and rent differences. The SEZ of Shenzhen has lower income tax rates for foreign high technology ventures and greater local autonomy to approve foreign investments (Leung,

*Table* 5.1  Nominal payroll per person engaged, by industry group, selected years

| Major division/ | Nominal index | | |
|---|---|---|---|
| industry group | 1981 | 1985 | 1990 |
| Mining and quarrying | 120.8 | 176.8 | 321.1 |
| Manufacturing | 138.4 | 212.2 | 389.4 |
| Electricity and gas | 171.3 | 299.6 | 566.1 |
| Wholesale, retail and import/export | | | |
| trades and restaurants and hotels | 155.6 | 229.2 | 426.2 |
| Transport, storage and communication | 142.9 | 241.6 | 435.1 |
| Financing, insurance, real estate | | | |
| and business services | 172.9 | 279.3 | 464.8 |
| Community, social and personal services | 148.3 | 222.2 | 408.5 |

*Note*:
Figures refer to December of the year.

*Source*: Employment and Earnings Statistics Section, Census and Statistics Department, Hong Kong.

1993: 277). The other SEZ of Zhuhai, adjacent to Macau, the open cities of Guangzhou and Zhanjiang and other individual cities in the Pearl River delta region such as Dongguan and Baoan, all have local, if variable, institutions to attract outside investors and facilitate local decisionmaking.

## The Shift in Manufacturing

The squeeze on manufacturing in Hong Kong has also to be seen within the context of the rising skill levels of the Hong Kong population. Between 1981 and 1991, the proportion of the population 15 years of age and older which had completed upper secondary increased from 21.3 to 26.7 per cent, while the proportion of those with degree-level education increased from 3.4 to 5.9 per cent. With continuing numbers going on to higher levels of education, the overall labour force participation rate has declined, further tightening the labour market. More important, with increasing levels of education, the population is less willing to undertake low paid and manual employment.

It is, however, deceptive to see Hong Kong as deindustrializing, with the sharp decline in numbers employed in manufacturing observed earlier. This decline is an artefact of the international boundary separating British-administered Hong Kong from China. What is emerging is an integrated

functional megacity, with Hong Kong as the service core and the industries being pushed towards the periphery as has been seen in the
spatial division of urban activities in core cities in developed countries. The evolving functional divisions of a 'greater Hong Kong' are
shown in a generalized form in Figure 5.2. The divisions essentially
represent declining land values away from the city centre, with three
bands of activity with service industries in the core, wholesale and
retailing in the semi-periphery, and manufacturing in the periphery.
Clearly, this is an idealized scheme, as there are subcentres within the
general bands of zonation that render the real pattern of activities much
more complex. Nevertheless by early in the twenty-first century it is
not unreasonable to expect an integrated urban area extending out
from Hong Kong well towards Guangzhou, which itself will form a
service subcentre in a continuous built-up area around the Pearl
River delta.

While the numbers employed in manufacturing in Hong Kong have
declined, those in China have increased. There are only estimates of
the numbers of workers employed in Hong Kong factories in Guangdong
Province. In 1990, these were in the range of 1 1/2–2 million workers,
rising to 3 million in 1991 (Hsueh and Woo, 1994: 708), three to four
times the numbers employed in manufacturing in Hong Kong at that
time. These same authorities estimate that over 90 per cent of Hong
Kong manufacturers participate in the outward processing in China
(Hsueh and Wu, 1994: 707). However, while agreeing that some 3 million
workers are employed directly or indirectly in Hong Kong companies
in Guangdong, a survey conducted by the Federation of Hong Kong
Industries in 1991 revealed that only about 40 per cent of their members had investments in other parts of the world, with over four-fifths
of that proportion having made investments in China (FHKI, 1991).

The shift in manufacturing into China may either be a direct shift of
a company's operation from Hong Kong into China or it may involve
an expansion of activities through subcontracting with Chinese-owned
or part-owned factories. Details are difficult to obtain, but a government survey of companies in Hong Kong in which there was some
overseas investment showed that half engaged in subcontracting, with
over half of these subcontracting to China. Subcontracting was most
common in the electronics and electrical products industries (Hong
Kong, 1992). The complete shift of manufacturing plants into China
can be seen as one extension of this process of subcontracting (Wong,
1994: 550).

No matter the exact proportion of Hong Kong manufacturers which

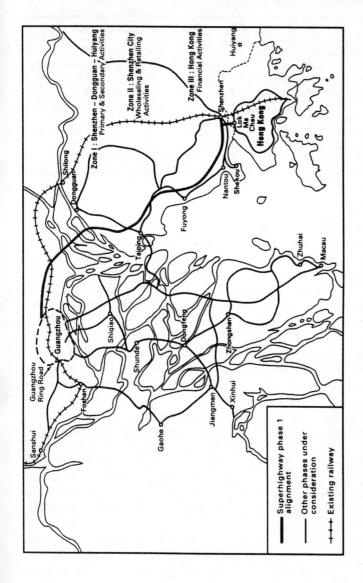

*Figure* 5.2  Hypothetical districts in the Pearl River delta by functional activity after 1997

*Source*: Nomura Research Institute (Hong Kong).

*Table* 5.2   Index of industrial production, 1988–93 (year-on-year rate of change, per cent, as at end of year)

|  | 1988 | 1989 | 1990 | 1991 | 1992 | 1993 |
|---|---|---|---|---|---|---|
| Wearing apparel | −1 | 1 | −2 | −3 | 1 | 2 |
| Textiles | −3 | 5 | −2 | 4 | 4 | −7 |
| Plastic products | −5 | −13 | −14 | −8 | −7 | −15 |
| Machinery and equipment | 19 | 1 | 1 | 9 | 15 | 13 |
| Consumer electrical and electronic products | 0 | −4 | 2 | −1 | −4 | −8 |
| Fabricated metal products | 20 | −10 | −11 | −2 | −5 | −9 |
| Overall manufacturing | 6 | 1 | −1 | 1 | 2 | −1 |

*Source*: Half-yearly economic reports, Financial Services Branch, Hong Kong Government Secretariat.

has interests in or has moved operations to China – very large numbers indeed have moved out of Hong Kong. This is clearly reflected in the statistics on industrial production. The year-on-year rates of change in production have been mainly negative since the middle of 1992, and particularly so for industries making plastic products, fabricated metal products, consumer electrical and electronic products and textiles (Table 5.2). Even as early as the late 1980s, it was estimated that between 70 and 80 per cent of the electronics and plastics industries had been moved to China (Feng, 1991: 499). As production in Hong Kong has declined, so too have domestic exports, while trade with China and re-exports of goods made in China have increased markedly. Domestic exports declined by 3.7 per cent in the first nine months of 1994, while total exports, including re-exports from China, increased by 10 per cent in volume. Commodity trade with China increased from only 9.3 per cent of Hong Kong's total commodity trade in 1978 to 32.4 per cent in 1991. The re-exports to China, however, increased from 1.6 per cent of total re-exports in 1978 to 28.7 per cent in 1991. The value of re-exports of goods made in China but exported to other countries through Hong Kong rose from $US781 million in 1978 to $US40.6 billion in 1991.[2]

From being the destination of exports from China before 1979, Hong Kong is now one of the principal outlets for China's trade to the outside world. From one point of view, Hong Kong has resumed its role as a conduit for China trade but, in effect, this is again a statistical artefact of the artificial nature of the boundary between Hong Kong and China, artificial in that it bisects an integrated spatial production unit and that 'greater Hong Kong' has emerged as an extended NIE and one of the most dynamic growth regions both in terms of manufacturing and in terms of services. As we will see below, the emergence of this powerful productive and administrative region is the fulcrum around which one of the perceived dynamic regions of a future world economy is evolving – Greater China.

While it is certainly the case that the majority of outprocessing in China has been carried out by small firms in the sense that these are essentially local Hong Kong companies rather than multinationals (Wu, 1994b), the decline in employment in manufacturing enterprises within Hong Kong itself was initiated by, and has been greatest among, the larger enterprises. For example, between 1983 and 1992, the numbers employed in manufacturing enterprises of 1000 workers or more declined by 44 per cent compared with an overall decline of 34 per cent. The decline for the companies with the greatest number of workers was from 1984, while that for the smallest size class of 1–9 employees commenced only after 1988 and registered only a 13 per cent decline. Hence, the larger Hong Kong firms were the earliest to take advantage of the opening up of China and the first to respond to the opportunities presented. The data on the trends on the establishments of intermediate size generally confirms a progressive delay in response to the opportunities in China with declining size of enterprise (Table 5.3).

**Capital Flows**

Important though the transfer of manufacturing from Hong Kong to China is for the development of southern China, and particularly the Pearl River delta, it is Hong Kong's role as a generator of finance that is even more significant. Of course, the transfer of industry itself directly reflects Hong Kong investment in China but the investment is much farther reaching than just the outward processing manufacturing sector. The Federation of Hong Kong Industries (FHKI) estimated that their members had invested over $US600 million in manufacturing in the Pearl River delta region alone up to 1991. The Hong Kong government keeps no record of direct investment overseas, although figures for investment in Asian countries are available from the Hongkong Bank. China is the overwhelming destination for Hong Kong's direct outward investment, accounting for almost 80 per cent, or some $US20.6 billion, during the decade of the 1980s (cited in Maruya, 1992: 135).

There was a surge of investment capital from Hong Kong to China

*Table* 5.3  Establishments and persons engaged in manufacturing industry, by employment size, 1983–92 (as at September of the year)

| Numbers of persons engaged | | 1983 | 1984 | 1985 | 1986 | 1987 | 1988 | 1989 | 1990 | 1991 | 1992 |
|---|---|---|---|---|---|---|---|---|---|---|---|
| 1–9 | Establishments | 31 368 | 33 022 | 32 827 | 32 987 | 34 354 | 35 066 | 34 802 | 35 915 | 33 888 | 31 261 |
| | Persons engaged | 118 192 | 124 413 | 121 291 | 123 787 | 128 079 | 133 425 | 129 666 | 130 957 | 121 870 | 111 753 |
| 10–19 | Establishments | 6 875 | 7 028 | 6 760 | 7 010 | 7 241 | 7 219 | 7 270 | 6 366 | 5 980 | 5 120 |
| | Persons engaged | 92 141 | 94 303 | 90 156 | 93 704 | 97 061 | 96 809 | 97 739 | 87 038 | 80 238 | 68 630 |
| 20–49 | Establishments | 5 108 | 5 342 | 5 040 | 5 084 | 5 336 | 5 032 | 4 735 | 4 219 | 4 018 | 3 501 |
| | Persons engaged | 157 434 | 164 478 | 154 161 | 156 457 | 164 012 | 154 807 | 145 104 | 136 092 | 122 565 | 106 157 |
| 50–99 | Establishments | 1 993 | 2 095 | 2 016 | 2 115 | 2 090 | 1 977 | 1 919 | 1 520 | 1 430 | 1 221 |
| | Persons engaged | 135 722 | 142 352 | 137 110 | 143 876 | 142 618 | 135 628 | 131 443 | 113 673 | 96 787 | 82 494 |
| 100–199 | Establishments | 938 | 942 | 904 | 889 | 869 | 828 | 741 | 668 | 602 | 524 |
| | Persons engaged | 127 159 | 128 684 | 122 734 | 120 249 | 118 898 | 112 678 | 100 345 | 91 280 | 81 596 | 70 323 |
| 200–499 | Establishments | 396 | 424 | 393 | 414 | 387 | 356 | 346 | 302 | 284 | 249 |
| | Persons engaged | 116 213 | 126 911 | 117 266 | 120 946 | 114 423 | 105 068 | 103 178 | 91 307 | 87 652 | 74 623 |
| 500–999 | Establishments | 107 | 104 | 99 | 93 | 104 | 105 | 88 | 77 | 56 | 45 |
| | Persons engaged | 70 926 | 71 362 | 67 257 | 64 348 | 71 210 | 71 949 | 58 611 | 50 173 | 37 064 | 30 703 |
| 1000 and over | Establishments | 32 | 35 | 26 | 31 | 28 | 23 | 26 | 20 | 18 | 17 |
| | Persons engaged | 47 286 | 52 206 | 38 925 | 46 386 | 38 949 | 34 211 | 36 896 | 29 697 | 26 891 | 26 499 |
| *Total* | Establishments | 46 817 | 48 992 | 48 065 | 48 623 | 50 409 | 50 606 | 49 926 | 49 087 | 46 276 | 41 937 |
| | Persons engaged | 865 073 | 904 709 | 848 900 | 869 753 | 875 250 | 844 575 | 802 983 | 730 217 | 654 662 | 571 181 |

*Source: Annual Digest of Statistics,* Hong Kong.

in the 1990s. From around $US3 billion a year in the late 1980s it reached $US4 billion in 1990, $US7 billion in 1991, $US40 billion in 1992 and a staggering $US75 billion in 1993 (unpublished figures, Hongkong Bank). These figures represent approved foreign direct investment (FDI), not the amounts actually utilized. There is a shortfall between the capital actually absorbed and that approved and committed, and so the real amounts actually moved into China are likely to be somewhat less than these figures. A recent Hang Seng Bank report recorded a total FDI transferred to China of $US91.2 billion to October 1994. Of this amount $US47.5 billion was from Hong Kong. Despite the variations in the figures they nevertheless indicate a tremendous surge in investment in the China market, which shows the interest of the international community, and particularly that of Hong Kong and the Chinese overseas, in the potential of a modernizing China. Not all of this capital was likely to have been generated in Hong Kong itself and it is not possible to trace the provenance of the funds, but all was funnelled to China through Hong Kong companies and institutions. This shows the growing importance of Hong Kong's role as a service centre for China, not just as a supplier of manufacturing activities.

To give an impression of the importance of investments in China from Hong Kong that were not related to outward processing manufacturing, Crédit Lyonnais Securities compiled details of the capital commitments of Hong Kong-listed companies to projects in China (Riddick and Cowan, 1993). The amounts of capital again refer to those funds committed in principle, not to the actual investment, and it is known that substantial proportions of the commitments were never realized (Riddick, personal communication, December 1994). While projects related to manufacturing were included in the Crédit Lyonnais compilation, these related to projects that were focused on China's domestic market rather than in re-exporting through Hong Kong. Their compilation showed that capital investment in non-outward processing manufacturing was relatively small compared with investments in infrastructure and in property. The results of this survey identified Hong Kong companies up to early 1993 having made commitments in China in projects that had a value of at least $US67 billion in 801 different projects. Approximately one-third of the project costs were to be directly attributable to the Hong Kong companies. The balance was to be met by mainland commitment or other parties through joint ventures. Of the total amount, some 47 per cent was invested in infrastructure projects, principally power plants (45 per cent), roads, bridges and railways (27 per cent) and container terminals and ports (27 per cent); 40 per cent was in property. Manufacturing, on the other hand, accounted for about 4 per cent of the investment, although spread among 223 projects, compared with only 58 in infrastructure and 396 in property.

## The Spatial Pattern of Hong Kong–China Linkages

The location of Hong Kong investment in China is concentrated over-whelmingly in areas close by. It is hardly surprising that up to 90 per cent of those companies surveyed by FHKI that had invested in China were concentrated in Guangdong Province, with a preponderance of activity concentrated in the crescent along the eastern Pearl River delta from Guangzhou through Dongguan to Shenzhen. The non-outward processing capital commitments surveyed by Crédit Lyonnais were also heavily concentrated in Guangdong Province, with 62 per cent of the committed value, and 51 per cent of the projects, located there. Again, Guangzhou, Shenzhen and Dongguan were the major destinations for that investment. Overall, Hong Kong has contributed between 50 and 60 per cent of all foreign investment to China and over half of these amounts are channelled into Guangdong Province. The other major destinations of Hong Kong investment are Shanghai (9 per cent), and Hainan Island (8 per cent), now a separate province in the southwest of the country and an open area in its own right. Perhaps surprisingly, the coastal province to the east of Hong Kong, Fujian, received only about 4 per cent of Hong Kong investment, showing that the develop-ment of that province is much more within the ambit of Taiwan, prov-ince of China.

What the figures do show is that, although coastal China is unques-tionably the region with the highest growth in the country, and this is dependent to a large extent on external linkages, the development within that region is concentrated in a few areas. The SEZ of Shenzhen had the highest gross values of industrial and agricultural output (GVIAO) in Guangdong at 42 359 yuan *per capita* in 1990, more than a thir-teen-fold increase since 1982. The vast majority of the counties and cities with high *per capita* GVIAO are in the Pearl River delta: in the counties of Foshan, Jiangmen, Baoan, Guangzhou, Huizhou and Shunde (Figure 5.3). The counties with the most marked increases in the pro-portions of employed population in industry are also mainly to be found in this region and particularly close to Shenzhen in Baoan, Dongguan, Huizhou, Foshan, Jiangmen and Shunde. The only major outliers of prosperity are Shaoguan in the interior, and Chenhai and Maoming at opposite ends of the Guangdong coastal region. Hence, the areas of

163

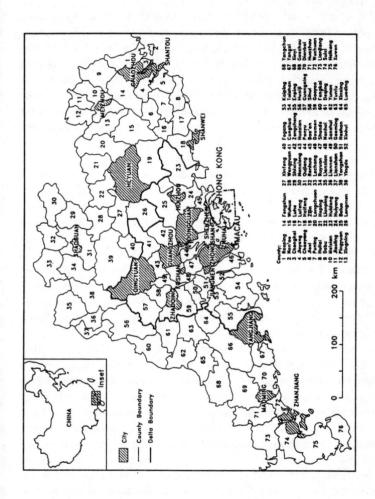

*Figure 5.3*   Administrative divisions of Guangdong, c. 1990

intense penetration of industrial development and resulting greater prosperity are still quite localized within the coastal region, and primarily
in the emerging megalopolis evolving around the Pearl River delta in
a triangle with its apex at Hong Kong and its base stretching from
Guangzhou to Macau.[3]

The Pearl River delta region received a major boost to its development efforts from the tour of the south by paramount leader Deng
Xiaoping in January 1993, which was followed a year later by the
visit of Premier Li Peng (Cheung, 1993). Both praised the types of
development occurring, which appeared to provide an official seal of
approval on the directions being followed. China's first nuclear power
plant, which has become operational at Daya Bay just to the northeast
of Hong Kong, provides power to both Hong Kong and the eastern
Pearl River delta region. Within the delta region, the Hong Kong dollar has become a *de facto*, if not a *de jure*, currency with, in early
1991, an estimated $US808 million circulation, some 16 per cent of
Hong Kong's total currency at the time (cited in Sung, 1994: 384).

The reasons why Hong Kong manufacturers either shift to particular
locations in Guangdong or subcontract in the immediate hinterland have
to do with much more than simple propinquity: a comprehensive investigation showed the importance of pre-existing kinship relations in
determining the precise location (Leung, 1993). These networks provide an environment of trust in which the Hong Kong entrepreneurs
can operate. They are often dealing directly with their home villages,
which re-emphasizes a point made earlier that, since 1979, Hong Kong
is being reintegrated back into its hinterland, not just economically
but also culturally. The period from the end of the Second World War
until 1978 was something of an aberration in terms of Hong Kong's
relations with southern China. That was the only time during which
the economies were operating separately, and the linkages, while not
entirely severed, were certainly more weakly maintained.

**The Demographic Consequences of the Linkages**

As seen above, a wave of migration into Hong Kong in the late 1970s
was attracted by the labour-deficit economy and allowed the persistence of manufacturing in the territory for a few years. Now, the transfer of the outprocessing manufacturing into the hinterland has been an
important factor in stimulating a massive migration into Guangdong
Province from elsewhere in China, and most particularly the contiguous
provinces of Guangxi and Hunan. The 1990 census of China provides

some insight into these flows, particularly when compared with the results from the 1987 1 per cent population survey. The comparison shows a marked increase in the importance of more long-distance interprovincial migration between the two five-year periods of 1982–7 and 1985–90. The number of migrants to Guangdong Province increased from 260 000 in the earlier period to 1.16 million in the later period (Li and Siu, 1994: 378–9). Migration to Guangdong accounted for more than 10 per cent of all interprovincial migration in China in the five-year period before the 1990 census, compared with only 4 per cent in the five-year period before 1987.

There are major problems in the definition of 'migration' in China and also difficulties in drawing comparisons between the results of the population census and those from the 1987 survey; hence, these figures must be seen as merely indicative. The major problem relates to short-term migrants, the so-called 'floating population', which has been, to all intents and purposes, omitted both from the census and from the survey. The figures from these sources on migration must therefore be seen as the tip of the mobility iceberg and the real number of job-seekers is very much higher. It has been estimated that, in the late 1980s, the number of short-term migrants in Guangzhou alone was in the region of 645 000 (Li and Siu, 1994: 380), although this is almost certainly a major underestimation. Other estimates place the total number of 'floating' people in all the major cities of China in the early 1990s as between 15 and 20 million, and after Chinese New Year in 1993, more than 1 million job-seekers were estimated to have arrived in the Pearl River delta, mainly through Guangzhou railway station (Taubman, 1993: 9–10).

Despite the difficulties with the various data sources, they do represent the most comprehensive data on migration in China available and can be used to draw out some important aspects of the development of south coastal China. Overall, interprovincial migration in China between 1985 and 1990, as identified from the 1990 census, was biased towards males, with 139 males moving for every 100 females. Yet, the migration to Guangdong Province was biased towards females, with only 86 male migrants to that province for every 100 females. There the demand is for young women in the labour-intensive activities established by Hong Kong entrepreneurs: a labour force that is often easy to exploit, easy to dismiss and that can be paid very low wages. The dangerous and hazardous conditions under which they work have been amply illustrated in the high death toll of young women in accidents and fires in factories in Shenzhen and elsewhere in the delta. Legislation needs to be enacted to protect workers and to guarantee their residential status should they wish to marry and settle down locally (Li, 1994: 274).

There are other aspects of population mobility that derive from the Hong Kong-Guangdong linkage. The first relates to retirement migration. It is likely that, in the late 1980s, some 20 000 persons a year who retired in Hong Kong or who were displaced from their jobs due to the structural transformation of the local economy returned to China to settle (Skeldon *et al.*, forthcoming). Hong Kong, with its spiralling property prices and increasing cost of living, is not a place in which to retire. While the retirees returning to their home areas may bring capital and, in some cases, regular retirement or welfare benefits from Hong Kong, the addition of older people to Guangdong's population will have future implications for the provision of welfare in the province, particularly in the areas of health care for the aged.

A final issue related to population mobility is the increasing movement between Hong Kong and its hinterland in China. In 1992, there were around 52.5 million person moves between Hong Kong and China, up from 25.7 million in 1986 and about 8 million in 1982. While the vast majority of these movements are for family visits and/or recreation, an increasing number of Hong Kong workers commute to China for work. In the second quarter of 1992, it was estimated that 64 200, or 2.3 per cent of Hong Kong's labour force, had worked in China at some time during the previous twelve months (Hong Kong, 1992). This figure represented an increase over the 45 600 who had been reported as working in China over a similar period in 1989. Most of these workers were mature males, with high levels of education, who were overseeing or managing enterprises in China. Again, these trends are an example of Hong Kong servicing business activities in China.

**China–Hong Kong Investment**

The diffusion of factors that generate growth is not simply outwards from Hong Kong into coastal China. The linkages are reciprocal, with much of Hong Kong's growth predicated upon development in China. China is the third biggest investor in Hong Kong's manufacturing industry, after the USA and Japan, with a total of about $US564 million up to the end of 1993, which represented 13.8 per cent of total foreign investment in industry. China's investment in other sectors is, however, more significant. Mainland companies are estimated to have invested over $US10 billion in property in Hong Kong in recent years and there are now over 20 000 registered companies in Hong Kong that are owned or controlled by mainland interests or nationals. While the number of companies incorporated in China but listed on the Hong Kong stock market (the so-called 'H' shares) is quite small (only fifteen so far), and small in terms of proportion of total market capitalization, the number of 'back-door' companies setting up in Hong Kong but doing business in China only would, when added together, account for a very significant part of the total market capitalization. Much more needs to be done in compiling information on this topic but, clearly, Hong Kong plays a crucial role in raising finance and loans for China (Sung, 1991: 94–9). The needs of China stimulate the demand for services in Hong Kong and the latter's prosperity is now very much dependent upon the continuing development of China.

## Other Consequences of Hong Kong–China Linkages

The linkages between Hong Kong and China are not simply made up of human and capital flows and the trade in goods and services, fundamental though these may be. There has been a profound impact on institutions and people's attitudes, which can affect the way in which development proceeds. In addition to significant job generation, the wave of FDI from Hong Kong and other foreign investors is having an impact on labour practices and labour market policies in China. Foreign-invested firms (FIEs) are introducing new management techniques and are pioneers in breaking away from traditional practices such as life-long employment contracts and nepotism in recruiting, i.e. giving priority to hiring employees' children and relatives. Experimentation with and diffusion of new employment practices are important as the country attempts to reform its labour market system to adapt it to a market economy. However, the situation varies across FIEs. While joint ventures with large multinationals have a good record, by Chinese standards, as concerns wages, working conditions and industrial relations, small and medium-sized foreign-owned enterprises seem characterized by poor wages, unjustified dismissals, unhealthy working environments, industrial accidents and allegations of child labour and other abuses (Zhu, 1995). According to Song (1995), this has led to tense industrial relations and strikes in a number of Hong Kong-invested plants, prompting the Chinese government to strengthen labour inspection and take measures to protect workers' rights in these enterprises. Song also notes that some Hong Kong investors have reacted to the minimum wage set by the government in Shenzhen by closing down their factories.

Another impact has been that associated with telecommunication systems: telephone, fax, television, radio, most of which emanate from, or through, Hong Kong. Hong Kong companies such as Hong Kong Telecom and Hutchison Whampoa are competing for business among the Hong Kong industrial interests in the Pearl River delta (Cheung, 1993: 18.18–18.19) One result of this activity has been the rapid spread of pagers throughout the delta region. The propagation of a Hong Kong Cantonese culture through films and television is a powerful image to influence the more than 60 million speakers of Cantonese dialects in southern China. This culture is reinforced by the many newspapers and magazines that are published in Hong Kong. When translated into consumerism through advertising, the images can play an important role in influencing tastes and behaviour which are ultimately reflected in the demand for new goods.

The linkages between Hong Kong and its hinterland can also have negative repercussions. A clear example relates to environmental deterioration. In some cases, the types of industries relocated across the border from Hong Kong are inefficient and those threatened with closure in Hong Kong under new environmental legislation in the territory. In China, conservation generally has a lower priority than development, and building and zoning legislation is poorly developed or ineffectually implemented, with the result that within the Pearl River delta area, in particular, there are serious problems of air and water pollution. A useful review of the main environmental issues in the Pearl River delta region can be found in Neller and Lam (1994). The rapid and often haphazard expansion of urban and industrial development has also led to the depletion or degradation of agricultural land, with implications for the supply of food to once self-sufficient areas. Official government statistics reveal that, within the Pearl River delta region, the area of arable land declined by 14 per cent between 1985 and 1991, and in the individual counties of Shenzhen, Baoan, Jiangmen and Foshan it was 30 per cent or higher (cited in Wu, 1997b). Whether these declines in area are being matched by increasing agricultural productivity elsewhere in the region is not yet clear. What is clear, however, is that adequate transport and distribution systems need to be created to ensure the supply of foodstuffs from outside the region.

The linkages that are developing between Hong Kong and southern China provide interesting comparisons and contrasts with the linkages developing between Singapore and Malaysia and Indonesia. Both the Singaporean and Indonesian governments have played an active role in developing infrastructure and managing labour (Kumar, 1994: 187), whereas the driving force in the movement of economic activities out of Hong Kong has been the private sector. The Hong Kong government has exercised little influence on the deconcentration of activities out of the territory. Yet, market forces in southern China are not operating entirely within a public policy vacuum as both central and regional governments in China have clearly been influential in fostering the linkages. The 'open door' policy that established the SEZs in southern China from 1979 and other local government, land, trade, tax and industrial policies has influenced the direction of development and establishment of infrastructure (Chen, 1994). The expansion of Hong Kong into southern China has, nevertheless, been a less formal affair and less subject to political factors than the case of Singapore. In addition, the return of Hong Kong to China on 1 July 1997 means that the region will exist within a single sovereign state, which should minimize political tensions, always assuming that the direction of China's reforms remains basically unchanged.

**Towards a Greater China**

Hong Kong is the major but not the only outside influence to have an impact on the development of south coastal China. Taiwan, province of China, is another major influence in the region. Its dealings with China are complicated by the lack of direct formal communication between their two governments, which means that interaction takes place primarily through Hong Kong. From late 1987, when Taiwan began to relax its restrictions on visiting China, up to the end of 1991 some 2 million Taiwan residents visited China, the vast majority of them through Hong Kong – a tremendous boost to the colony's business and tourism activities (Hsiao and So, 1994). Distance and lack of official support make it much more difficult for the businessman from Taiwan to move offshore into China compared with those from Hong Kong, Taiwan is nevertheless the third most important source of FDI in Guangdong Province, after Hong Kong and Macau, and the second most important source in Fujian after Hong Kong (cited in Wu, 1994). Like Hong Kong, it uses kinship and friendship linkages and, like Hong Kong, it is the smaller and medium-sized enterprises which are set up on the mainland. However, unlike Hong Kong, there are few joint ventures and most enterprises are single owner, mainly due to the difficulties that Taiwan residents have in doing business officially with China (Hsiao and So, 1994). While labour-intensive industries, particularly the shoe industry, have been moved almost entirely into the Pearl River delta region, the main sphere of influence of Taiwan is in Fujian Province. Here, the historical and cultural ties are closest and, if and when official linkages are re-established, the geographical distances too will be closest. These facts notwithstanding, over 1000 Taiwan based firms have interests in Shenzhen and accounted for almost one-quarter of total production in the SEZ, 44 per cent of its exports and employed 7 per cent of its labour force (Kao and Lin, 1994: 20–1). Three general spheres of outside influence in China have been identified: south coastal China centred in Guangdong but stretching into Fujian, where Hong Kong influence operates; an eastern coastal region, centred in the SEZ of Xiamen but stretching north from Fujian through Zhejian to Jiangsu, where the influence of Taiwan is growing; and a northern zone, including Shandong and parts of Liaoning and Jilin, where the influence of South Korea is penetrating (identified in Wu, 1997; see also Sung, 1994). Of the spheres of activity, by far the most intense is that of Hong Kong in the south.

The combined influence of Hong Kong and Taiwan, each with their global linkages to Chinese overseas in southeast Asia, North America and Australasia, provides the basis for one of the wealthiest, and thus most powerful, regional groupings in the world. This grouping has been given various spatial definitions and various names: 'Great Chinese Economic Circle' (Hsiao and So, 1994: 24); 'Greater China' (Shambaugh, 1993; Harding, 1993); and 'Greater China and the Chinese Overseas' (*Fortune* magazine, October 31, 1994). It is this unit that some analysts see as the 'Southern China Growth Triangle' (Chen and Ho, 1994). The foreign reserves of Hong Kong, Singapore and Taiwan make up around $US212 billion, dwarfing the $US106 billion of Japan, and their combined trade (exports *plus* imports) make them the third most important trading group in the world (*Fortune* magazine, October 31, 1994). When combined with the rapidly developing coastal regions of China, the resultant economy is being seen as one of the future global engines of growth. Nevertheless, despite the importance of business networks in Chinese economic development (Hamilton, 1991; Redding, 1990), this grouping is not yet a single monolithic body but a fairly diffuse entity of conflicting interests and political and economic goals. Looked at as Chinese peoples as a whole, the networks and business interests are impressive indeed. There are, however, still significant national, regional and cultural divisions amongst these peoples. A fundamental aim of any future study of regionalism in Asia will be to examine the centripetal and centrifugal tensions within this Greater China entity. How the three spheres of influence identified earlier will, first, interact with the wider global community, secondly, will expand and relate to mainland China and, thirdly, will develop identities on their own right will be of critical importance for future development in the Asia-Pacific region.

## Notes

1. The open door policies in Guangdong Province are reviewed in Maruya (1992), with an assessment of their impact on China as a whole in Chen and Maruya (1992).
2. All these figures are from official government sources and cited in Hsueh and Woo (1994: 696–697). For an earlier version of the work of these scholars, see Hsueh and Woo (1991) and see also Ash and Kueh (1993).
3. Assessments of the importance of this region will be found in Lam *et al.* (1989), Cheung (1993), Cheng and MacPherson (in press) and Sung *et al.* (in press).

## References

Ash, R.F. and Y.Y., Kueh (1993), 'Economic Integration within Greater China: Trade and Investment Flows Between China, Hong Kong and Taiwan', *The China Quarterly*, 136: 711–45.

Chan, K.Y. (1990), 'The Role of Migration in China's Regional Development: A Local Study of Southern China' (Department of Geography and Geology, University of Hong Kong) (M Phil dissertation).

Chen, D. (1994), 'Chinese Public Policy and the Southern China Growth Triangle', in M. Thant, M. Tang and H. Kakazu (eds) *Growth Triangles in Asia: A New Approach to Regional Economic Cooperation* (Hong Kong: Oxford University Press): pp. 94–113.

Chen, E.K.Y. and A. Ho (1994), 'Southern China Growth Triangle: An Overview', in M. Thant *et al.* (eds) *Growth Triangles in Asia: A New Approach to Regional Economic Cooperation* (Hong Kong: Oxford University Press): 29–72.

Chen, E.K.Y. and T. Maruya (eds) (1992), *A Decade of 'Open Door' Economic Development in China, 1979–1989* (Hong Kong and Tokyo: The University of Hong Kong, Centre of Asian Studies, and Institute of Developing Economies).

Cheng, J. and S. MacPherson (eds) (in press), *The Fifth Dragon: Reform Strategies and Development Issues in the Pearl River Delta* (Hong Kong: Longman).

Cheung, P.T.-Y. (1993), 'Pearl River Delta Development', in J. Cheng and M. Brosseau (eds), *China Review 1993* (Hong Kong: The Chinese University Press): 18.1–18.29.

Feng, B.Y. (1991), 'The Role of Hong Kong in China's Modernization', in E.K.Y. Chen, M.-K. Nyans and T.Y.C. Wong (eds), *Industrial and Trade*

*Development in Hong Kong* (Hong Kong: The University of Hong Kong, Centre of Asian Studies): 497–509.

FHKI (1991), *Hong Kong's Industrial Investment in the Pearl River Delta*: (Hong Kong: Federation of Hong Kong Industries).

Hamilton, G. (ed.) (1991), *Business Networks and Economic Development in East and Southeast Asia*, (Hong Kong: The University of Hong Kong, Centre of Asian Studies).

Harding, H. (1993), 'The Concept of 'Greater China': Themes, Variations and Reservations', *The China Quarterly*, 136: 660–86.

Hong Kong (1992), *1992 Survey of Overseas Investment in Hong Kong's Manufacturing Industries* (Hong Kong Government, Industry Department).

Hopkins, K. (ed.) (1971), *Hong Kong: The Industrial Colony* (Hong Kong: Oxford University Press).

Hsiao, H.-S.M. and A.Y. So (1994), 'Taiwan – Mainland Economic Nexus', The Chinese University of Hong Kong, Hong Kong Institute of Asia-Pacific Studies, *Occasional Paper* 37.

Hsueh, T.T. and T.O. Woo (1991), 'The Changing Pattern of Hong Kong–China Economic Relations since 1979: Issues and Consequences', in E.K.Y. Chen, M.-K. Nyan and T.Y.C. Wong (eds), *Industrial and Trade Development in Hong Kong* (Hong Kong: The University of Hong Kong, Centre of Asian Studies: 464–96.

Hsueh, T.T. and T.O. Woo (1994), 'The Development of Hong Kong–China Economic Relationship', in B.K.P. Leung and T.Y.C. Wong (eds), *25 Years of Social and Economic Development in Hong Kong* (Hong Kong: The University of Hong Kong, Centre of Asian Studies: 689–727.

Kao, C.H.C. and S. Lin Chu-chia (1994), 'The Economic Impact of Taiwan's Investment in the Mainland', *Issues and Studies*, 30(6): 16–27.

Kumar, S. (1994), 'Johor–Singapore–Riau Growth Triangle: A Model of Subregional Cooperation', in M. Thant, M. Tang and H. Kakazu (eds), *Growth Triangles in Asia: A New Approach to Regional Economic Cooperation* (Hong Kong: Oxford University Press): 175–217.

Lam, K.C. *et al.* (eds) (1989), 'Special Issue: Spatial Development in the Pearl River Delta', *Asian Geographer*, 8(1–2).

Leung, C.K. (1993), 'Personal Contacts, Subcontracting Linkages, and Development in the Hong Kong–Zhujiang Delta Region', *Annals of the Association of American Geographers*, 83(2): 272–302.

Li, E.B.C. (1994), 'Welfare Provisions', in Y.M. Yeung and D.K.Y. Chu (eds), *Guangdong: Survey of a Province Undergoing Rapid Change* (Hong Kong: The Chinese University Press): 259–76.

Li Si-ming and Siu Yat-ming (1994), 'Population Mobility', in Y.M. Yeung and D.K.Y. Chu (eds), *Guangdong: Survey of a Province Undergoing Rapid Change* (Hong Kong: The Chinese University Press): 373–400.

Maruya, T. (ed.) (1992), *Guangdong: 'Open Door' Economic Development Strategy* (Hong Kong and Tokyo: The University of Hong Kong, Centre of Asian Studies, and Institute of Developing Economies).

Neller, R.J. and K.C. Lam (1994), 'The Environment', in Y.M. Yeung and D.K.Y. Chu (eds), *Guangdong: Survey of a Province Undergoing Rapid Change* (Hong Kong: The Chinese University Press): 401–28.

Redding, S.G. (1990), *The Spirit of Chinese Capitalism* (Berlin: De Gruyter).

Riddick, A. and K. Cowan (1993), *Capital to China*, (Hong Kong Research, Crédit Lyonnais Securities).

Shambaugh, D. (1993), 'Introduction: The Emergence of "Greater China", *The China Quarterly*, 136: 653–9.

Sinn, E. (forthcoming), 'Emigration from Hong Kong Before 1941: General Trends', in R. Skeldon (ed.), *Emigration from Hong Kong: Tendencies and Impacts* (Hong Kong: The Chinese University Press).

Skeldon, R. (1986), 'Hong Kong and its Hinterland: A Case of International Rural-to-urban Migration?', *Asian Geographer*, 5(1): 1–24.

Skeldon, R. *et al.* (forthcoming), 'An Assessment of Available Data Sources for the Analysis of the Trends in Migration', in R. Skeldon (ed.), *Emigration from Hong Kong: Tendencies and Impacts* (Hong Kong: The Chinese University Press): 79–109.

Song, Xiaowu (1995), 'Labour Market Interaction Between Hong Kong and China Coastal Areas', paper presented at the IILS/ROAP Meeting on Regionalization and Labour Market Interdependence in East and South-East Asia, Bangkok 23–26 January).

Sung, Yun-wing (1991), *The China–Hong Kong Connection: The Key to China's Open-Door Policy* (Cambridge: Cambridge University Press).

Sung Yun-wing (1994), 'The Economic Integration of Hong Kong, Taiwan and South Korea with the mainland of China', in R. Garnaut and P. Drysdale (eds), *Asia–Pacific Regionalism: Readings in International Economic Relations* (Pymble, NSW: Harper Educational Publishers): 381–99.

Sung, Y.W. *et al.* (in press), *The Fifth Dragon: The Emergence of the Pearl River Delta* (New York: Addison-Wesley).

Taubmann, W. (1993), 'Socio-economic Development and Rural–urban Migration in China since the Beginning of the 1980s', University of Macau, China Economic Research Centre, *Discussion Paper Series*, CERC/DP9300.

Turner, H.A. (1980), *The Last Colony: But Whose? A Study of the Labour Market and Labour Relations in Hong Kong* (Cambridge: Cambridge University Press).

Vogel, E.F. (1991), *The Four Little Dragons: The Spread of Industrialization in East Asia* (Cambridge, MA:, Harvard University Press).

Wong, T.Y.C. (1994), 'Hong Kong's Manufacturing Sector: Transformations and Prospects , in B.K.P. Leung and T.Y.C. Wong (eds), *25 Years of Social and Economic Development in Hong Kong* (Hong Kong: The University of Hong Kong Centre of Asian Studies): 533–59.

Wu, C.T. (1994), 'NIEs and their Cousins: Transnational Investments and their Regional Impacts', paper presented at the Fourth Asian Urbanization Conference (1–5 January) (Taipei).

Wu, C.T. (1997), 'Globalization of the Chinese Countryside: International Capital and the Transformation of the Pearl River Delta', in P.J. Rimmer (ed.), *Pacific Rim Development: Integration and Globalization in the Asia-Pacific Economy* (St Leonards, NSW: Allen & Unwing), pp. 57–82.

Zhu, Ying (1995), 'Major Changes under Way in China's Industrial Relations', *International Labour Review*, 134, (1): 37–49.

# 6 Recent Developments of Growth Triangles and the Implications for Labour Mobility in Asia

Min Tang and Myo Thant[1]

## INTRODUCTION

One of the most important developments in the Asian regional economy in the 1990s has been the emergence of subregional economic cooperation. One form of cooperation which has attracted particular attention are 'growth triangles' which are transnational economic zones spread over well defined, geographically proximate areas usually covering three or more countries. Differences in factor endowment and economic complementarity are exploited by the growth triangle to promote external trade, domestic and foreign investment, tourism, natural and human resource development, and infrastructure development.

The term 'growth triangle' came into common use after the then Deputy Prime Minister of Singapore, Goh Chok Tong, used it in December 1989 to describe the subregional economic cooperation involving Singapore, the southern part of Johor in Malaysia and Batam Island in Riau Province in Indonesia (SIJORI). The economic cooperation between Hong Kong, Taiwan, China and the southern part of the People's Republic of China (mainly parts of Guangdong and Fujian provinces) has been referred to as the Southern China Growth Triangle (SC-GT). The Tumen River Area Development Programme, which includes parts of Jilin province in the People's Republic of China (PRC), parts of Siberia in Russia, and the Democratic People's Republic of Korea (DPRK), has also been referred to as a growth triangle. Japan, Mongolia and Republic of Korea are also involved in this growth triangle in terms of natural and financial resource inputs. The Indonesia–Malaysia–Thailand Growth Triangle (IMT-GT) has also been established and consists of the northern states of Malaysia, Northern Sumatra in Indonesia

174

and Southern Thailand. A similar type of cooperation exists in the Greater Mekong subregion which includes Cambodia, Lao PDR, Myanmar, Thailand, Vietnam and Yunnan Province of the PRC. A new growth triangle, the Brunei Darussalam–Indonesia–Malaysia–Philippines East ASEAN Growth Area (BIMP-EAGA) is also being developed.

The growth triangle concept seems to be a particularly relevant solution to the operational problems of regional cooperation among Asian countries which are at varying stages of economic development. However, despite the growing interest in growth triangles in Asia, and the actual design and formation of new growth triangles, there are still many unresolved issues relating to their development. Issues which need to be clarified include the identification of the key factors underlying the success of a growth triangle and the mix of public-and private-sector policies necessary for its development. A major issue which needs to be addressed, and with which the present chapter is primarily concerned, is the impact of growth triangles on labour mobility.

The chapter is presented in six parts. The next section describes the evolution of growth triangles in different parts of Asia. The conditions necessary for the successful development of growth triangles are then discussed, followed by consideration of the prospects for extension of the growth triangle concept to other parts of Asia. Labour mobility is then evaluated in the context of three growth triangles: Southern China, SIJORI and the IMT-GT. Finally some conclusions are drawn.


## EVOLUTION OF GROWTH TRIANGLES IN ASIA

Regional economic cooperation initiatives in the form of growth triangles have emerged rapidly all over Asia, particularly since 1989. Compared with other forms of regional cooperation, particularly the European Union (EU) or the North American Free Trade Agreement (NAFTA), the growth triangle arrangement has some unique advantages. First, unlike the EU and NAFTA which require changes in nationwide institutional and administrative arrangements, a growth triangle is only a localized arrangement and usually involves only selected areas of the countries, thereby reducing the political and economic risks associated with cross-country economic cooperation. Second, because a growth triangle covers only a limited area at the initial stage, it can be established at a lower cost and in less time than a formal large-scale regional cooperation venture. Third, a country can simultaneously participate in several growth triangles to test various approaches to cooperation. Fourth, a growth triangle has an export-oriented structure for which the size of the internal market of the growth triangle is relatively unimportant. This characteristic makes growth triangles particularly appropriate for Asia, whose internal markets are much smaller than those of North America and Europe. Finally, growth triangles are also capable of extending economic benefits to non-member countries, by offering market access and by allowing foreign investment. It is therefore consistent with the promotion of free trade and greater efficiency in the use of global resources. However, despite some fundamental common features, growth triangles can differ greatly in terms of objectives, scope, focus and problems encountered (see Table 6.1). The first and the most established growth triangle is the cooperation among Hong Kong, Taiwan, China and Southern China, mainly parts of Guangdong and Fujian provinces (SC-GT). The second major growth triangle centres on an area contained by Singapore, the southern part of the Malaysian state of Johor, and the islands of Riau Province of Indonesia, SIJORI (see Table 6.2). The SC-GT is discussed extensively in Skeldon's Chapter 5 in this volume. In this section, the SIJORI growth triangle and the evolution and history of triangles which are at the planning or design, are discussed.[2]

### Singapore–Johor–Riau Growth Triangle

A major growth triangle centres on an area contained by Singapore, the southern part of the Malaysian state of Johor, and the islands of Riau Province of Indonesia (see Table 6.2). Although a growth triangle as a formal concept was recognized only in late 1989, the shift of labor-intensive industries from Singapore to Johor has been taking place for some time. The basic premise is that as production costs in Singapore increase, manufacturing plants will move from Singapore to Johor and the Riau Islands. The products of these plants would then be designed, marketed and distributed by service industries located in Singapore where they would benefit from the existing developed infrastructure and external marketing and distribution capacity. The growth triangle concept capitalizes on the availability of low-cost land and labor in the Riau Islands and of semi-skilled labor in Johor. The triangle allows a wider manufacturing base with different factor inputs which facilitates both economies of scale and vertical integration. The Riau Province–Singapore portion of the triangle is more recent than the Johor–Singapore portion, its emergence dating back only from the signing of an agreement between Indonesia and Singapore in August 1990.

*Table* 6.1  Growth triangles in Asia, 1980s–1994

|  | Hong Kong, Taipei, China and Southern China | Singapore–Johor–Riau | Tumen River Area Development | Indonesia–Malaysia–Thailand | Brunei Darussalam–Indonesia–Malaysia–Philippines |
|---|---|---|---|---|---|
| Date of Inception | Early 1980s | 1989–90 | 1991 | 1993 | 1994 |
| Participating areas | Hong Kong, Taipei, China and Guangdong and Fujian Provinces of PRC | Singapore, Johor Province of Malaysia and Riau Province of Indonesia | Jilin Province of PRC, Northern part of North Korea and Far East part of Russia | Northern Sumatra Province of Indonesia, Northern Malaysia and Southern Thailand | Brunei, North Sulawesi, East and West Kalimantan Province of Indonesia, Sarawak, Sabah and Labuan Province of Malaysia, and Mindanao in Philippines |
| Approximate Area (sq km) | 430 000 | 20 000 | n.a | 180 000 | 700 000 |
| Population (million) | 120 | 6 | n.a | 22 | 24 |
| Focus | Export of labor intensive goods and economic development zones | Export of manufactured goods | Infrastructure development, free trade zones and joint natural resource development | Expansion of trade and investment; joint development of infrastructure and tourism; cooperation in agriculture and fishery, and increasing factor mobility | Sectoral cooperation; infrastructure development; mineral, forest and marine resource development; trade and investment |

*Note:*
n.a.  Non-available.

Table 6.2 Basic indicators in the Southern China and SIJORI growth triangles

| Indicators | Southern China | | | | | Singapore–Johor–Riau | | | |
| --- | --- | --- | --- | --- | --- | --- | --- | --- | --- |
| | Hong Kong | Taipei, China | Southern Guangdong | Eastern Fujian | Total | Singapore | Johor | Batam | Total |
| Area (sq km) | 1 075 | 36 000 | 18 000 | 12 000 | 67 075 | 639 | 18 914 | – | 19 553 |
| Population (million) | 5.7 | 20.4 | 62.8 | 30.0 | 118.9 | 2.8 | 2.2 | 0.1 | 5.1 |
| Per capita GNP ($ 1991) | 13 200 | 3 070 | 535 | 350 | n.a. | 12 890 | 3 594 | 500 | n.a. |
| Total GDP ($ billion) | 59.7 | 180.3 | 33.6 | 10.5 | 284.1 | 34.6 | 4.3 | . . .[a] | 38.9 |
| GDP growth rate (1991) | 3.9 | 7.3 | 17.3 | 15.4 | n.a. | 6.7 | 9.0 | n.a. | n.a. |
| Unskilled labor cost ($ per month) | 708 | n.a | 103 | n.a. | n.a. | 350 | 150 | 90 | n.a. |
| Land cost ($/sq m/month) | 24.7 | n.a | 1.9 | n.a. | n.a. | 4.3 | 4.1 | 2.3 | n.a. |

Notes:
[a] $0.045 billion.
n.a. Not available.
. . . Rounded to zero.

Source: Chia and Lee (1992).

The creation of this growth triangle has led to outward investment and relocation of industries from Singapore to Johor and Riau, especially labor-intensive industries. Singapore firms invested more than $600 million in Johor between 1990 and 1993 and nearly $350 million in the Riau Islands over the same period. The largest impact of the triangle has been on the Riau Islands which had previously been largely untouched by economic development. The most dramatic changes have occurred on Batam island where eight industrial estates have been established, the most important of which is the Batam Industrial Park which in 1994 had 32 000 employees and $600 million worth of exports. In late 1994, the three governments concerned formalized SIJORI by signing a formal memorandum of understanding on the growth triangle. The governments agreed that a private-sector umbrella body would be created to coordinate business activities within SIJORI which was also officially renamed the Indonesia–Malaysia–Singapore Growth Triangle (Teal, 1995).

## Tumen River Area Development Programme

A future growth triangle in Asia centres on the Tumen River Area in Northeast Asia where a plan to transform a remote coastal area at the convergence of the borders of DPRK, the PRC and Russia is being drawn up with financing from the United Nations Development Programme (UNDP). The rationale for the triangle is that natural resources from Siberia and Mongolia could pass through the PRC and DPRK where low cost labour would process the minerals, which would then be shipped to markets in Japan, the Republic of Korea and industrial countries. The triangle would also be strategically located since it would be at one pole of the trans-Siberian land bridge between Europe and Asia, which is only 13 000 km. long compared to the 21 000 km trip via the Suez Canal.

In July 1991, the two Koreas, the PRC, Japan and Mongolia concluded a joint proposal to cooperate on the Tumen Project. Russia joined later and, in September 1992, a major study to develop a master plan for the area was initiated. A number of concrete steps have already been taken to realize the triangle, most notably the Rajin–Sonbong Free Economic and Trade Zone created by DPRK. Foreign investors in the zone are offered a five-year tax holiday before being subject to a maximum 14 per cent corporate tax. The PRC has supported the triangle by creating a special economic zone (SEZ) at Hunchun in Jilin province. As of late 1994, the regional development strategy for the

Tumen River Area Development Programme (TRADP) had been endorsed by all participating countries and an investment profile and resource mobilization strategy prepared. Further, agreement for the establishment of a Northeast Asia consultative commission had been reached.

Despite these achievements, the Tumen growth triangle faces a number of problems. First and foremost is the problem of poor, or non-existent, physical infrastructure. To alleviate this, large amounts of capital will be required, but given the risks and uncertainties involved, funding from the private sector is likely to be limited. A continuation of the present political and economic problems in DPRK will hinder the inflow of large-scale capital even more. A second problem is that there is as yet no agreement as to which areas investment should be channelled. PRC wishes to transform Hunchun into a major port by dredging the last 18 km of the Tumen River which presently blocks its access to the open sea. Other collaborators including UNDP object to such a plan because of the high cost of dredging the river, and suggest instead the use of the ports at Vladivostock, Nhaborsk, Chongjing and Rajin (Kakazu, 1994).

### Indonesia–Malaysia–Thailand Growth Triangle

The Indonesia–Malaysia–Thailand Growth Triangle (IMT-GT) consists of the states of North Sumatra and DI Aceh in Indonesia, the four states of Perak, Penang, Kedah and Perlis in Northern Malaysia, and the five provinces of Songkhla, Satun, Yala, Narathiwat and Pattani in Southern Thailand (see Table 6.3). The IMT-GT area displays significant differences in natural resource endowments, giving rise to numerous potential trade and investment complementarities. Northern Malaysia's land scarcity is offset by the substantial availability of land in northern Sumatra and in southern Thailand for both agricultural and industrial activity. Southern Thailand has greater availability of fruits and vegetables than the other two subregions. Ample parawood reserves in Songkhla province and in other areas of Thailand provide a stable supply of inputs for wood processing industries. Northern Sumatra's supply of oil and gas products is a clear relative advantage, making it a potential supplier of these products to Malaysia and Thailand. It also has a relative advantage in fishery reserves, and vegetable and food crop production.

The overall goal of the IMT-GT is to accelerate private-sector-led economic growth and facilitate the economic development of the sub-

*Table 6.3*  Basic indicators in the I-M-T growth triangle

| Country/Subregion | Total population (000) 1990 | Area (sq km) | Population density/sq km 1990 | Average annual growth rate of population (%) 1980–91 | Real GDP[a][b] ($ billion) 1992 | Real GDP per capita ($) 1992 |
|---|---|---|---|---|---|---|
| Indonesia | 179 380 | 1 904 600 | 94 | 1.8 | 109.481 | 572.69 |
| *Northern Sumatra* | 13 667 | 127 070 | 108 | 2.3 | 5.525[a] | 404.8[c] |
| North Sumatra | 10 252 | 71 680 | 143 | 2.1 | n.a. | n.a. |
| DI Aceh | 3 415 | 55 390 | 62 | 3.0 | n.a. | n.a. |
| Malaysia | 17 760 | 329 800 | 54 | 2.6 | 53.474 | 2 845.90 |
| *Northern Malaysia* | 4 658 | 32 257 | 144 | 1.6 | 5.239[a] | 1148.5[a] |
| Perak | 2 040 | 21 005 | 97 | n.a. | n.a | n.a. |
| Penang | 1 133 | 1 031 | 1 099 | n.a. | n.a | n.a. |
| Kedah | 1 301 | 9 426 | 138 | | | |
| Perlis | 184 | 795 | 231 | | | |
| Thailand | 56 080 | 513 100 | 109 | 1.9 | 89.391 | 1 547.62 |
| *Southern Thailand* | 2 840 | 20 809 | 136 | 2.0 | 2.2[c] | 769[c] |
| Songkhla | 1 148 | 7 394 | 155 | n.a. | n.a. | n.a. |
| Satun | 217 | 2 479 | 88 | n.a. | n.a. | n.a. |
| Yala | 364 | 4 521 | 81 | n.a. | n.a. | n.a. |
| Narathiwat | 545 | 4 475 | 122 | n.a. | n.a. | n.a. |
| Pattani | 566 | 1 940 | 292 | n.a. | n.a. | n.a. |

*Notes:*

[a]  Base year of real GDP used: Indonesia, 1990; Malaysia, 1990; and Thailand, 1988.

[b]  Average exchange rates per US $ in 1992: 2029.9 Indonesian Rupiah; 2.5474 Malaysian Ringit; and 25.4 Thai Baht.

[c]  Data for 1988

n.a.  Not available.

*Source:* Naseem (1996).

regions by exploiting underlying economic complementarities and comparative advantages, enhancing subregional competitiveness for investment and exports, lowering transport and transaction costs arising from geographical proximity, and reducing production and distribution costs through greater economies of scale. Further, through the creation of employment opportunities, the welfare of indigenous populations and women of the subregions will be enhanced. The higher rate of economic growth and creation of employment opportunities will also lead to significant regional economic development since the areas included in the IMT-GT are not the most developed parts of their respective countries.

The proposed IMT-GT development plan has several noteworthy features. First, the IMT-GT is to be created through policies, projects, programmes and institutional arrangements. The master plan has outlined nearly 100 proposals. The full development of these proposals is expected to cost at least $15 billion over the next ten years. Second, the IMT-GT is to be created through full collaboration of the private and public sectors. The private sector is to be the engine of growth but the role of the public sector is no less important, especially in the earlier stages of development when the rules and conditions for cooperation are being established. The public sector's role in disseminating information and knowledge, which will ultimately lead to lower business transaction costs, is also highlighted. Third, as with other growth triangles, there are major proposals for improving physical infrastructure, particularly in northern Sumatra (the Medan–Belawan corridor) and the Thai–Malaysian border area which is expected to be the locus of many IMT-GT activities.

## Greater Mekong Subregional Economic Cooperation

At the request of the governments of the six countries in the Greater Mekong Subregion (Cambodia, Lao PDR, Myanmar, Thailand, Vietnam and Yunnan Province of the PRC), the Asian Development Bank in 1992 implemented a study on the Greater Mekong Subregional Economic Cooperation (GMSEC). The six countries through which the Mekong river flows share borders and vast natural resources, and have cultural links. Economic interaction among them has, however, been very limited so far and the development potential of the area, with the exception of Thailand, has not been realized. Following global political changes in the late 1980s, both the willingness and possibility for cooperation have improved in the region. Some cooperative efforts–mainly on a bilateral basis–are already under way for pursuing development opportunities or overcoming impediments to trade. The challenge is to advance such efforts and use them as building blocks towards greater economic cooperation among the countries in the subregion. The most urgent need is to improve the transportation system, and energy is a major sector that has substantial possibilities for cooperation.

Although GMSEC is still being designed, it is likely to differ from the IMT-GT in at least three significant ways. First, due to the weakness of the private sector, the relative importance of the public sector in implementing economic cooperation is likely to be greater in GMSEC. Second, given the lack of previous economic linkages and the long period of political turmoil, physical infrastructure in the GMSEC area is still rudimentary. Physical projects and particularly those related to transport and communication, are therefore likely to be much more important than in the IMT-GT. Finally, because of the large numbers of countries involved, many GMSEC projects will be strictly bilateral, albeit under the GMSEC framework.[3]

## Brunei Darussalam–Indonesia–Malaysia–Philippines East ASEAN Growth Area

Brunei Darussalam–Indonesia–Malaysia–Philippines East ASEAN Growth Area, BIMP-EAGA, (see Table 6.1) is still in the design and development stage. The potential for cooperation in this region is enormous due to its rich natural resources including forestry and timber products, marine products, oil, gas, gold, diamond and crystal sand. However, although economic exchange between the people of these regions has long been established, it remains limited and rudimentary. Much of the existing trade and commerce is informal, clandestine or illegal. The main constraint to development is the lack of infrastructure. The subregions are also among the least developed in their respective countries, partly because of physical remoteness from the national capitals.

## KEY FACTORS FOR THE SUCCESS OF A GROWTH TRIANGLE

It is perhaps appropriate now to review the major factors which underlie the success of a growth triangle. Available evidence indicates that they are economic complementarity, geographical proximity, political commitment, policy coordination, and infrastructure development.[4]

**Economic Complementarity**

Economic complementarity derives from the participating countries' different stages of economic development or different factor endowments. Both the SC-GT and the SIJORI growth triangles contain fairly well-developed urbanized areas and less developed, low income areas.

Southeast Asia's leading urban centres–Hong Kong, Singapore and Taiwan, China–have strong, high tech industrial sectors, well developed financial markets, fairly advanced infrastructure facilities, well-trained labour forces and high quality management. The abundance of 'soft technology' (Chen and Ho, 1994) in Hong Kong's service sector has been one of the main reasons for its development into an international financial centre and a conduit for capital flowing into the region. Taiwan, China is particularly rich in 'hard' and 'soft' technology in the industry sector. In Singapore, both the manufacturing and service sectors are capable of serving a wider economic and geographic base, and neighbouring areas can benefit from Singapore's managerial, operational and logistical networks. Their limited supply of unskilled labour and the scarcity of land have, however, pushed up labour costs and property prices, reducing their competitiveness in the global economy. In contrast, many of the neighbouring areas, which lack capital and managerial skills, have an ample supply of both labour and land. Thus, a relocation of labour-intensive industries from the well developed to relatively less developed areas would be mutually beneficial.

An even broader basis for economic complementarity can be found in the Tumen River Delta area which allows for the integration of the capital and technology of Japan and the Republic of Korea, the natural resources of the former Soviet Union and DPRK, and the abundant labour and agricultural resources of the PRC.

**Geographical Proximity**

Empirical studies have shown that countries tend to trade with their neighbours if transportation and communication costs can be minimized (Summers, 1991). Hence, it is not surprising that geographical proximity is one of the most compelling factors for capital from Hong Kong to move to Guangdong, for investment from Taiwan, China to flow to Xiamen, or for Singaporean companies to relocate in Johor and Batam. Moreover, similarities in language and cultural background, which often prevail between geographically proximate areas, and lower transaction costs of doing business are conducive to better understanding and closer business relationships. A good example is the Southern China Growth Triangle, where interpersonal bonding and business trust have been fostered by linguistic affinity.

## Political Commitment and Policy Coordination

The political commitment of the governments involved and policy coordination among the parties are also key factors for the success of a growth triangle. At the national level, there is a need to implement appropriate policies relating to tariffs, employment regulations, real estate, finance, foreign investment and foreign exchange. All such policy directives and initiatives must be strongly supported and implemented by both central and local governments. For example, high level government commitment was critical to the relaxation of Indonesian regulations on foreign direct investment in Batam, where new policies are being implemented such as allowing 100 per cent foreign equity ownership, local processing of investment applications, and the private-sector establishment of industrial estates (Chia and Lee, 1992). To date, progress in the Tumen River Delta area has been possible only because of political commitment at the highest political levels. An advantage of such commitment is that it allows multilateral development organizations, such as UNDP, to play a catalytic role by providing initial financing for project study and design while maintaining a non-partisan role.

Compared with the SIJORI and Tumen River Delta Area triangles, formal policy coordination among the members of the Southern China Growth triangle is relatively weak, with the development of the triangle having been spurred largely by market forces and private sector initiatives.

## Infrastructure Development

Infrastructure development may be the single most important factor in the creation of an economic environment conducive to the development of a growth triangle. In the Greater Mekong Subregion, the transportation sector was identified as the most important sector for cooperation. The lack of adequate transport connections among the subregions is also a significant constraint to IMT-GT development. Therefore, eliminating infrastructure bottlenecks is one of the priorities in the IMT-GT development plan and a number of projects to physically integrate the three subregions have been proposed. In the Southern

China Triangle, the development of the four SEZs involved large-scale land development and capital construction. While infrastructure is relatively well developed in the Johor area, large infrastructure projects are still required to develop the Batam Industrial Park and the Bintan Integrated Development Project. Infrastructure development is likely to play an even more important role in the Tumen River Delta Area growth triangle, where it is almost non-existent.

## PROSPECTS FOR EXTENSION OF THE GROWTH TRIANGLE CONCEPT

The Asian experience in subregional economic cooperation suggests that the growth triangle is an appropriate form of regional cooperation for many Asian countries which could be complementary to, and an interim arrangement leading to, other forms of regional cooperation such as ASEAN or the APEC. The output of the growth triangle is largely for export and a large portion of the capital invested in the area emanates from areas outside the growth triangle. Therefore, economic complementarity should not be limited to the geographical areas of the growth triangles; neither should it be limited to trade issues. Economic cooperation in non-tradable sectors such as infrastructure, joint promotion of foreign investment, human resource development can be as important in the growth triangle framework.

Given this broader definition of economic complementarity, the growth triangle concept is thought to be particularly relevant in at least three situations. First, existing growth triangles could be expanded to cover larger areas within the countries involved. The Southern China Growth Triangle is a good example. Initially, investment and economic ties were limited to the areas of the SEZs, but after a few years of operation the PRC Government decided to apply the special policies governing the SEZs to the entire Pearl River Delta area, and later to fourteen coastal cities. Regional commercial linkages are now being observed in many inland provinces.

Second, the growth triangle concept is particularly appropriate for countries in the process of transition from a centrally planned to a market-oriented economy such as the PRC, DPRK, Vietnam, Lao PDR, Cambodia, Mongolia and the Central Asian Republics. A gradual approach to opening up the economy and changing economic systems is made possible by the growth triangle concept, minimizing political risks and undue economic hardships.

Third, for countries which are essentially market-oriented but which have only recently discarded serious biases against exports, e.g. South Asian countries, a growth triangle could be an effective means of promoting outward-oriented and export-led growth strategies. Aside from being a testing ground for new and untried policies, the growth triangle could lead to increases in foreign investment and exports which could offset losses suffered in the transition to a new economic system.

## LABOUR MOBILITY AND GROWTH TRIANGLES

The basic premise of the economic analysis of migration is that people move from one area to another in response to expected differentials in income and living conditions (Massey *et al.*, 1994). Large-scale, economically motivated movement of population is not new to Asia. In the postwar period, since the two oil shocks of the 1970s, there has been a massive volume of migration to the Middle East from Asia, which was a direct result of the phenomenal increase in oil revenues, ambitious development plans and the human capital profile of the oil exporting states (Quibria and Thant, 1989).

There have also been significant increases in labour movement within Asia. This movement has several unique features. First, it is composed of several different streams. At one end is the movement of approximately half a million persons from other Asian countries, primarily from the Republic of Korea, Bangladesh, Philippines, Pakistan, and Thailand, to Japan. There is also a significant amount of labour movement to other high level economies such as Singapore and Hong Kong. Singapore employs an estimated 300 000 foreign workers while the employment of Filipino maids alone in Hong Kong is estimated to number in the tens of thousands. At the other end are migrants who move into neighbouring countries to work in jobs which the indigenous population do not find attractive, as evidenced by the presence of an estimated 2 million Filipinos and Indonesians in Eastern Malaysia and the large numbers of people from Myanmar, Lao and Cambodia in Thailand.

Second, a large proportion of the labour movement is illegal. More than half of the Asian labourers in Japan are thought to be illegal, either as overstaying tourists or abusing student visas. Very few of the estimated 300 000 foreign workers in Thailand have employment permits. It is, therefore, useful to review labour migration experiences in the growth triangles, and prospects in other regional cooperation schemes including the IMT-GT.

## Labour Mobility in the Southern China and SIJORI Growth Triangles

Closer regional cooperation could be expected to lead to increased labour mobility. It allows labour-exporting countries to fully utilize their resources and reduce unemployment pressure, and labour-importing countries to access a broader category of work-power that is not available domestically. In this respect, labour migration within a regional cooperation framework is attractive since it gives importing countries greater control over labour inflows while permitting the labour-exporting countries to derive benefits on a sustained and fairly predictable basis.

The experience of the two existing regional economic cooperation efforts, Southern China and SIJORI, however, suggests that the potential benefits of labour migration have yet to be fully tapped and that non-economic considerations such as the possibility of conflict, culture and social welfare, etc. may overshadow economic logic and thereby reduce actual labour flows. Furthermore, to the present at least, movement of capital has been more important than that of labour, as it is far less constrained.

In the SC-GT, the relocation of Hong Kong manufacturing concerns to the PRC had two major impacts on labour and employment conditions in the region. In Hong Kong, employment in the manufacturing sector declined from over 1 million in the early 1980s to under 600 000 in 1992. On the other hand, a corollary to the reduction of the absolute size of employment in manufacturing in Hong Kong was the creation of an estimated 3 million jobs in the Pearl River Delta of the PRC. This induced large-scale domestic movement as labour from the inland provinces responded to perceived differences in employment opportunities and income differentials by moving to the Pearl River Delta area (Chen and Ho, 1994).

The SIJORI regional cooperation was motivated by many of the considerations present in the Southern China growth triangle, although purposive planning and design were in much greater evidence in SIJORI. Labour availability has been a major issue in Singapore which has a small population base, and both skilled and unskilled foreign workers have played an important role in the Singaporean economy. Foreign labour has been useful not only as a buffer for seasonal variation in labour market demand but also for fluctuations in the health of the Singaporean economy as a whole (Sullivan *et al.*, 1992). Regional cooperation, especially as a means of obtaining access to a large pool of low wage labour, became more attractive, particularly after average wages rose significantly as a result of deliberate policies designed to affect industrial and service sector upgrading.

Despite fundamental differences in economic philosophy, labour mobility within SIJORI is similar to the Hong Kong–Southern China situation in several key aspects. First, movement of labour into the capital-abundant country is strictly controlled. In both Hong Kong and Singapore, however, there were some exceptions and some labour movement was allowed, the majority for family reunions or relieving labour shortages in specific sectors such as domestic helpers and construction workers.

Second, this movement of capital induces a large amount of labour movement over considerable distances within the capital-receiving country. To cite an example, in the PRC labour numbering in the millions moved from Sichuang, Hunan and other inland provinces to the Pearl River Delta area where higher income were offered and more job opportunities available. In the SIJORI growth triangle, while Singapore has restrictions on the entry of unskilled workers, a large amount of labour migration poured into the Batam and Johor areas from the other parts of the countries to capture income differential.

Third, these movements in labour may be influenced by regional labour policies such as wage distribution policies and controls on physical movement to areas included in the growth triangle. In Southern China, there is a special entry permit for workers working in the SEZs, the core areas of the SC-GT. Hiring rural labour from other parts of the country requires approval from the labour bureau. However, working permits for other parts of the Pearl River Delta are relatively easier to obtain. In the SIJORI growth triangle, a large proportion of the labour force on Batam Island in Indonesia is recruited from Java and Sumatra on two-year contracts. Labour migration is being controlled by recruitment agencies; only migrants with residence permits are allowed while the permits are issued only to people who have secured jobs in the island. In order to prevent high labour turnover, workers seeking a new job must be assured of employment by their previous employers.

Finally, labour mobility even within the capital-receiving country may encounter problems. In the Shenzhen SEZ in the PRC, there are not enough skilled technicians and the scarcity is exacerbated by administrative restrictions on employment of technicians and skilled workers (Wang, 1994). Fears about social problems associated with large-scale labour movement have been expressed in both Southern China and SIJORI, particularly as they bring about large changes in cultural and ethnic mix in the labour-importing areas. In Batam, the influx of workers from Java and Sumatra brings into play ethnic and religious differences which need to be carefully addressed. Similarly, the migration of mostly Malay single female workers to industrial locations in Johor may lead to social problems in both urban and rural areas (Kumar, 1994).

## Labour Mobility in the IMT-GT

In addition to, and largely because of, subregional differences in wage rates and labour market conditions, labour migration is a prominent element of the IMT-GT economies. There are substantial differences in the wage rates in the IMT-GT area which may generate some incentives for labour mobility. The average daily labour cost is about US$2 in North Sumatra, while the wage rate of unskilled labour in Penang, Malaysia is as high as US$8.50/day. In Southern Thailand, the minimum wage for unskilled labour is approximately US$4.30/day. Traditionally, most of the labour movement in the region is derived from family ties and cross-border trade relationships. Recently, however, labour migration has increased in pursuit of better economic opportunities. Most such migration is from northern Sumatra and southern Thailand to northern Malaysia, much of it undocumented. Estimates of the size of the undocumented labour force in Malaysia range from 0.5 million to 1.5 million individuals. In the Thailand–Malaysia border area, there are a large number of the workers who obtain daily passes and work in Malaysia.

The major policy constraint affecting cross-border labour migration is the lack of consistency in policies governing labour flows from the 'labour-exporting' countries, Indonesia and Thailand, to Malaysia, and the delays in processing foreign labour employment applications in Malaysia. This situation has led to increasing illegal migration as well as to delays in the legal entry of foreign workers.

Indonesia's fiscal clearance policy (*de facto* exit tax) appears to be one of the factors influencing the illegal entry of Indonesians to Malaysia for employment purposes. Most low wage labourers prefer to enter Malaysia illegally – which is quite easy to do over the Strait of Malacca – rather than have to pay a high exit tax for which they cannot claim a refund since they generally do not pay income taxes. Potential migrants also have to apply for an overseas work permit, take various skills tests, get clearance from the Ministry of Labour, and obtain travel documents – all before immigration authorities grant the necessary travel permits. This is exacerbated by high fees charged by private recruitment agencies and difficulties in obtaining passports by unskilled workers.

Given these problems, the goal of the labour mobility strategy within the IMT-GT study is to facilitate and regularize labour flows to support the overall IMT-GT industrial development strategy. There are four objectives: (i) facilitate the daily movement of labour across the Thai–Malaysian border; (ii) reduce formalities for employment of foreign professional and technical labour; (iii) regularize and streamline procedures for inflow of unskilled and semi-skilled labour into Malaysia, in accordance with the industrial strategy and national priorities; and (iv) enhance Malaysian foreign labour employment policies in accordance with the IMT-GT development strategy. To address the problem of lack of adequate information on labour flows, the recently completed study on the IMT-GT includes specific proposals for a regional labour data bank in the IMT-GT area. The data bank will help to facilitate labour recruitment by providing regional information on labour demand and supply, employment trends and wages.

**Prospects of Labour Mobility in Asia**

Labour mobility in Asia in the future will be strongly and positively affected by three factors. The first is differences in the time and path of the demographic transition. Asian countries began their demographic transitions at different times and the extent to which they have made progress toward low fertility and mortality varies. This in turn implies a wide diversity in current and projected labour supply conditions. In Japan, Singapore, the Republic of Korea and Taiwan, China, where fertility declines were swift, labour force growth rates have already slowed and current labour shortages will become more severe. These shortages along with the aging of the labour force will push labour costs higher, thereby causing industrial restructuring through increased foreign direct investment outflows and importation of labour (Bauer, 1990). At the same time, declines in fertility rate, which started later elsewhere in Asia, mean that strong labour force growth and low wages will continue to be the rule for many years to come. The difference in labour force growth between countries which are well into their demographic transition and others which are further back on the transition path is a powerful incentive for large-scale movement of labour.

The second major factor promoting labour movement is regional economic cooperation for a couple of reasons. First, new cooperation schemes may explicitly address labour migration issues at the design stage. For example, the IMT-GT consciously takes labour mobility issues into account. Second, even if the general liberalization of labour movement does not occur, greater cross-border investment will lead to greater amounts of travel for business reasons or in designated areas such as the Thai–Malaysian border under the IMT-GT scheme.

The third major factor is that when regional cooperation involves areas which are undeveloped relative to other parts of the country of which it is a part, greater investment from within the growth triangle as well as elsewhere may gradually push up wage levels, thereby attracting labour from other regions within the same country; this will offset external migration.

## CONCLUSION

Compared with other forms of regional cooperation, the growth triangle approach seems to be a particularly effective solution to the operational problem of regional cooperation among Asian countries at different stages of economic development. The benefits of cooperation are not restricted to participating countries, but may extend to non-participating countries as well, through market access and greater investment opportunities.

This chapter has noted that labour mobility has occurred on a substantial scale in most of the countries engaged in regional economic cooperation activities. A large proportion of this labour is, however, of a non-legal nature. Both Hong Kong and Singapore have strict restrictions on labour movement particularly for unskilled labour. The predominant result of regional cooperation in both Southern China and SIJORI has been the greater movement within rather than across national boundaries.

The participating areas of the IMT-GT have experienced substantial and discernible movements of labour movement, within as well as across national borders. If the IMT-GT comes into being as envisioned in the master plan, domestic movement within countries should accelerate. In the case of Thailand, there should be more movement particularly from Northeast Thailand to a few key towns on the Thai–Malaysian border, while in the case of Indonesia, more movement to the Medan–Belawan agro-industrial belt is likely. Substantial cross-border movement of labour, on the other hand, is unlikely given existing political and social concerns. Much can, however, be done to make existing labour migration more efficient and to regularize the employment of existing non-legal labour.

Increased labour mobility presents both opportunities and challenges to planners and policymakers. For the labour exporter, migration is a safety valve and source of remittances. For the labour-importing country, the existence of large numbers of low cost, mobile labour allows industrial restructuring. However, social and political issues are never too distant from considerations about labour movement and it is highly improbable that decisions concerning labour mobility, domestic or external, will be solely based on economic grounds. Notwithstanding this, policymakers will still have to design and implement labour policies which allow for increased flows of labour. A key issue which needs to be addressed is the provision of information on labour supply and demand conditions to improve efficiency of labour movement.

The issue of illegal labour migration also needs to be addressed, especially if problems in this area are not to affect the general progress in regional cooperation. Both labour importers and exporters need to agree upon a set of minimum social, health and labour standards which apply to legal as well as illegal labour. Policy makers in labour-exporting countries also need to devise means of channelling labour remittances to socially desirable investment and minimizing the costs of re-entry into the domestic labour market of returning workers.

### Notes

1. This chapter is based on a paper presented at the Meeting on Regionalization and Labour Market Interdependence in East and Southeast Asia (23–26 January 1995) (Bangkok, Thailand). The authors thank J.M. Dowling and D.H. Brooks for their excellent comments and Beth Leuterio, Ludy Pardo, Pat Baysa and Helen Buencamino for their invaluable assistance. The views expressed in the paper are those of the authors and do not necessarily reflect the views and policies of the Asian Development Bank.
2. Readers who desire more detailed information on the Southern China, SIJORI and the Tumen River Growth Triangles should consult Thant *et al.* (1994), which contains several essays on each. For more detailed information on the Indonesia–Malaysia–Thailand Growth Triangle, see Asian Development Bank (1995).
3. For more detailed information on the GMSEC, see Asian Development Bank (1994).
4. Conceptual issues concerning growth triangles are extensively discussed in (Asian Development Bank, 1994b, chapter 1).

194     *Growth Triangles and Labour Mobility*

## References

Asian Development Bank (1994a), *Economic Cooperation in the Greater Mekong Subregion: Toward Implementation* (Hong Kong: Oxford University Press for the Asian Development Bank).

Asian Development Bank (1994b), *Growth Triangles in Asia: A New Approach to Regional Economic Cooperation* (Hong Kong: Oxford University Press for the Asian Development Bank).

Asian Development Bank (1995), 'Indonesia–Malaysia–Thailand Growth Triangle: Theory to Practice' (Manila 1996) (Asian Development Bank).

Bauer, J. (1990), 'Demographic Change and Asian Labor Markets in the 1990s', *Population and Development Review*, (4): (December) 615–45.

Chen, E.K.Y. and A. Ho (1994), 'Southern China Growth Triangle, An Overview', in M. Thant, M. Tang and H. Kakazu (eds), *Growth Triangles in Asia: A New Approach to Regional Economic Cooperation* (Hong Kong: Oxford University Press).

Chia, S.Y. and T.Y. Lee (1992), 'Subregional Economic Zones: A New Motive Force in Asia-Pacific Development', paper presented at the 20th Pacific Trade and Development Conference (September) (Washington, DC.).

Kakazu, H. (1994), 'Northeast Asian Regional Economic Cooperation', in M. Thant, M. Tang and H. Kakazu (eds), *Growth Triangles in Asia: A New Approach to Regional Economic Cooperation* (Hong Kong: Oxford University Press).

Korner, H. (1991), 'Future Trends in International Migration', *INTERECONOMICS* (January/February).

Kumar, S. (1994), 'Johor–Singapore–Riau Growth Triangle: A Model of Subregional Cooperation', in M. Thant, M. Tang and H. Kakazu (eds), *Growth Triangles in Asia: A New Approach to Regional Economic Cooperation* (Hong Kong: Oxford University Press).

Massey, D.S. *et al.* (1994), 'An Evaluation of International Migration Theory, the North American Case', *Population and Development Review*, 20 (December).

Naseem, S. (1996), 'The IMT-GT Area: Problems and Potentials', in M. Thant and M. Tang (eds), *Indonesia–Malaysia–Thailand Growth Triangle: Theory to Practice* (Manila: Asian Development Bank).

Quibria, M.G. and M. Thant (1989), 'International Labor Migration, Emigrants Remittances, and Asian Developing Countries: Economic Analysis and Policy Issues', *Asian Industrialization: Changing Economic Structures*, Vol. 1 (Part B): (JAI Press) 287–311.

Sugimoto, T. (1992), 'The Dawning of Development of the Tumen River Area', International Institute for Global Peace, *Policy Paper*, 75E.

Sullivan, G., S. Gunasekaran, and S. Siengthai (1992), 'Labor Migration and Policy Formulation in a Newly Industrialized Country: A Case Study of Illegal Thai Workers in Singapore', *ASEAN Economic Bulletin*, 9 (1): (July) 66–84.

Summers, L.H. (1991), 'Regionalism and the World Trade System', paper presented at the conference paper at US Fed Reserve Conference (August).

Takeuchi, J. (1992), 'Changing Labor Market in ASEAN and Growing Need for Human Resource Development', *RIM Pacific Business and Industries*, IV: 2–16.

Tang, M. and M. Thant (1994), 'Growth Triangles: Conceptual and Operational Considerations', in M. Thant, M. Tang and H. Kakazu (eds), *Growth Triangles in Asia: A New Approach to Regional Economic Cooperation* (Hong Kong: Oxford University Press).

Tang, M. and M. Thant (1995), 'Indonesia–Malaysia–Thailand Growth Triangle – Opportunities and Challenges', in M. Thant and M. Tang (eds), *Indonesia–Malaysia–Thailand Growth Triangle: Theory to Practice* (Manila: Asian Development Bank).

Teal, G. (1995), 'The Johor–Singapore–Riau Growth Triangle', paper presented at the Meeting on Regionalization and Labour Market Interdependence in East and Southeast Asia (23–26 January) (Bangkok, Thailand).

Thant, M., M. Tang and H. Kakazu (eds) (1994), *Growth Triangles in Asia: A New Approach to Regional Economic Cooperation* (Hong Kong: Oxford University Press).

Wang, J. (1994), 'Expansion of the Southern China Growth Triangle', in M. Thant, M. Tang and H. Kakazu (eds), *Growth Triangles in Asia: A New Approach to Regional Economic Cooperation* (Hong Kong: Oxford University Press).

# Part IV

# Labour Policy

# 7 Thailand in the Regional Division of Labour

Voravidh Charoenloet

## INTRODUCTION

At the approach of the twenty-first century, Thailand finds itself at a crossroads. What was traditionally an agrarian economy has, in the last ten years been transformed into a vibrant FDI-led export-oriented manufacturing base, with real GDP growth rates for the most part above 8 per cent in the last five years and the manufacturing sector contributing over 28 per cent to GDP in 1992, a larger contribution than any other sector. Despite these impressive figures, Thailand may discover that the role that it currently plays in the regional division of labour is incompatible with its long-term development objectives.

Thailand has been an attractive location for labour-intensive production activities due to its abundance of low cost, low skilled labour. The boom in investment and economic growth, however, is having the consequence of raising wages, and with the appearance of new sources of cheap manufacturing labour in other emerging economies in Southeast Asia, Thailand will eventually lose its initial comparative advantage in low-cost labour. In preparation for this eventuality, the country has had to redefine its role in the regional division of labour. The policy initiatives undertaken at this stage will be vital in configuring the Thai economy for the future so as to reduce its dependence on low labour costs for export growth, to take on more skill-intensive and technologically sophisticated economic activities, and to develop new, less transient sources of competitive advantage, which should be based more on innovation and quality of production.

This chapter will begin with an analysis of the conditions and policies that have led to the present position that Thailand enjoys in the East and Southeast Asian (ESEA) regional division of labour. It will proceed by assessing the sustainability of this position. Finally, it will conclude with the policy alternatives that Thailand faces.

THE IMPORT SUBSTITUTION PHASE OF
INDUSTRIALIZATION IN THAILAND IN THE 1960s AND 1970s

**Industrialization Policy**

In 1960, Thailand was still an agrarian economy. The main exports
were dominated by agricultural commodities and raw materials, namely
rice, tin and teak. With the exception of the central plains surrounding
Bangkok, which were used for agricultural activities integrated into
the commercial export sector, however, much of the agricultural production was for subsistence purposes. The agriculture sector accounted
for 39 per cent of GDP, and employed 82 per cent of the economically active population while the manufacturing sector accounted for
11.5 per cent of GDP and employed only 3 per cent. Trade and taxation policies favoured the agricultural sector and resource based production, primarily for domestic consumption but also for export (World
Bank, 1993).

From the very beginning, the state has played a leading role in
Thailand's industrialization process. In the late 1950s, on the advice
of the World Bank, the Thai government began to institute a series of
programmes for economic development which gave some priority to
attracting private foreign investment. In addition, an import substitution
strategy for industrialization was adopted. The state worked closely
with foreign capital in order to provide the conditions for import-
substitution industrialization in Thailand. The Board of Investment was
created in 1960 to implement the investment incentives and strategy, and
to safeguard domestic production (World Bank, 1993). Moreover, the First
Five-Year National Economic Development Plan, implemented in 1961,
focused on infrastructure development. Government resources were channelled into the construction of roads and communication facilities, the
generation of electricity and the further irrigation of the central plains.

It was hoped that the import-substituting industries, which were highly
protected, would create employment through forward and backward
linkages. Furthermore, it was thought that through its tax policy the
state could push the industries to increase the local content of their
product, which would improve the balance of payments, accelerate the
transfer of technology and eventually lead to the capacity to produce
intermediate and capital goods. Given a population of over 35 million
in 1960 and a birth rate of over 3 per cent and, therefore, a potentially
large domestic market, the choice of an import-substitution strategy
seemed justified.

It was also during this period that the government sought to put in place institutional conditions which allowed new state interventions in the labour market, including tight control over the labour movement. In 1958, the military government abolished the Labour Act of 1956, thereby banning all trade union activities and the freedom of association. Working conditions were poor, with workers working long hours, while being paid very little (8–10 bahts a day or between US$ 0.38 and US$0.47 at the 1958 exchange rate).

Import substitution was intensified in the 1970s. Tariffs on consumer goods were increased, while capital and intermediate goods' imports were protected in an effort to benefit domestic production. In addition, the agricultural sector and export production suffered. The sectors that were promoted included textiles, pharmaceuticals and auto assembly.

Although during its import-substitution period Thailand did achieve high growth rates of between 7 and 8 per cent on average, this model of industrialization was, as elsewhere, not successful in equitably distributing wealth and thus led to high levels of frustration which, along with political tensions, culminated in the 1974 students' uprising against the military dictatorship. In fact the import-substitution strategy of industrialization was less effective than expected for a number of reasons. For example:

- As in other developing countries that adopted the import substitution strategy, the import substitution policy in Thailand led to an increase in imports, rather than to a reduction in foreign imports as had been expected. Although fewer luxury goods were imported than previously, the country became increasingly dependent on the import of intermediate and capital goods, especially machinery and equipment. This, coupled with a deterioration in the terms of trade between the primary products exported and the equipment goods imported, resulted in a balance of payments crisis which became quite serious during the Third Five-Year Plan (1971–6). The government had to resort to external financing, borrowing especially from the World Bank. The amount borrowed increased enormously from about US$ 1.3 billion during the Third Five-Year Plan to about US$ 7.2 billion during the Fourth Five-Year Plan. By 1983, the long-term debt accumulated totalled US$ 9.5 billion and the debt service ratio was as high as 20 per cent.
- The very skewed distribution of income and relative poverty in the rural areas imposed a limit on demand and therefore on the extent of the local market, which in turn acted as a barrier to expanding industrial growth.

- In addition, the large-scale manufacturing through foreign direct investment did not generate the high levels of employment that had initially been expected due to the capital-intensive nature of production involved in import-substituting industrialization.
- It was this less than adequate creation of jobs compounded by the differences in income earnings between the urban and rural areas that set in motion large-scale rural–urban migration. The total number of migrants from regions around the country to Bangkok grew from 128 811 between 1955 and 1960 to 312 850 between 1965 and 1970. Furthermore, the lack of employment creation of higher paying jobs resulted in outmigration. In 1982, the number of Thais working outside the country was 108 519.

## The Labour Movement and the Development of Democracy in the 1970s

The Thai trade union movement's experience in the 1970s can be characterized as reflecting a pattern of 'strong' bargaining. There were many interlinked factors which contributed to make this unique. First, the cessation of the military regime in 1974 allowed a certain degree of democratization to occur. At this time, political and economic concerns were closely connected whenever the workers articulated their demands to the employers. Low wages were often cited as the negative side of Thai capitalism and a new, just, society was envisioned. So much so that the government began accusing the workers of being influenced by 'outside' elements.

A second factor was the existence of a marked imbalance between Bangkok with its advanced industrial structure and the outlying provinces, which were economically and socially under-developed. The massive rural–urban migration led to a concentration of the work-force in and around Bangkok, which was ready to be organized.

A third factor was that although the 1974 oil crisis had contributed to economic difficulties, Thailand did not record double-digit unemployment rates, unlike some European countries. The large agricultural base made open unemployment less pronounced.

A fourth factor was the emergence of public-enterprise workers in collective bargaining. Despite the fact that the law prohibited the state enterprise workers from striking, they had a strong bargaining position which derived from their general economic status, which can be characterized as secure (with regard to job security, earnings, welfare and other benefits), and also their high unionization rates.

The 1970s were marked by the highest number of labour disputes and strikes. The bargaining pattern was to conduct strikes first, where possible, and negotiate later. A minimum wage was enacted in 1973 and was set at 12 bahts per day. In 1975, in an effort by the government to build social consensus, the minimum wage was indexed to the price level to cope with the inflationary pressures created by the 1974 oil crisis. This social consensus, however, did not last. The change in government after the 1976 coup d'etat brought the collective bargaining process to a halt. The new government proclaimed martial law, banning employers from closing down factories and employees from striking. All labour disputes that could not be settled under the conciliation of the Labour Department were to be mediated at a higher level. A committee on labour relations was set up to undertake centralized bargaining. The tripartite system was reintroduced but in form only. As only one worker from each union was elected to tripartite bodies, giving each union only one vote, this system did not allow for the accurate representation of the variety of unions and their members, and led eventually to a more fragmented labour movement, encouraging the proliferation of small trade unions.

## RESTRUCTURING THE THAI ECONOMY AND THE EXPORT-ORIENTED STRATEGY OF INDUSTRIALIZATION

Even if not reflected in open unemployment, Thailand was severely hit by the two oil shocks. As the economy had been overly dependent on oil imports, the shocks resulted in balance of payments crises. Owing to its low level of foreign borrowing prior to the oil shocks, Thailand was able to continue borrowing to cover its expenditures. The crises, however, provided the impetus for macroeconomic adjustment and the transformation of the Thai economy from import-substitution to export-orientation.

The World Bank mission of 1980 prescribed measures required to restore the economy to its previously high rates of growth. This mission listed a number of serious economic problems: the trade deficit, inflation, wealth and income disparities, high tariff barriers, an inward-looking industrialization strategy, stagnation in the agricultural sector, failure to utilize a 'comparative advantage' in cheap labour, and restrictive foreign exchange regulations. The Bank's recipe for overcoming these problems was 'structural adjustment'. The basic changes demanded were the following: an increased export orientation, reductions in the level of protection, a devaluation of the currency, an expansion of the tax base, large-scale privatization, and liberalization of foreign exchange. For domestic firms, this sudden exposure to the international economy meant that either they had to compete by reducing production costs and increasing efficiency, or go out of business.

After the adoption of the export-led growth strategy in 1985, the integration of the Thai economy into the world economic system was greatly accelerated by the 1987–90 economic boom which was mainly supported by a combination of foreign markets, foreign capital and foreign tourists. Restructuring the economy for export-led growth was also aimed at attracting foreign investment to Thailand, a condition deemed necessary for growth and employment. Foreign investment increased by about 300 per cent in 1988 compared to the previous year. Furthermore, the Code of Investment of 1977 was amended in 1991 to give guarantees and grant privileges to foreign investment. Being given special preferences by the Board of Investment, new foreign investments were drawn into export-oriented, labour-intensive industries so as to use abundant and cheap Thai labour to produce goods competitively for the world market. Thus in recent years the Thai economy has been carried by a massive increase in exports, the most impressive in all of Asia: exports, in fact, increased by 20.7 per cent in 1986 and 28.8 per cent in 1987. In 1988, the country exported goods valued at 400 billion bahts or US$ 15.85 billion, an increase of 33.9 per cent over the previous year. Despite a fall in the growth rate of exports in 1992 and 1993, in 1993 Thailand exported US$ 36.8 billion worth of goods. The growth of exports was back up to 20 per cent in 1994 (EIU, 1994). The average annual growth rate of exports between 1980 and 1993 was 15.5 per cent (World Bank, 1995).

While continuing to export the traditional agricultural commodities and raw materials, rice, rubber and sugar-cane, Thailand has become a major exporter of canned food (sardines) and pineapple. Moreover, the country has begun producing a series of consumer goods such as textiles, ready-made garments and confections, exported mainly to the USA and the European Community. Other manufactured goods exported include precious stones and jewelry, integrated circuits, footwear and ball bearings. In addition, recently, some industries have been set up to produce intermediate products, especially auto spare parts and engines. In 1993, over 70 per cent of the country's exports consisted of manufactured goods, whereas in 1960 it was only 2.4 per cent. Indeed, labour-intensive, foreign-owned, export-oriented industries have played a major role in the recent industrialization of Thailand. This has not, however, reflected a move to higher value added production.

## STRUCTURAL CHANGE AND THE SECTORAL DISTRIBUTION OF EMPLOYMENT

Rapid industrialization in Thailand has brought about structural change in the economy. The share of manufacturing in GDP was 17.6 per cent in 1970, 21.6 per cent in 1987 and 28.8 per cent in 1992. The share of agriculture, in the meantime, has declined progressively, from 39.8 per cent in 1960 to 20.9 per cent in 1987 and 13.4 per cent in 1992. This shows that industry is becoming an increasingly important source of growth, attracting foreign direct investment (FDI) and creating employment in the country.

Along with this, there has also been a significant shift in the sectoral distribution of employment. Thailand's population at the end of 1993 reached about 58.6 million. The labour force stood at over 33 million. The number of employed persons was about 32 million (EIU, 1994), of which the majority, 59 per cent, was still in agriculture in 1993; this was, however, down from 78.3 per cent in 1970. The manufacturing sector's share in total employment has increased steadily from 3 per cent in 1960 to 10 per cent in 1988. The share of commerce and services also increased considerably during the 1980s. In 1988, the service sector accounted for 29 per cent of total employment.

In the process of industrialization, there has also occurred the rapid integration of women into economic activities. In 1988, female employment grew at a rate of 7.9 per cent over the previous year, a higher rate than the growth in male employment, 5.4 per cent. With regards to the rest of Asia, Thailand's female labour force participation rate is one of the highest. The female share of the labour force was 44 per cent in 1993 (World Bank, 1995).

The evolution of different components of the labour force in Thailand confirms that the country is in the process of modernization. The transition from an agriculture society to an industry based society has, however, been tempered by the fact that a large number of people still make their living in the countryside. In addition, in the present situation, where firms have to operate increasingly in the international environment, stiff competition from abroad has pushed many firms to adopt cost-cutting strategies. Thus, in recent years, Thailand has witnessed a decline in the quality of employment and the development of a large informal sector.

## INDUSTRIALIZATION AND THE DEVELOPMENT OF NON-WAGE LABOUR

The rapid growth of the Thai economy under the export-oriented strategy has not led to a 'trickle down' effect, but has tended to generate an increasing concentration of wealth among the rich (the share of wealth among the affluent, the (richest 20 per cent), rose from 49.3 per cent in the 1970s to 54.9 per cent in 1988 and 59 per cent in 1994. The share of the poorest 20 per cent fell from 4.5 per cent in 1988 to 3.5 per cent in 1994), and the hyperurbanization of Bangkok – the only metropolis attracting investment – has led to the marginalization of the poor and the rural areas. In other words, it has not solved the problems associated with the previous import-substitution strategy.

### The Informal Sector

As a strategy for 'survival', many people have had to find alternative employment in the 'informal sector'. This sector is not registered with the authorities or regulated by laws and its activities range from street vending, garbage collecting and motor bike rentals to manufacturing. It is estimated that no less than 4–5 million workers are employed in some kind of informal activity. Workers employed in the informal sector are usually young, in their teens or twenties, low paid and are not awarded any form of social protection.

Many informal-sector activities originate from subcontracting arrangements organized by firms in the formal sector. Subcontracting is particularly prevalent in the ready-made garment industry, where it is not uncommon for home based or small-scale shops to supply the export market. In recent years, investment from Hong Kong and Taiwan (POC) has been increasing significantly. This has coincided with the strategy to relocate labour-intensive industries away from the Newly Industrialized Economies (NIEs) so as to use ASEAN countries as a cheap base for production. However, due to the volatility, uncertainty and competitive nature of the world market, firms in the formal sector have tended to rely on a network of subcontractors as a way of reducing costs and risks. When there are many subcontractors in the informal sector competing for a limited number of orders, this can lead to a situation where exploitation of workers becomes quite commonplace, as workers in the informal sector are not organized as a group.

## Employment Flexibility

Along with the adoption of an export-oriented strategy, there has been a gradual shift away from a state-dominated market to a freely competitive market in which labour costs are defined by the market and respond quickly to changes. This has meant that the hiring of permanent employees, where the firm has to bear 'permanent' costs (wage, welfare and seniority), has become less frequent while the hiring of workers on a short-term basis has become increasingly preponderant. This reflects another form of flexibility, in addition to subcontracting.

Short-term employment is widespread in the textile, hotel, food and beverage industries. A survey of the employment situation in 1988 showed that 18.5 per cent of the total 32 062 employed persons in the Prapradaeng area were temporary employees. In this area, in 6 out of the 46 establishments surveyed, 40 per cent or more of those employed were temporary employees. The short-term employment situations in Omnoi and Omyai areas are the most serious. In 31 establishments, 60 per cent of the total 9377 employed persons were employed on a temporary basis. In Rangsit and nearby areas about 15 per cent of the total employees were also temporary.

Although the demand by workers for the abolition of temporary work had been accommodated by the previous government, the Interior Ministerial Announcement No. 11 (1993) eliminates the difference between permanent and temporary employees by introducing a fixed or broader term 'employee', which refers to all workers, whether or not they work for wages. Employers, however, usually get around the law by employing workers on short-term contract work. The employment is terminated before the contract expires and the workers are re-hired on new contracts.

Although this strategy is directed at minimizing costs of production and creating flexibility of employment in the face of fluctuations in the world market, it is also a means of controlling labour. It creates insecurity among workers as employers can dismiss them at any time without compensation. In addition, it creates divisions between workers and weakens the strength of the trade unions. The higher the proportion of workers in this category, the more reduced is the ability of trade unions to recruit new members and the more difficult it is for the trade unions to gain consensus or make unified demands on employers. The new flexibility model encourages the undermining of a collective approach to industrial relations and accentuates the divisions in Thai society. Such an approach may produce short-term benefits to employers at the expense of workers at large. It cannot be the basis for long-term and stable economic growth.

**Privatization**

Privatization has re-emerged as a major public policy issue in Thailand in recent years. It is thought that by changing the nature of ownership, from public to private, the efficiency of the enterprise will be greatly enhanced. In the past, state enterprise trade unionists have put up firm resistance to the privatization schemes of the government. Much of the workers' strength as a group came from state enterprise unions.

On 19 April 1991, the state enterprise trade unions were effectively abolished, in that they were allowed to function as associations but without any trade union rights. This paved the way for the implementation of an extensive programme of privatization. The abolition of state-enterprise unions also weakened the labour movement as an organized social force. According to recent statistics, on 1 July 1992, 707 trade unions were registered with the Labour Department but only 250 000 or 5.56 per cent of workers in the private sector hold union membership. By contrast, 57.3 per cent of the 700 000 workers employed in the state enterprises were unionized. The abolition of state-enterprise unions, therefore, substantially weakened the bargaining power of the organized workers' movement.

## THAILAND IN THE REGIONAL DIVISION OF LABOUR

So far, the products exported from Thailand have been based on cheap labour, which has been traditionally abundant. The private sector has tried to maintain its competitive advantage and to keep the cost of labour low by relying on the casualization of labour and by extending subcontracting into the informal sector. However, at present, the evolution of the labour force in Thailand is such that there is a trend towards the development of labour shortages. This is because Thailand's population growth rate has declined substantially, from above 3 per cent per annum during the late 1950s to about 1.5 per cent per annum at present. There has also been a change in the age structure of the population. Within the next ten years, the proportion of the population in the under-15 age group will decrease from 32.7 per cent to 26.7 per cent, while the population between 15 and 59 will increase from 61 per cent to 65 per cent and the proportion of the population over 60 from 6.2 per cent to 7.8 per cent. This means that the size of the labour force will continue to grow but at a slower pace, leading eventually to a smaller labour force.

Already labour shortages have been felt in some sectors such as construction and fruit cultivation. Many firms have been forced to re-locate to the provinces in search of labour. If the Thai economy keeps growing as it has, there may be many more examples of labour short-ages that are filled by illegal immigrants.[1] There has been a cry from the business sector to liberalize the flow of immigrants, i.e. to allow the import of legal labour from neighbouring countries. Businessmen support this because it keeps the cost of labour down so as to allow them to maintain cost-competitiveness in the international market. However, reliance on a supply of cheap labour is likely to favour the tendency of firms in Thailand to under-invest in skill development, training and technological and organizational improvements.

Such a tendency is reflected in the features of most export-oriented and high volume production processes. The common characteristics of labour-intensive industries are Tayloristic production lines, where cheap, docile and unorganized predominantly female workers are employed to perform monotonous and repetitive tasks, involving economies of scale and the production of standardized goods for export primarily to developed countries. In this framework, wages are a determining fac-tor of competition. However, in a situation characterized by labour shortages, increased demand for labour and the gradual democratiza-tion of the political system, there is a proclivity for wages to rise. Indeed, in recent years, the minimum wage has been rising very fast, thus exhausting the comparative advantage that Thailand had regard-ing labour costs. The purchasing power of industrial wages or real wages, calculated as the ratio of nominal wages to the consumer price index, increased at an average rate of 9.7 per cent annually between 1985 and 1990. This is a very rapid increase by international stand-ards, implying that Thailand may lose its comparative advantage in labour-intensive industries relative to other locations in the region.

**Asian Regional Integration**

In the last decade or so, there has been a large-scale expansion of trade and investment within the Asian region. As has been discussed in Chapter 4 in this volume, Japan has been a large source of that expansion and for the regional integration of East and Southeast Asia. In terms of foreign direct investment in Thailand, inflows from Japan but also from the NIEs have come to represent the core of foreign investment. Following Japan, which was the largest investor in 1987 with about 42 per cent of the net private FDI inflows in Thailand, the largest Asian NIE investor the same year was Hong Kong, with 22 per cent, followed by Taiwan with almost 9 per cent and lagging behind was Singapore with less than 3 per cent. Together, the three NIEs represented the most important investment inflow behind Japan, progressively substituting the FDI from Western countries, which represented less than 25 per cent of total FDI inflows in 1987. The FDI that came into Thailand in the 1980s was investment in search of lower production costs. This corresponded to the boom in Thai exports of textiles and garments.

While Japan remains the major foreign investor in Thailand (with 37 per cent of the foreign project applications to the Board of Investment in the first half of 1993 and 38 per cent in the first half of 1994), Europe has sharply increased its participation (27 and 27.4 per cent respectively), the proportion of US projects has declined (11.6 and 11 per cent respectively), and Taiwanese and Hong Kong projects together represent just under 25 per cent. This might reflect a new pattern of investment in the globalization process. Joint consortia between US, Japanese and European companies are becoming a more frequent form of investment abroad.

## Thailand at a Crossroads

The recent changes in the regional division of labour suggest that in the not too distant future Thailand may have to phase out the traditional labour-intensive industries, such as textiles, garments, leather and shoes, etc. as the country loses its comparative advantage in low labour costs to newcomers in Asia such as Vietnam, Indonesia and China.

There are three strategies available to Thailand; (1) to shift labour-intensive production to the frontier to employ cheap, foreign migrant, especially Burmese, labour; (2) to introduce new technology that would facilitate the production of higher quality and higher value added products; or (3) to continue the downward pressure on 'flexibility' to maintain the initial comparative advantage.

At this stage of development, it would be appropriate for Thailand to upgrade its industries and the skills of its labour force. In order to compete effectively, Thailand ought to adopt an 'offensive' strategy, i.e. the production process should have access to and involve technologically advanced inputs and skilled labour so as to produce goods for higher market niches. This may mean entering the realm of electronics and machinery original equipment manufacturing and becoming part of the global production network. Whether Thailand will succeed in upgrading its industries remains to be seen. There are some constraints that may hamper Thailand's efforts towards modernization. The pressing problem for Thailand is not only the lack of technological infrastructure but also the lack of skilled labour: over 80 per cent of workers in the manufacturing sector have no more than primary school education.

**Policy Implications for Thailand**

There are many policy areas that could be targeted to ensure Thailand's future in the continuously evolving regional division of labour, and each of the actors – the government, the workers and the employers – has a significant role to play. The government ought to make its presence in the economic sphere more effective. With the process of globalization under way and the programmes of economic liberalization which are being adopted by many countries, capital is becoming increasingly mobile across national borders. The restructuring of the world economy under the auspices of multinational corporations has led to the emergence of a new international division of labour. At one end, there has developed a network of enterprises producing high value products for a differentiated market, relying on skilled workers and technological innovation. At the other end, there is high volume production, which works on the principle of the assembly line, utilizing cheap labour. The latter is reflective of the pattern of industrial development in much of Asia, particularly Southeast Asia. The future of Thailand depends on the ability of the country to configure itself to participate in the higher value added production chain rather than the high volume, labour-intensive production chain.

To this end, the role of the government is very important in terms of investment in social infrastructure. In the short run, training and retraining schemes have to be implemented in order to prepare for the redeployment of workers discharged from the labour intensive industries. A Skill Development Fund ought to be set up to upgrade the skills of workers. Human resource development can be achieved, however, only if workers feel secure in their work. Therefore, labour protection legislation needs to be strictly enforced, while certain laws such as those covering short-term employment should be reformed. Additionally, it is necessary to strengthen the role of trade unions, and to encourage different forms of labour force participation.

Furthermore, the present government's policy, emphasizing the re-location of industries to the countryside, ought to be accompanied by a decentralization of political power. Local communities need to be revived and given a key role in decision-making and in the development process.

The private sector ought to seek internal flexibility, i.e. the promotion of skill based development. It is vital to reform assembly line production so as to humanize the working conditions of employees. In Thailand, the cost of labour is about 15–20 per cent of the total cost of production; the proportion is, thus, small. Price competition therefore needs to give way to more productive uses of capital and resources, and to the efficient management of stocks.

It is important that trade unions overcome their fragmentation. At present, workers seem to realize that to be a social force they have to unite but they should also be independent as a movement. Recently, there has been increasing cooperation among three Labour Councils, especially on the more pressing issues such as the social security law, 90-day maternity leave, and the campaign to return trade union status to state-enterprise workers. While the vertical structure of unions needs to be strengthened and democratized, horizontal relations also have to improve in order to accommodate the demands of workers from various sectors and to create a genuine workers' movement. Collective bargaining could place more emphasis on positive issues at the current level of industrialization such as improvement in skills, social benefits, and health and safety in the workplace. Awareness can be drawn from the experience of the NIEs with regard to environmental degradation. The labour movement may also be linked to other social movements to form a more broady based progressive force in society as a whole.

Finally, Asian regional integration should not be unidimensional, taking into consideration only the economic aspects involved in integration. Rather, it should consider the social dimensions as well. Competition among ASEAN countries, especially to attract foreign investment that seeks low skills and low labour costs and introduces only a low level of technology, will lead to a general decline in the condition of work and the quality of life of the workers throughout the region. Cooperation among ASEAN countries to pool resources for the development of technology and the upgrading of skills will benefit all.

**Note**

1. The number of illegal foreign workers in Thailand is estimated to be about 500 000. Of these, 200 000 are Burmese, working mostly in the fishing industry.

**References**

Charoenloet, V. (1991), 'Thailand in the Process of Becoming a NIC: Myth or Reality?' *Journal of Contemporary Asia*, 21(1): 31–41.
Economist Intelligence Unit (EIU) (1995), *Thailand: EIU Country Profile, 1994–95* (London: The Economist Intelligence Unit).
Koniya, R. *et al.* (eds) (1994), *Interdependence among East Asian Economies* (Tokyo: MITI and CERC).
Limqueco, P., B. McFarlane and J. Odhnoff (1989), 'Industry in ASEAN', *Journal of Contemporary Asia Publishers*.
Mounier, A., K. Kaewthep and V. Charoenloet (1994), 'Thailand: Export Oriented Industrialization in a Historical Perspective' paper prepared for the Political Economy Forum, Faculty of Economics, Chulalongkorn University.
Pitayanon, S. (1985), 'Labour Markets, Labour Flows and Structural Change in Thailand', paper prepared for the ASEAN–Australia Joint Research Project on Labour Market Behaviour.
World Bank (1993), *The East Asian Miracle: Economic Growth and Public Policy* (London and New York: Oxford University Press).
World Bank (1995), *The World Development Report 1995* (New York: Oxford University Press).

# An Employer Response

Niphant Simakrai

### INDUSTRY DEVELOPMENT

In general, industrial development can be divided into five stages, each of which is related to government policy, the industry itself and the labour force. At each stage of development, all the sectors mentioned above need to be aware of the changes that occur at each stage and need to plan and prepare for the coming era.

(1) Government policy needs to address the issues of improving infrastructure, technology, education and workers' skills, etc.
(2) Each industry needs to improve its nonefficiency through better management, etc.
(3) The labour force as a group or the trade union should pull together to be better organized and genuinely work for the overall benefits of the workers. Each individual should adopt self-discipline and an open willingness to learn new techniques.

In the current globalization process, success depends very much on all parties having access to information, and reacting quickly to adapt and improve.

The stages of the industry development are summarized below, giving each stage a name for easy reference:

**Stage I: 'Bull'**

At this early stage of industrial development, workers are readily available at low wages. Investment and operating costs are also at the most competitive level.

**Stage II: 'Dog'**

This is a critical stage. Sometime after the 'Bull' period, industry becomes developed and starts to face a shortage of labour, especially of

214

skilled workers. This causes wages to rise. The investment and re-investment (expansion) costs increase, in addition to operating costs. This situation forces industries again to seek the conditions that existed during the 'Bull' stage in order to survive and prosper further.

**Stage III: 'Cat'**

The industries at the 'Dog' stage, under strong pressure to maintain their competitive edge in the market place, are prompted to relocate (either onshore or offshore). Industries in this stage, the 'Cat' stage, will have the advantages of the 'Bull' stage and, to a certain extent, experienced management and skilled workers.

**Stage IV: 'Dat'**

Some industries at the 'Dog' stage may decide to retain the original base and set up in new locations. This is a mixture of 'Dog' + 'Cat' = Dat.

**Stage V: 'Dog Plus'**

This is perhaps the most critical condition. The industries which had been under the 'Dog' stage and did not diversify to 'Cat' would continue to face more pressure. The situation which the 'Dog Plus' industries face is characterized by:

• Extremely high labour costs
• Acute labour shortages
• High operating cost
• Demands for better working conditions, health care and ecologically sound production practices.


## THAILAND IN THE REGIONAL DIVISION OF LABOUR

The majority of industries present in Thailand today, based on Professor Charoenloet's analysis, if categorized by these five stages of development, would be found to be at the 'Dog' stage: textile and garment, leather and shoes or so called 'high volume production goods'. At the same time, some industries are still at the 'Bull' stage: autos, electrical appliances, electronics, etc.

Several manufacturers at the 'Dog' stage have undergone the transformation to the 'Cat' or 'Dat' stages. However, the relocation is still mainly onshore, thereby creating a new wave of work force migrants (workers moving to the central part of Thailand (industrial zone 2 and the eastern region (industrial zone 3).

1. The onshore relocation of the manufacturing base may benefit the local and nearby work force but offer little or no advantages to the migrant workers whether they work around Bangkok or anywhere other than where the factory is located.
2. As long as there are differences between the economic structure of one location and another, movement of the work force or migration of workers is inevitable. This is evidenced in both onshore and offshore. The offshore work force (migrants working abroad) was recorded at 108 519 in 1982 and the inflow of workers at about 500 000. While the outgoing migrants include legal and illegal workers the incoming migrants are as yet entirely illegal.

   The outflow workers move to more developed economics mainly in East Asia, Europe and the USA. The inflow workers are from impoverished neighbours and West Asia.

Globalization offers opportunities to industries which adopt offensive strategies, while hampering those that ignore the changes. The emergence of the newcomers in Asia (in the East, Vietnam, Indonesia, China and in the West, Sri Lanka, Bangladesh and India) will put even more pressure on industries in Thailand, especially industries at the 'Dog' stage, due to the wide gap in wages rates. Among the 'Dog' category industries, the most labour-intensive industry is the sewing industry (garments and shoes) which is likely to be affected faster than others. The sewing industry also has the largest female work force.

## THAILAND AT THE CROSSROADS

Charoenloet's analysis indicates that Thailand may have to phase out labour-intensive industries in the not too distant future. He suggested that there were three alternatives:

1. To shift production out
2. To introduce new technology and to produce better products
3. To allow developments to continue along the current path

The first alternative, in the case of moving production offshore, will hurt the unskilled workers, as they will be totally replaced by the unskilled workers of the new manufacturing countries. The second alternative would offer by far better benefits, although there is still a possibility that some unskilled workers may lose their jobs.

The policy implications of industrial development globalization for Thailand, which were mentioned briefly at the beginning of Charoenloet's chapter, will be discussed here.

## Government Sector

Charoenloet's analysis suggest that the government should become more involved in the economic sphere and investment more in social infrastructure. While the training, retraining and upgrading of skills of workers in Thailand is progressing at a very slow pace, especially and surprisingly in the most vulnerable industry, the garment industry, progress in this field is occurring much faster amongst the newcomers as the following examples show:

- *India*: National Institute of Fashion Technology (NIFT) established during 1980s with collaborative assistance from Fashion Institute of Technology, New York.
- *Sri Lanka*: The Clothing Industry Training Institute (CITI) established in September 1984 with financial support from the World Bank and technical assistance from the UK.
- Looking at a more advanced economy, *Hong Kong*: The Clothing Industry Training Authority (CITA) was established in September 1975.
- *Thailand*: The initiative for a Textile Institute occurred some ten years ago but obtained government approval only in mid-1995 with a start up budget of 50 million Baht.

## Private Sector

Each industry needs to upgrade its production and management capability, so called 're-engineering'. At the same time, efforts need to be made to improve the quality of the products to appeal to the up-market segment of consumers by adding features, updating the design and using higher technology.

**Labour Force**

Two main obstacles have to be overcome:

1. Seasonal employment – there are a sizable number of workers who still work in the agricultural sector as their main employment and work in the manufacturing industry during the off season. This creates waves of enormous seasonal absenteeism in the industrial sector which badly affects the consistency of production output.
2. *Resistance to Change* – there must be a sincere willingness on the part of workers to adapt to changing production and management techniques.

In short, under the guidance of the government sector, all sectors should try to adapt and make the necessary efforts to keep Thailand competitive, harmonizing industry and labour activities to avoid abrupt changes.

# A Worker Response
## Sakool Zuesongdham

One of the most controversial issues concerning Thai economic development today is how Thailand will counter diverse social problems as well as the constraints imposed by the current condition of infrastructure, skill formation, and technological know-how, while maintaining the high growth rates it enjoys at present and given the trend towards globalization. A main task is to formulate and implement a comprehensive human resource development policy/strategy.

### TIME TO RE-ENGINEER THE LABOUR MARKET

Employment in Thailand boomed in the 1980s when Japan and the Asian NIEs moved their manufacturing activities to Thailand, due to the appreciation of their currencies. Those employed by Japanese investors worked in metal related and machinery plants, including electrical appliances and electronics factories. Meanwhile, Taiwanese and Korean investors employed semi-skilled and unskilled workers to work in their food processing, textile and garment factories. During this period, Thailand encountered various problems, among them the lack of skilled workers and infrastructure facilities, which slowed down the influx of foreign investment in the early 1990s.

In the current situation, when the economic growth rate is faster than labour expansion, Thailand needs to re-engineer its manpower development structure, to be more competitive and ready for the next century. Some problems and threats which need immediate attention from both the public and private sectors include the following:

1. Thailand should concentrate on acquiring using and diffusing appropriate foreign technology, rather than trying to develop it. Thailand's lack of technological capacity is reflected in the low priority given to Research & Development in the national budget, currently only 0.3 per cent of the country's GDP. It must develop a strong capability to assess, select, adapt and improve technology, all of which requires

knowledge and skill. Students at the university level, therefore, should be given full financial support by both sectors, and the number of scholarships should increase in line with the increase in the number of experts required by industries. The state policy to expand compulsory education from six to nine years before the end of this century is appropriate, but it should also emphasize apprenticeship training throughout the country by allocating more for the Labour Skill Development Institutions located in the provinces. Less than 10 per cent of investment in training goes to blue-collar workers at present.

2. Compared with its neighbours, Singapore and Malaysia, Thailand is far behind as regards its low standard products. While in Singapore and Malaysia more than 300 and 2000 plants, respectively, have reached the ISO 9002 standard, only a few plants in Thailand have received such certificates. These figures suggest that Thai industries are not as competitive as their ASEAN counterparts in developed country markets.

3. Thailand enjoys GSP status provided by the USA and other developed countries, whereby exporters from selected countries receive a greater margin through tax and tariff exemption given by the importing countries. Most of the products exported are labour-intensive such as textiles, garments, leather products, agro based products, wood and wood products, electrical appliances, integrated circuits and plastic products. In anticipation of the time when Thailand will no longer enjoy GSP privileges, it is necessary to identify the demand for skilled and semi-skilled workers in order to shift to more advanced production activities. Furthermore, where production problems arise due to the shortage of unskilled workers, such as in fishery, rubber cutting, farming and cottage factories, the government should legalize the use of migrant workers from neighbouring countries like Cambodia, Laos and Myanmar. However, this measure must be applied with strict controls, to guard against labour exploitation.

4. The present government wants Thailand to focus on the auto industry, financial institutions, and communications. This is not impossible provided that most of the resources come from the private sector, while the government concentrates on facilitating and planning and overcoming human resource bottlenecks.

5. Workers in free trade zones must be given the right of association, the right to set up a union of their own choosing and to codetermine their working conditions, as endorsed by ILO Conventions. Deregulation should not affect trade union rights in the industrial zones.

# UNIFYING LABOUR, MANAGEMENT AND GOVERNMENT

Economic growth which brings better living standards for the majority in society is what is desired. In the Asia-Pacific region, the endorsement of APEC non-binding investment principles has to be followed up by governments and the parties concerned, not only on paper but in practice. The division of labour within the region will mean nothing if workers in those countries are still far from an equitable distribution of wealth. With the strong belief that economic development cannot proceed without the full participation of society, the democratic grouping from people of various occupations must be fully supported by the government.

## The Labour Movement

Most governments in the region, including Thailand's, have treated the workers' movement as a core pressure group to stir up political instability, while the trade unions' actual objectives are to seek and protect fairness, basic human rights and the rights of association. Until today the government has employed a 'divide and rule' approach, which has been the main obstacle to trade union unity and development. There are eight national centres in the trade union movement so far; none of them is strong enough to form and conduct concrete long-term policy on labour development to complement the government's economic reform plan. There should be greater dialogue between government authorities and prominent trade unionists to get correct and first-hand information, and direct suggestions. They should seek ways and means to solve the problems that fall within their responsibility. Without unity in the labour movement, the government will find it difficult to implement and follow the development plan.

The government should seek the amendment of the present labour laws to allow the labour councils to merge into one, or at the most two, congresses. A group of well known unionists has already proposed that the number of founder members for a trade union congress should not be less than 15 federations, or 50 unions and the number of individual members must reach 30 000. Another factor which creates a rift among unions is the process of electing representatives to tripartite bodies. Equal representation of government, employer, and employee alone is not enough. Free and fair elections must occur in the selection of workers' representatives, taking into account the number of individual members in each union to be represented, rather than the current 'one union, one vote' system, whereby each union has only one vote in the tripartite bodies.

## Labour–Management Relations

Present business operations are increasingly dominated by competition at the regional or global level. Labour–management cooperation is increasingly important for Thai firms in order to maintain a good image, be competitive and prosper in the climate of dynamic change resulting from global competition.

Strikes or lockouts in any business may have a chain effect in the industry, and spoil the investment climate. Aggressive labour relations policies and the exploitation of unorganized workers must be contained. Both management and labour should pay more attention to long-term working conditions; compromise with sincere respect for the equal rights of all; hold more social activities and functions to ensure better understanding; assess measures to guarantee health and safety in the workplace and set up a joint committee for this task; and encourage more intermediate and advanced skill and professional training. This strategy would help strengthen economic growth and political stability at the industry, national and regional level.

## Cooperation and Government Policy

Labour issues in Thailand fall under the mandate of a number of ministries. General labour policy comes under the Ministry of Labour and Social Welfare. Labour issues are also addressed, though less directly, by the Ministry of Interior on the formation process and some trade union activities, by the Ministry of Health on the workers' health, by the Ministry of Industry on workers' safety, by the Ministry of Education and University Bureau on a national plan for education, and by the Ministry of Commerce on consumer prices and import–export investment, and so on. These ministries should coordinate their activities to promote human resource and industrial development.

Coordination with the private sector should also be pursued in implementing a human resource development strategy. Private-sector firms are now paying more attention to training programmes, but do not like to shoulder the cost. While in the process of adapting its human resources policy to the new requirements of competitiveness in the region, the government should encourage the private sector to do more training at the intermediate and advanced professional level, by treating these expenses for such activities as capital investment and exempting them from taxation. Workers who participate in the training programmes should do so on a paid-leave basis, and be eligible for promotion to higher levels of responsibility.

Thailand is preparing for many changes in the face of global competition. The report of the National Economic and Social Development Board, 'Thailand 2000 – A Guide to Sustainable Growth and Competitiveness', states the government's policy objectives for the near future. Emphasis is placed on human resources and infrastructure development, particularly in urban areas and in transport and communications, rural development, making technology more accessible, reshaping the role of public administration and poverty eradication. The report also points to regional cooperation as being important in preparing Thailand for the future. How these worthy objectives are going to achieved or carried out is still unclear, however.

The regional division of labour is just one aspect of cooperation among countries within the Asian-Pacific region. It is a good test of the possibility of constructive cooperation. If we succeed in creating the right balance in the division of labour in the region, productivity in all member countries will rise, making them competitive and bringing sustained prosperity and wealth to communities and people from all walks of life. Some issues that could be addressed on a regional basis include the free movement of labour; the terms of investment; following up APEC's resolution on human resource development, in terms of providing quality basic education, relevant skill training, and analyzing country needs in terms of human resources; the classification of markets, common currency and the establishment of a regional trade organization that could coordinate with the World Trade Organization (WTO).

### References

APRO-FIET (1994), *APRO-FIET Faces the Future*, background paper for APRO FIET 7th Regional Conference (Malaysia).

Wehmhorner, A. (ed.) (1993), *NICs in Asia – A Challenge to Trade Unions* (Singapore: Friedrich Ebert Stiftung).

National Economic and Social Development Board (1994), *Thailand 2000 – A Guide to Sustainable Growth and Competitiveness* (Bangkok: Office of the Prime Minister).

Chiasakul, S. (1994), *Industrial Development Toward the Year 2000* (Chulalongkorn University, Faculty of Economics).

# 8 The Philippines in the Regional Division of Labour

Aniceto C. Orbeta, Jr and
Maria Teresa C. Sanchez[1]

## INTRODUCTION

The Philippines is a country rich in natural and human resources. Agriculture has traditionally been and is still very important for the Philippine economy. In addition, the country boasts one of the highest tertiary enrolment rates in the region, even paralleling some of the high income economies. Yet, despite progress in the last couple of years, the economic performance of the Philippines has been disappointing relative to the other economies in East and Southeast Asia. The average annual GDP growth rate and the growth rate of exports between 1980 and 1993 were far lower than its ASEAN counterparts. In the international and regional division of labour, moreover, rather than attracting the higher value added, more skill-intensive jobs, the Philippines is competing with Thailand, Indonesia and Malaysia, countries with lower overall school enrolment rates, for foreign investment which seeks cheap and low skilled labour (see Table 8.1).

The Philippine experience can be distinguished from the East Asian model and the development experience of the other ASEAN countries for a number of reasons. First, postwar Philippine political history has been turbulent, characterized by dictatorships, coups d'etat and only recently democracy. In this environment, economic and industrial policy reflected uncertainty and varying degrees of commitment towards the prevailing development policies and strategies. Secondly, unlike the East Asian NIEs, there was a great reluctance to adopt and follow an export-oriented strategy, and the type of import-substituting strategy that was implemented, i.e. emphasizing capital-intensive activities, was not suited to local conditions. Thirdly, labour force migration has been a prominent issue. Since the latter part of the 1970s, the Philippines

*Table* 8.1   Basic economic indicators, 1973–90

| Country | Average annual GDP growth rate 1980–93 (%) | Average annual FDI inflows 1973–90 (US$ million) | Enrolment at the secondary level 1992 (% of age group) | Enrolment at the tertiary level 1993 (% of age group) |
|---|---|---|---|---|
| Philippines | 1.4 | 182 | 74 | 28 |
| Indonesia | 5.8 | 316 | 38 | 10 |
| Thailand | 8.2 | 428 | 33 | 19 |
| Malaysia | 6.2 | 859 | 58 | 7 |

*Sources*: World Bank (1995); Aldaba (1994).

has been exporting labour, in proportionately larger numbers than other similar countries, to the Middle East and other more developed Asian countries. Overseas migration of workers reached its peak in the 1980s as new labour market opportunities opened up in other countries. While this has levelled off, it is still relatively high. Finally, in the 1980s, the economic crisis and the accompanying political instability caused foreign direct investment (FDI) to dwindle. In the ASEAN region, the Philippines had the lowest share of FDI during this period. The change in government in 1986, with the promise of improved economic growth and greater political stability, provided the impetus for the renewed interest of foreign investors in the country and the declining trend in FDI was arrested. Since the late 1980s and the early 1990s there has been a resurgence in the flow of FDI, which has had implications for the flow of overseas contract workers.

The purpose of this chapter is to analyze the role of the Philippines in the regional division of labour, addressing the issue of why the country has not fared better and examining the outlook for future growth. It starts with a brief account of postwar Philippine development, highlighting export growth, FDI, and the flow of overseas contract workers (OCWs), presenting a review of past and present policies, and the political events which have affected economic performance and have been integral in defining the role of the Philippines in the regional division of labour. The chapter then looks at the impact of foreign-led industrial development, focusing on the labour-intensive electronics and garment industries. An attempt is made to identify the labour market consequences arising from FDI and the changing organization of production in the region. Prospects and policy implications are presented in the final section.

## POSTWAR PHILIPPINE DEVELOPMENT

### The Political Environment and Policy-making

Policymaking in the Philippines has, until recently, been dictated by the country's precarious political situation, exacerbated by the inherent weakness of the institutional structure and state. This has led to often misguided and incoherent development strategies for which the country is still paying. The Philippines was under martial law throughout the 1970s. Although lifted in 1981, there was hardly any change in the power structure until the People Power Revolution in 1986. The restoration of democratic processes after the Marcos era was accompanied by a series of politically and economically destabilizing coups d'etat. At present, the country is showing signs of an enduring political stability under the Ramos Administration. The economic and political events, and the policies towards FDI that were likely to have affected investors' confidence are summarized in Table 8.2.

Two areas that have been neglected in the postwar era are the agricultural sector and land reform, precisely those that have been vital to the success of other East Asian economies (World Bank, 1993). High productivity and the growth of agricultural output enhanced by extensive land reform, investment in new agricultural technologies and investment in infrastructure and irrigation characterized the agricultural sectors in the Taiwan (POC), Japan, the Republic of South Korea, Malaysia and Indonesia. In the Philippines, as there was a perceived trade off between industrialization and agricultural growth, the labour-intensive agricultural sector was given very low priority. In addition, the leadership was supported and controlled by the landowning elite, who were unwilling to allow their position to be diminished. As a result, there was no political will to undertake significant land reform until the Ramos administration took over (World Bank, 1993: 169). This delay has perpetuated the income inequality in the country and created a situation where a large percentage of the population, despite being highly educated, are unable to share in the growth of the country and some are even forced to leave in order to find employment. Furthermore, the fact that the fertility rate in the Philippines is still relatively high and the population growth rate has only declined to 2.3 per cent in 1993 from 2.5 per cent in 1970, ensures that the Philippines is going to have a larger labour force and more mouths to feed in the future.

With respect to industrial policy, during the 1960s the country adopted

*Table* 8.2 The Philippines, chronology of significant economic and political events, 1970–94

| Year | Event |
|------|-------|
| *1970* | Balance of Payments (BOP)/BOP crisis.<br>*RA 6135: Export Incentives Act* This Act was the first step towards redirecting investments away from import-substituting industries that had dominated the Philippine economy. It followed the same rules on foreign ownership as RA 5186 and provided almost the same incentives granted to firms registered under RA 5186 in addition to tax credit on duties and taxes paid on raw materials and additional deduction of the sum of direct labor cost and raw materials used. |
| *1972* | Declaration of Martial Law.<br>*PD 66: Export-Processing Zones* RA 5490 of 1969 was passed to pave the way for the country's first export-processing zone (EPZ) in Bataan, but no real progress was made until PD 66 was issued. Total production of firms must be entirely geared for exports; in certain instances, however, and subject to the approval of the EPZ Authority, 30 per cent of production may be sold in the domestic market. Foreign ownership was permitted up to 100 per cent; however, only promoted industries were allowed to be set up. |
| *1974* | Expiration of Laurel–Langley Agreement. |
| *1980* | *Trade liberalization programme* Under a World Bank SAL, the government embarked on a programme to reduce the level and dispersion of tariff rates and remove quantitative restrictions over a period of five years ending in 1985. The Programme proceeded broadly on schedule until the 1983 BOP crisis. |
| *1981* | Lifting of Martial Law.<br>*PD 1789: Omnibus Investments Code of 1981* This consolidated into a single code all incentive measures to investments, agriculture and exports contained in separate pieces of legislation, but did not alter their overall thrust. |
| *1983* | *BP 391: Amendment of PD 1789* This reduced the number of incentives under PD 1789. It did away with some of the capital cheapening measures such as accelerated depreciation and expansion reinvestment allowances. It also gave strong preference to exports and substituted performance based for capital based benefits.<br>Aquino assassination.<br>BOP crisis. |
| *1984–5* | Trade liberalization postponed due to BOP crises.<br>Holding of massive demonstrations participated in for the first time by the urban middle class and the business community. |

*continued on p. 228*

*Table* 8.2   *continued*

| Year | Event |
|---|---|
| *1986* | February People Power Revolution.<br>July coup attempt.<br>November coup attempt. |
| *1987* | *EO 226: Omnibus Investments Code of 1987*   Regulated the entry of foreign investment in enterprises not registered under Book 1 of the Code whenever their equity participation exceeded 40 per cent (instead of 30 per cent in the old Code). The new Code simplified and consolidated previous laws and provided two important additions: income tax holiday for enterprises engaged in preferred areas of investment and labor expenses allowance for tax deduction purposes.<br>August coup attempt. |
| *1989* | Nearly successful December coup and persistence of rumours of further conspiracies. |
| *1990* | *Build-Operate-Transfer Act*   Encouraged private sector participation in government investment programme. |
| *1991* | *RA 7042: Foreign Investment Act*   Liberalized the existing regulations by allowing foreign equity participation up to 100 per cent in all areas not specified in the Foreign Investment Negative List (FINL). The FINL has three component lists: A, B and C. List A covers areas where foreign participation is excluded or restricted by the Constitution or specific legislations. List B contains activities where foreign investment is limited for reasons of defence, risk to health and morals, and protection of local small and medium-scale enterprises. List C contains areas of investment in which there already exists an adequate number of enterprises to serve the needs of the economy and further foreign investment is no longer necessary. Foreigners who do not seek incentives and/or whose activities are not included in the negative list can invest up to 100 per cent equity simply by registering with the Securities and Exchange Commission (SEC). They can also invest up to 100 per cent in enterprises that export at least 60 per cent (instead of 70 per cent under EO 226) of their output, provided these do not fall within List A and B.<br>*EO 470*   Designed within a four-year phasedown period from July 1991 to July 1995, EO 470 aimed to lower the maximum tariff rate to 50 per cent and reduce the number of tariff tiers within the range of zero minimum for raw materials to 50 per cent (with some exceptions) for finished products. |
| 1992 | *Foreign Exchange Liberalization*   Including (1) increase in retention of export receipts by commodity from 2 per cent to 40 per cent; (2) increased access of exporters to the foreign |

*Table* 8.2   *continued*

| Year | Event |
|------|-------|
| | currency deposit system; and (3) liberalization of non-trade foreign exchange regulations. Election of Ramos. |
| *1993* | *Land Lease Law*   Extension of land lease period up to 75 years. *Further Foreign Exchange Liberalization*   Including: (1) Totally lifted all mandatory surrender requirements on export receipts and removed all quantitative restrictions on current account transactions; (2) allowed full and immediate repatriation of capital and remittance of dividend, profits and earnings; (3) Abolition of US$50 000 minimum deposit requirement for non-residents in offshore banking units. *Banko Sentral ng Pilipinas*   Established with new charter bestowing strengthened authority to conduct independent monetary policy and free from the burden of huge losses incurred by the previous Central Bank. |
| *1994* | *RA 7721: Entry of Foreign Banks*   Granted permission to foreign banks to operate branches in the Philippines. Granted permission to foreign banks to buy into existing local banks. *Multilateral Investment Guarantee Agreement*   Philippine accession ratified by Senate. *GATT-Uruguay Round*   Philippine accession ratified by Senate. |

*Sources*: Aldaba (1994); Lamberte (1994); Soriano (1992).

an import-substitution policy regime. Export promotion was initiated in the 1970s with the establishment of export-processing zones (EPZs) under Presidential Decree (PD) 66 in 1972 (see Table 8.2). Until the late 1980s, however, trade and investment policies still favoured the inward-looking industries. Studies on Philippine postwar economic policies are unanimous in pointing to import-substituting policies as the main culprit in the country's failure to develop rapidly (Bautista and Power and associates, 1979; Medalla, 1990; Medalla *et al.*, 1994). In the 1980s, the country embarked on a series of trade liberalization programmes which were interrupted several times due to concurrent economic and political crises and natural disasters.

There was an ambivalent attitude towards FDI in the 1960s and the 1970s that was mainly due to the controversy over the role of FDI in the development of a host country. The idea that FDI thrives where there are relatively low factor costs, mainly labour and natural resources, spawned the criticism that it is exploitative. As elsewhere, however, this attitude has changed with the demonstration of its role in export-led

*Table* 8.3   Distribution of central bank-registered FDI, by source, cumulative flows, 1973–93 (million US$)

| Country | 1973 | 1980 | 1990 | 1993 |
|---|---|---|---|---|
| *North America* | *64.59* | *58.54* | *55.66* | *45.30* |
| USA | 64.25 | 54.60 | 54.07 | 44.08 |
| Canada | 0.34 | 3.94 | 1.58 | 1.22 |
| *Asia* | *10.99* | *22.22* | *23.72* | *30.78* |
| Japan | 9.66 | 16.79 | 15.29 | 20.25 |
| Hong Kong | 1.33 | 4.32 | 6.12 | 6.65 |
| South Korea | 0.00 | 0.46 | 0.49 | 1.56 |
| Singapore | 0.00 | 0.41 | 0.65 | 1.09 |
| Taiwan | 0.00 | 0.21 | 0.83 | 0.92 |
| Malaysia | 0.00 | 0.03 | 0.34 | 0.32 |
| *Europe* | *18.87* | *15.06* | *17.38* | *19.46* |
| *Other countries* | *5.55* | *4.19* | *3.25* | *4.46* |
| *Total* | *100.00* | *100.00* | *100.00* | *100.00* |

*Sources*: Aldaba (1994); basic data.

development in the Asian NIEs. Beginning in the late 1970s, the attitude towards FDI thus became more receptive. Since then, many policies have been implemented to attract foreign investment and liberalize the conditions that regulate it. Table 8.2 lists some of the more important policies.

In the Philippines, the flow of FDI was traditionally determined by political relations. Consequently, FDI in the country was mainly of US origin. On a cumulative basis, the US still dominates, however, Japan, European countries and the Asian NIEs have now become increasingly important sources of FDI in the recent past (Table 8.3).

The government's commitment to the export-led development strategy was reinforced by the ongoing structural adjustment programme, defined in Executive Order (EO) 470 (1991). The four-year programme which ended in 1995 aimed at a progressive reduction in tariff rates. Tariff reduction in the textile and garment industries as well as in the industries producing their chemical inputs was accelerated. The accession to the GATT–Uruguay Round Agreements in 1994 is a further addition to these liberalization efforts.

The liberalization of the foreign exchange market which started in 1992 was highlighted by the removal of mandatory surrender requirements for exporters. In 1994, foreign banks were allowed to establish branches in the country or to buy into existing domestic banks. As part of the free competition policy, the government also dismantled barriers to entry in long protected key industries such as telecommunications, land, sea and air transport and cement. The privatization of government-owned and controlled corporations (GOCCs) has also been under way. In 1993 alone, nineteen GOCCs composed of several large corporations such as Petron, Philippine Shipyard and Engineering Corporation and Oriental Petroleum and Minerals Corporation were privatized.

These policies have been designed to gear the economy toward an outward-looking strategy based on the country's comparative advantages. In fact, the twin pillars of the current development strategy are world competitiveness and sustainable human resource development.

## Economic Growth and Employment

The effects of the policies outlined above become more apparent by looking at indicators such as economic growth, export performance, FDI and the flow of overseas contract workers.

The high rates of economic growth in the 1960s and 1970s, brought to a virtual halt in the mid-1980s, showed a tentative resurgence in the late 1980s, and a more complete recovery in the 1990s. For the first time in many years, the economy surpassed the government-set gross national product growth targets in 1994, registering a relatively strong 5.5 per cent growth rate. The projections for future years are equally, if not more, upbeat.

The employment performance of the economy, meanwhile, has been unimpressive. Employment growth was hampered by a long-persisting policy bias against the agricultural sector and the country's most abundant resource, labour. This is reflected in the change in the sectoral contribution to output and employment (Tables 8.4 and 8.5). For instance, the industrial sector which contributed a steadily increasing share of output, reaching as high as 41 per cent in 1980, absorbed no more than a little over 20 per cent of workers. A striking case in the industrial sector is the manufacturing industry. Its output contribution between 1970 and 1990 was more than 25 per cent but its employment contribution for the same period declined from 12 to 10 per cent. The agricultural sector, on the other hand, which has contributed a declining share of output, still employs as much as 45 per cent of the workers. While the contribution of the service sector to output is relatively stable at about 40 per cent, its contribution to employment has been increasing steadily, reaching 35 per cent in 1990. This indicates that the service

*Table* 8.4    Shares in real GDP, by industry, 1970–94 (per cent)

| Sector | 1970 | 1980 | 1990 | 1993 | 1994[a] |
|---|---|---|---|---|---|
| Agriculture, fishery and forestry | 28.18 | 23.50 | 22.38 | 22.76 | 22.41 |
| Industrial sector | 33.70 | 40.52 | 35.59 | 34.35 | 34.84 |
| Mining and quarrying | 1.44 | 1.50 | 1.54 | 1.58 | 1.44 |
| Manufacturing | 27.07 | 27.60 | 25.61 | 24.73 | 25.13 |
| Construction | 4.06 | 9.39 | 5.83 | 5.28 | 5.54 |
| Electricity, gas and water | 1.13 | 2.03 | 2.60 | 2.76 | 2.99 |
| Service sector | 38.12 | 35.98 | 42.03 | 42.89 | 42.69 |
| Transport, communications and storage | 4.14 | 4.78 | 5.72 | 5.88 | – |
| Commerce | 23.92 | 22.14 | 24.36 | 25.05 | – |
| Services | 10.05 | 9.06 | 11.94 | 11.96 | – |
| GDP (million) | 343 162 | 609 768 | 718 069 | 733 097 | 766 086 |

*Note*:
[a] 1994 data are advance estimates.

*Sources*: *Philippine Statistical Yearbook* (various issues), National Statistical Coordination Board, Economic and Social Statistics Office.

sector has absorbed much of the surplus labour. The unemployment rate of the country is one of the highest in the region. Contributing largely to this is the failure to bring down fertility rates and the consequent high annual growth rate of the labour force, currently at 4 per cent. An ILO report pointed out that the country should attain about 8–10 per cent growth in output in order to absorb those who are openly unemployed (ILO, 1990).

## Export Performance

The country's total exports were valued at about US$ 1 billion in 1970. By 1993, total exports had increased to US$ 11.4 billion (Table 8.6). Total exports grew by 18 per cent between 1970 and 1980. That growth rate was not sustained in the early to mid-1980s but recovered in the late 1980s and early 1990s.

Despite the mixed performance in the 1980s, there has been a clear shift in the composition of exports by commodity, from traditional agricultural and natural resource-based exports like coconut, sugar, forest and mineral products (copper and gold) and abaca fibre to manufactured, non-traditional exports (Table 8.6). Garments, electrical parts

*Table* 8.5  Proportion of employed persons, by major industry, 1970–94

| Major industry group | Census 1970 | 3rd quarter 1980 | October 1990 | October 1993 | January 1994 |
|---|---|---|---|---|---|
| Total (000) | 11 775 | 16 434 | 22 532 | 24 443 | 24 673 |
| Agriculture, fishery and forestry | 53.80 | 51.44 | 45.20 | 45.80 | 45.20 |
| Industry | 20.80 | 20.00 | 20.07 | 21.07 | 21.28 |
|   Manufacturing | 11.80 | 11.04 | 9.71 | 10.04 | 10.05 |
|   Mining and quarrying | 0.45 | 0.57 | 0.59 | 0.53 | 0.52 |
|   Electricity, gas and water | 0.29 | 0.35 | 0.40 | 0.43 | 0.44 |
|   Construction | 3.92 | 3.58 | 4.32 | 4.51 | 4.64 |
|   Transportation, storage and communications | 4.35 | 4.45 | 5.05 | 5.56 | 5.62 |
| Services | 23.67 | 28.53 | 34.66 | 33.08 | 33.48 |
|   Wholesale and retail trade | 7.32 | 10.10 | 13.96 | 13.97 | 14.14 |
|   Financing, insurance, real estate and business services | 1.79 | 2.04 | 1.97 | 2.03 | 1.95 |
|   Community, social and personal services | 14.57 | 16.39 | 18.73 | 17.08 | 29.55 |
| Industry not adequately defined or reported | 1.65 | 0.04 | 0.07 | 0.05 | 0.03 |

*Source*: Labour Force Surveys.

and equipment, and new agricultural (primarily frozen fish and fruits) and mineral exports dominated the non-traditional export category.

An instructive way of looking at export performance involves the classification of goods by factor intensities. Exports can be classified as agriculture and forest resource-intensive, mineral-intensive, unskilled labour-intensive, human capital-intensive, and technology-intensive goods. The export of agricultural resource-intensive goods and mineral-intensive goods declined significantly between 1975 and 1990, from 69 per cent to 25 per cent and 16 per cent to 12 per cent respectively. On the other hand, the share of unskilled labour-intensive goods (garments, furniture, electrical machinery and apparatus) increased from 13 per cent in 1975 to 52 per cent in 1990. In addition, during the same period, the export shares of the human capital-intensive goods increased from a negligible amount to more than 5 per cent of the total as did the share of technology-intensive goods from 12 to 17 per cent. High export potential in the human capital-intensive goods category was found in the telecommunications and sound recording subindustries.

There has also been a notable diversification in the destination of Philippine exports. The US and Japan accounted for 70 per cent of

*Table* 8.6    Shares of Philippine exports, by major commodity group, 1970–93 (per cent)

| Commodity groups | 1970 | 1980 | 1990 | 1993 |
|---|---|---|---|---|
| I   Traditional exports, of which: | 91.53 | 53.01 | 17.55 | 12.26 |
| 1. Coconut products | 19.68 | 14.01 | 6.06 | 4.34 |
| 2. Sugar and products | 18.46 | 11.35 | 1.62 | 1.13 |
| 3. Forest products | 26.18 | 7.34 | 1.15 | 0.40 |
| 4. Mineral products | 20.43 | 15.86 | 4.41 | 3.16 |
| 5. Fruits and vegetables | 2.45 | 1.92 | 1.98 | 1.64 |
| 6. Abaca products | 1.41 | 0.47 | 0.20 | 0.17 |
| 7. Tobacco unmanufactured | 1.32 | 0.50 | 0.24 | 0.23 |
| 8. Petroleum products | 1.60 | 1.55 | 1.89 | 1.20 |
| II  Non-traditional products | 2.35 | 44.30 | 81.05 | 85.95 |
| A   Non-traditional manufactures, of which | 1.13 | 33.15 | 73.23 | 79.39 |
| Electrical and equipment and parts/ telecommunications | 0.00 | 11.59 | 23.99 | 31.22 |
| Garments | 0.00 | 8.67 | 21.70 | 19.97 |
| Textile yarns/fabrics | 0.56 | 1.28 | 1.14 | 1.04 |
| Furniture and fixtures | 0.09 | 1.33 | 2.31 | 1.78 |
| Chemicals | 0.47 | 1.54 | 3.19 | 2.30 |
| B   Non-traditional commodities of which: | 1.22 | 11.14 | 7.82 | 6.56 |
| Nickel | 0.00 | 2.38 | – | – |
| Iron ore agglomerates | 0.00 | 2.04 | 0.99 | 0.55 |
| Bananas | 0.47 | 1.97 | 1.82 | 1.99 |
| Fish, fresh or simply preserved | 0.19 | 1.85 | 3.59 | 3.02 |
| III Special transactions | 1.98 | 0.21 | 0.23 | 0.33 |
| IV  Re-exports | 0.38 | 0.07 | 1.16 | 1.45 |
| *Total value* (million US$) | 1 062 | 5 788 | 8 186 | 11 375 |

*Sources*: 1970 and 1980 figures were computed from Lamberte *et al.*; 1988–93 figures were computed from Department of Economic Research, Bangko Sentral ng Pilipinas.

total exports in 1970. Their share decreased to about 50 per cent in 1990, while the share of the EEC and other ESCAP countries increased considerably.

## Foreign Direct Investment

Table 8.7 shows the great fluctuations in the level of FDI since 1970. The lower flow of FDI into the country relative to neighbouring countries may not, however, be attributable to differential incentives. Manasan

*Table* 8.7   Net FDI flow in the Philippines, 1970–93 (million US$)

| Year | New foreign investments | Reinvested earnings |
|------|------------------------|---------------------|
| 1970 | 4 | 0 |
| 1971 | 3 | 0 |
| 1972 | 2 | 0 |
| 1973 | 83 | 0 |
| 1974 | 64 | 0 |
| 1975 | 116 | 0 |
| 1976 | 91 | 67 |
| 1977 | 130 | 78 |
| 1978 | 60 | 62 |
| 1979 | 62 | 58 |
| 1980 | 75 | 39 |
| 1981 | 91 | 62 |
| 1982 | 25 | 44 |
| 1983 | 119 | 26 |
| 1984 | 32 | 15 |
| 1985 | 9 | 10 |
| 1986 | 17 | 20 |
| 1987 | 34 | 22 |
| 1988 | 81 | 17 |
| 1989 | 93 | 56 |
| 1990 | 171 | 28 |
| 1991 | 130 | 34 |
| 1992 | 234 | 42 |
| 1993 | 334 | 43 |

*Note*:
'Net foreign direct investment' inflow is the sum of new foreign equity investments, reinvested earnings, debt conversion, technical fees converted into equity, imports converted into investments *plus* capital withdrawn from the Philippines.

*Source*: Aldaba (1994).

(1988), using the user cost of capital and internal rate of return as indicators, concludes that the ASEAN countries are as competitive with each other before and after the incentives. Alburo, *et al.* (1992) also conclude that FDI flows increased dramatically even if there were no significant changes in incentives granted. Some explanation can be found in the differences in trade policies. While economic liberalization was simultaneously being pursued by the four ASEAN countries starting in the mid-1980s, its implementation in the Philippines had stalled. Given the depressed economic conditions and political instability during the waning years of the Marcos regime and during the process of restoring democracy that followed, the country had to postpone the implementation of trade liberalization because of impending balance of payments crises. Furthermore, the exchange rate policy was not used aggressively. The overvaluation of the peso was calculated to be as much as 30 per cent if free trade prices were used as the benchmark (Medalla *et al.*, 1994). In addition, policies favoured the predominance of inward-looking FDI.

It is notable that the flow of FDI seems to be directed at the non-export-oriented, non-labour-intensive sectors. The sectoral concentration of cumulative FDI between 1973 and 1993 is shown in Table 8.8. It is evident that since 1973, manufacturing has been the favoured sector and within it chemicals and chemical products, food processing, transport equipment, and machinery and appliances. Another sector which receives large FDI flows is the mining sector. Banks and other financial institutions rank third, having had the highest share in 1973. FDI in textile and garments, on the other hand, appears to have been stagnant between 1973 and 1993, while FDI in machinery and appliances, which includes electronics, has increased significantly in the early 1990s.

Looking at effective protection rates (EPRs), Aldaba (1994]) points out that FDI in the Philippines has tended to be concentrated in highly protected sectors. The manufacturing sector received the highest protection compared to mining and agriculture, fishery and forestry. Within the manufacturing sector, before the 1980 tariff reform, EPRs for chemicals were between 15 to 227 per cent, for food, 495 per cent, metal products, 84 per cent, textile and garments, 106 per cent, transport, machinery and appliances, 118 per cent, and for petroleum and coal, 38 per cent before the 1980 tariff reform. Even after the tariff reform programme, the EPRs are still high in textiles, chemicals, basic metal products and processed food. These observations are more pronounced if one looks at EPRs using price comparisons which, in addition to tariffs, reflect the impact of non-tariff barriers (NTBs). Finally, Aldaba (1994) highlights the fact that even Board of Investment approvals of foreign equity participation, which are supposed to encourage exports, follow the same pattern of hiding behind high protection walls.

**Overseas Contract Workers**

One unique feature of Philippine development is the large number of workers employed abroad. While neighbouring countries have attracted FDI and been able to keep their workers within their borders, the Philippines continues to send workers abroad as opportunities at home are

*Table* 8.8  Distribution of Central Bank-registered foreign equity investment, by sector, 1973–90 (per cent)

| Industry | 1973 | 1975 | 1980 | 1985 | 1990 | 1993 |
|---|---|---|---|---|---|---|
| Banks and other financial institutions | 45.44 | 35.12 | 18.81 | 12.25 | 12.15 | 11.69 |
| Banks | 40.36 | 26.85 | 11.47 | 7.24 | 7.25 | 5.94 |
| Other financial institutions | 5.07 | 8.26 | 7.34 | 5.01 | 4.90 | 5.75 |
| Manufacturing | 39.18 | 44.80 | 50.42 | 49.10 | 48.66 | 53.02 |
| Chemicals and chemical products | 3.65 | 5.18 | 14.71 | 13.02 | 13.16 | 12.26 |
| Food | 2.41 | 5.37 | 6.90 | 10.85 | 9.54 | 8.21 |
| Metal and metal products | 1.39 | 12.40 | 7.96 | 6.45 | 5.24 | 4.48 |
| Textiles and garments | 4.98 | 3.66 | 2.83 | 2.14 | 2.47 | 2.70 |
| Transport equipment | 2.33 | 1.36 | 4.28 | 3.86 | 3.55 | 4.36 |
| Petroleum and coal | 16.37 | 6.20 | 2.32 | 3.04 | 2.51 | 5.10 |
| Mach. app. appl. and suppl. | 1.04 | 1.38 | 3.04 | 2.79 | 4.75 | 9.21 |
| Non-metallic mineral products | 1.24 | 0.64 | 1.05 | 1.29 | 1.50 | 1.53 |
| Others | 5.78 | 8.62 | 7.33 | 5.66 | 5.94 | 5.17 |
| Mining | 3.25 | 7.81 | 17.57 | 26.44 | 26.06 | 20.43 |
| Petroleum and gas | 0.10 | 0.21 | 14.31 | 24.28 | 22.64 | 16.90 |
| Copper | 2.35 | 4.92 | 2.37 | 1.67 | 1.32 | 0.99 |
| Iron ore | 0.22 | 2.22 | 0.73 | 0.36 | 0.28 | 0.21 |
| Nickel | 0.58 | 0.35 | 0.11 | 0.05 | 0.07 | 0.06 |
| Others | 0.00 | 0.12 | 0.06 | 0.08 | 1.74 | 2.27 |
| Commerce | 2.55 | 5.76 | 6.49 | 4.36 | 5.29 | 5.10 |
| Wholesale | 1.57 | 2.79 | 5.07 | 3.23 | 3.30 | 2.86 |
| Real estate | 0.90 | 2.35 | 0.93 | 0.96 | 1.38 | 1.78 |
| Others | 0.07 | 0.62 | 0.50 | 0.16 | 0.61 | 0.46 |
| Services | 0.18 | 1.70 | 2.55 | 3.96 | 4.28 | 5.68 |
| Business | 0.16 | 0.83 | 1.92 | 2.62 | 2.46 | 2.17 |
| Others | 0.01 | 0.86 | 0.63 | 1.34 | 1.82 | 3.51 |
| Public utility | 6.76 | 3.20 | 1.51 | 1.31 | 1.26 | 2.18 |
| Communication | 0.62 | 0.68 | 0.30 | 0.48 | 0.56 | 1.28 |
| Land transport | 6.12 | 2.33 | 0.71 | 0.40 | 0.32 | 0.24 |
| Others | 0.02 | 0.20 | 0.50 | 0.43 | 0.38 | 0.65 |
| Agriculture, fishery and forestry | 2.49 | 1.44 | 1.27 | 1.74 | 1.63 | 1.23 |
| Agriculture | 0.14 | 0.23 | 0.34 | 1.14 | 1.32 | 1.00 |
| Others | 2.36 | 1.21 | 0.92 | 0.60 | 0.31 | 0.23 |
| Construction | 0.08 | 0.05 | 1.34 | 0.83 | 0.66 | 0.66 |
| Transport facilities | 0.00 | 0.00 | 0.58 | 0.40 | 0.32 | 0.24 |
| Infrastructure | 0.00 | 0.00 | 0.56 | 0.60 | 0.48 | 0.40 |
| Others | 0.08 | 0.05 | 0.20 | −0.17 | −0.13 | 0.02 |
| Others | 0.08 | 0.13 | 0.04 | 0.02 | 0.02 | 0.01 |
| *Total value* (million US$) | 146 | 391 | 1 281 | 2 601 | 3 275 | 4 396 |

*Sources*: Aldaba (1994); basic data.

*Table* 8.9   Distribution of unemployed persons, by highest grade completed (per cent), selected years

| Year | Total | No grade | Elementary | | High school | | College | | Not reported |
|------|-------|----------|------------|-----------|-------------|-----------|---------------|-----------|--------------|
| | | | 1–5 | Graduated | 1–3 | Graduated | Non-graduated | Graduated | |
| 1961 | 6.36 | 5.80 | 31.20 | 21.30 | 18.10 | 12.70 | 10.40 | 0.50 | 0 |
| 1965 | 6.16 | 6.30 | 26.80 | 28.30 | 13.30 | 12.70 | 12.20 | 0.50 | 0 |
| 1976 | 4.25 | 2.31 | 15.13 | 21.79 | 17.05 | 16.79 | 14.23 | 11.67 | 1.03 |
| 1980 | 5.05 | 3.58 | 15.27 | 16.15 | 16.77 | 19.38 | 17.27 | 10.21 | 0.67 |
| 1985 | 7.12 | 1.42 | 8.64 | 13.75 | 13.87 | 23.71 | 20.64 | 17.89 | 0.08 |
| 1990 | 8.13 | 2.80 | 12.40 | 14.80 | 14.20 | 24.80 | 14.70 | 15.90 | 0.50 |

*Source*: Labour Force Survey Series.

limited. While there are important signals that this trend is changing, it is instructive to analyze the flow of OCWs.

In the 1960s, the contract workers were of three types. Professionals and technical workers went to the US mainland; skilled workers and craftsmen were hired by construction firms and logging companies for projects in Southeast Asia, and entertainers went to Japan and Hong Kong. By the 1970s, the flow had shifted to the Middle East and was dominated by blue-collar workers servicing the construction boom. By the 1980s, with the decline in the demand for construction workers in the Middle East, the composition of OCWs by occupation gradually shifted to professional and skilled workers. Furthermore in recent years, the neighbouring Asian countries have become an increasingly important destination (Abrera-Mangahas, 1989). Since the mid-1980s with the surplus of educated labour at home, professionals and middle-level managers have found employment in the growing neighbouring economies. In fact, comparing the occupational distribution of OCWs with the composition of domestic employment, proportionately the country is fielding twice as many professional workers abroad as it is employing domestically. This can easily be understood given that domestic open unemployment rates have not spared even the highly educated (Table 8.9).

Contributing to this flow of OCWs have been supportive government policies and the mushrooming of private recruitment agencies. Through the 1974 Labour Code, the government established the Philippine Overseas Employment Programme making it state policy to promote overseas employment for Filipinos. As the volume of overseas workers grew and official agencies were unable to handle the increasing volumes of OCWs, private intermediaries were allowed to proliferate to handle the recruitment and placement of OCWs (Abella, 1988). By 1990, there were 683 officially recognized recruitment agencies in operation, a dramatic increase from the 71 in 1977.

Contract workers were particularly recognized as playing an important role in the development of the country when the performance of the country faltered and remittances provided a steady flow of the much needed foreign exchange. More than 2 per cent of the GNP was contributed by OCWs during the difficult period in the mid-1980s. These figures consider only those remittances which are documented and may be grossly understated. Given the increasing trend in the composition of OCWs towards professionals and technical workers, and the liberalization of foreign exchange transactions, the flow of remittances has been increasing steadily, surpassing 4 per cent of GNP by 1992. Subsequently, the government has removed the remaining barriers to the movement of OCWs into and out of the country.

## EVOLUTION OF THE PHILIPPINES IN THE REGIONAL DIVISION OF LABOUR: FOREIGN-LED INDUSTRIAL DEVELOPMENT

Electronics and garments are the leading exports of the country, and there is a sustained world demand for these industries' products. Both industries are labour-intensive and their exports are mostly on a consignment basis.[2] FDI is more dominant in the electronics industry relative to the garments industry. However, the role of the Philippines in the regional division of labour is reflected in both industries.

### The Garment Industry

The origins of the garment industry can be traced back to the late 1950s when cottage-level enterprises began to replace the traditional tailors and dressmakers. Over the years, larger, export-oriented firms have joined the industry which has made it the second largest non-traditional exporting industry in the country. Garment exports became the greatest contributor to the total export of consumer manufactures, with a share estimated at 62.81 per cent in 1990. Moreover, a sizable proportion of garment exports consists of finished embroidered goods, apparel and clothing (using imported raw materials) which are exported on a consignment basis. This subgroup accounted for 60.55 per cent of garment exports in 1990.

The garment industry has contributed significantly to the manufacturing sector in terms of labour absorption. The employment share of the industry relative to total manufacturing employment is higher than its output share. Moreover, garment industry employment is probably underestimated, as the garment industry is characterized by the prevalence of subcontracting in multi-level arrangements and official statistics do not cover contractors and home workers. Employment in the garment industry has grown steadily over the years. The proportion of employment accounted for by the industry was estimated at 16.59 per cent in 1988, and grew at an average annual growth rate of 13.56 per cent between 1975 and 1988. Moreover, the Philippines has the highest proportion of garment industry employment relative to total manufacturing employment among ASEAN countries.

**The Electronics Industry**

The Philippine electronics industry was established in the 1960s. Its primary function was to assemble consumer electronics products such as television sets and transistor radios for the domestic market. This segment of the industry was composed of Filipino-owned independent third-party subcontractors producing specific types of products and relied on contracts with American and European manufacturers. The production of semiconductors was carried out by subsidiaries of foreign electronics multinational corporations and was primarily export-oriented. The industry was heavily dependent on imported raw materials and was sensitive to changes in the international markets. In contrast to the Republic of South Korea, Taiwan (POC) and to a lesser extent Malaysia and Thailand, where consumer electronics comprise at least 20 per cent of output, the focus of the Philippine electronics industry was basically on components' manufacturing. Protectionist policies contributed to confining consumer electronics firms to the domestic market and, consequently, to their limited growth (Medalla *et al.*, 1994).

In the 1970s and 1980s, the export-processing zones (EPZs) were established granting fiscal incentives to foreign firms whose production activities were labour-intensive and export-oriented. By 1993, the Philippines had become an important export base with the share of the electronics industry's exports to total exports reaching 31 per cent, with semiconductor devices accounting for 90 per cent of total electronics exports in 1988. Other electronics products such as appliances and telecommunication and sound recording equipment continued to be domestically-oriented, although their contribution to exports has increased slightly in recent years. The electronics industry also contributed significantly to the manufacturing sector's output. In addition, employment in the electronics industry grew significantly in the 1980s. Its share of total manufacturing employment was 6.35 per cent in 1988.

The computer software services industry includes programming services, data entry and data processing services. Besides the provision of these services domestically, the country also exports computer professionals who work abroad on individual contracts. The data show that this contributed 2 per cent of the US$ 2 billion output of the industry in 1991. The growth of this industry has been enhanced by the 11 per cent of the country's tertiary schools, 110 offering computer education. At least one tertiary school offering computer training is present in every region of the country. While the majority of college graduates still opt for commerce and business management, there is a steadily increasing proportion of graduates in the information technology field.

## The Mactan Export-Processing Zone (MEPZ)[3]

Recent developments in the Cebu Province which have resulted in new and better prospects for investment have attracted the attention not only of policymakers but also of foreign investors. The establishment of the Mactan Export-Processing Zone (MEPZ) in 1979 and the upgrading of the nearby Mactan airport to the standards of an international airport have largely contributed to the rapid development of the province as one of the industrial centres in the country and have also provided an institutional set-up for the Philippines' integration and role in the regional division of labour, with Cebu as a node.

As in most EPZs, industries in the MEPZ, are labour-intensive, export-oriented, light, and non-pollutant. Establishments in the zone include those which manufacture electrical components, semiconductors, computer software, garments, watches, gloves, costume jewellery, luggage, toys, plastic and metal components, furniture and wood products.

The first two firms established in the zone were both electronics firms – TMX Philippines and Fairchild (National Semiconductor, Inc.). In 1985, only six firms were operating in the zone employing 3243 workers, but by 1991, a large proportion of the zone's total land area was already occupied. Lamberte *et al.* (1993) attribute this to the overall incentive package such as low land lease/sale rates, cheap utilities, and low wages. In 1994, 44 firms were operating in the zone employing 22 410 workers. The MEPZ has had the highest employment growth of all the EPZs in the country (Tiukinhoy, 1991).

The zone has the highest proportion of wholly-owned foreign firms relative to the zones in Bataan and Baguio. In 1989, 68.8 per cent of the establishments in the MEPZ were wholly foreign-owned, 11.4 per cent were partly foreign-owned while the remaining 20.0 per cent were fully Filipino-owned. The Japanese account for 50 per cent of total foreign equity in the zone.

In Mactan, as in most EPZs, the majority of workers in the zone are blue-collar workers (over 76 per cent in 1988), young, female (80 per cent in 1994), and highly educated, (i.e. having completed high school). Most of the jobs in the zone, however, require only a low-level of skills, implying massive underemployment. Training and apprenticeship programmes are few.

The majority of the zone's production workers are employed on a regular or permanent basis, but the proportion declined from 99.50 per cent in 1986 to 80.59 per cent in 1988. This decline was accompanied by an increase in the proportion of workers employed on a contractual or probationary basis from a negligible number in 1986 to 3.55 per cent in 1988. In addition, while almost all the firms in the zone pay the wage rates required by law, very few firms pay wage rates above the minimum.

It is also notable that there is an absence of labour unions in the zone; this is due to a deliberate attempt by the Zone Authority and the firms to keep the zone free of unions. The Zone's Chamber of Manufacturers and Exporters is supposed to ensure that labour laws and standards are upheld and that the workers rights are safeguarded (Tiukinhoy, 1991). The absence of labour unions in the MEPZ, however, eliminates the workers' opportunity to bargain for higher wages and other employment concerns.

The findings of the study by Lamberte *et al.* (1993) show that in a broader context, the employment contribution of the MEPZ has been insignificant. Due to the dominance of subcontracting arrangements in the zone's garments industry, however, a significant number of jobs may have been created in the neighbouring communities. The MEPZ's significant employment contribution to the local community may also be reflected in improved living standards of the workers. An important impact of the MEPZ has been in the form of the rising number of micro service related enterprises in the area, particularly in food and transportation, which cater to those who work in the zone. This reflects a strong consumption linkage with the local community.

On the whole, the industries in the MEPZ are found to have weak linkages with the local economy. For instance, as the electronics industry relies heavily on imported materials and produces for the export market, it has very little impact on domestic production activities. Lamberte *et al.* (1993) point out the potential for the garment industry to have a strong backward linkage with the local textile, fibre and spinning industries. The garment industry also, however, relies on imported raw materials which are cheaper than domestic raw materials. This has been attributed to the heavy protection granted to domestic textiles and other related industries and their consequent under-development (Mercado, 1986).

## THE PHILIPPINES IN THE REGIONAL DIVISION OF LABOUR: PROSPECTS AND POLICY IMPLICATIONS

At present, the Philippines plays two primary roles in the regional division of labour, one of an exporter of cheap skilled and unskilled labour and the other of a low cost location for assembly-type activities. The mismanagement of policy has resulted in the misallocation of the Philippines' abundant resources. Despite the high level of education of the domestic labour force, the country is catering to an investment market for which its labour force is over-qualified and it is unable to provide enough domestic employment to keep its labour force occupied at home. While the Ramos government has gone a long way to liberalize the economy and encourage FDI, much still needs to be done to ensure that in the long run the Philippines has a secure and beneficial position in the regional division of labour. A firm commitment to a more equitable distribution of the gains from development and the Philippines' role in the regional division of labour would be a start. What lies ahead, therefore, depends very much on the policy choices now made.

### The Role of Labour Provider: Overseas Contract Workers

The rapid growth of the country's population and labour force accompanied by trade and macroeconomic policies which were biased against labour-intensive industries, and the political instability that interrupted economic growth, have resulted in a labour surplus. The labour surplus, especially in terms of unskilled workers, was minimized by the opening of new opportunities for work in the neighbouring developed and ANIEs, and the Middle East. The role of the Philippines as labour provider to these countries, although not as profound as in the 1980s, is most significant.

What are the prospects for the flow of OCWs? If the economy

continues to grow, economic incentives for working abroad will decline rapidly for blue-collar workers. Soon, the wage differential may not be large enough to cover the social and other costs of adjusting to different cultures and locations. Given the geographical proximity and the similarity of cultures, which implies lower adjustment costs, blue-collar workers that remain overseas will be those in the nearby Asian countries. In addition, if FDI continues to flow into the country under a more politically stable and a more economically conducive environment, the demand for semi-skilled workers in the domestic market and special economic zones will increase.

The case of professional and technical workers, however, is more complex. First, the wage differential between foreign and domestic employment opportunities is larger. Second, this class of workers is less prone to exploitation by employers. Finally, in the next few years both the higher demand for professional and technical workers abroad and the lure of gaining experience in sophisticated work environments may become important factors that will keep these workers in their overseas jobs and likewise attract those who have just finished tertiary schooling. Thus in contrast to blue-collar workers, many of the professional and technical workers will continue to work abroad in the near future even if the domestic economy continues to improve.

### The Role of Providing a Low-cost Location for Foreign Direct Investment

In particular industries such as the export-oriented electronics and garment industries, the Philippines has evidently assumed the role of providing cheap, unskilled, and efficient labour. Over time, the inflow of capital and technology from abroad has led to employment creation. However, the types of employment created through this regional division of labour are highly sensitive to relative production costs and technological development (Edgren, 1990). Labour market conditions such as low wages, which serve as an instrument to attract capital inflows, have an ambiguous impact on workers' welfare. Competitiveness based on low labour costs and the precarious nature of work created by low wage–low skill, export-oriented investments have restricted the ability of workers to unionize and have left little room for the improvement of the workers' living standards or, as in the Mactan EPZ, for the development and utilization of proper institutions to address their grievances concerning working conditions, employer–employee relations, etc.

As elsewhere, export-oriented zones in the Philippines, as was illustrated by the case of the Mactan EPZ, have not been as effective as originally expected either at creating sufficient employment or at improving the working conditions and living standards of those who work there. Given that the nature of production activities of export-oriented firms, particularly in the electronics industry, consists mainly of assembly and testing types of operations which generate little value added, skill upgrading and technical training may be limited.

## Policy Implications

The present trend in the division of labour in the Asian region has resulted in subregional divisions of labour wherein the more industrialized countries continue to upgrade production technology and to move to higher value added and skill-intensive production, leaving other countries, like the Philippines, to specialize in the assembly types of operation. Production technologies and labour processes have been upgraded in terms of their quality and complexity in countries like Hong Kong and Singapore. This is seen as the result of increasing labour costs and the availability of well trained scientists, engineers, and technicians. With technological upgrading, production activities are carried out with higher levels of precision.

Recognizing this trend, the Philippines can position itself to take on the higher value added activities that the more developed countries in the region leave behind. The country should train its manpower for the higher stages of production activities not only to qualify skilled workers to work in developed countries but also to prepare for the future shifts toward higher skill-intensive domestic production activities.

The future for the garment industry is in export niches in upscale apparel, and high value added types of garments (Austria, 1994; NEDA, 1994). It can no longer count on the cheaper end of the garment export market because labour cost advantage has allowed countries like China to capture this. Domestic producers, therefore, should move on from being design and order takers to creating innovative designs that capture the fancy of the world market. In this regard, the industry needs to upgrade its equipment, invest in manpower training, and invest in Research & Development to face up to this emerging challenge. This is a role that can be filled by FDI. In addition, the more intense competition that will be brought about by the opening up of the economy and increased export orientation is expected to force stronger linkages between the garment industry and the domestic textile industry, which the past structure of protection did not encourage.

The country's comparative advantage as host to semiconductor firms has been enhanced by the liberalization of the economy and the establishment of special economic zones (SEZs) such as the one in Mactan. However, labour costs are getting to be higher than those in Indonesia, China, and Pakistan. Thus, the country needs to start moving away from the production of semiconductors into higher value added activities such as original equipment and design manufacturing (Intal, 1994). The highly educated labour force is a plus factor in this move. Furthermore, the educational system is responding positively to this emerging challenge, which is a welcome shift for a system that has been known to over-produce in disciplines where there is limited demand. However, if the move towards higher value added activities is not realized, these technicians may be forced again to find remunerative jobs overseas. An important task of the government, therefore, is to encourage the acquisition of new technology by the private sector.

The prospects for the appliance as well as the telecommunications and sound recording equipment industries lie in export markets. The small size of the domestic market should provide the necessary push. The removal of protection under the current trade liberalization efforts will provide the other impetus. A competitive parts industry (Lapid, 1994) and the software and data processing service industry are other bright areas.

Government intervention in the EPZs has made investment opportunities more profitable while the low cost work force has played a large role in attracting foreign investment. Attention should now turn to attracting foreign investment in high value added production activities and to creating domestic employment for the professional and technical workers who are forced to go overseas. Only proper policies, which address the inequalities and biases that have hampered economic growth until now, can ensure this transition. In addition, political stability and proof that the political will exists to implement tough policy measures, including land reform, are vital in gaining investors' confidence.

### Notes

1. The authors gratefully acknowledge the assistance of Ms Consolacion Chua and Ms Mildred Belizario.
2. 'Consigned exports' are those exports in which the buyer supplies the raw materials while labor and other processing costs are provided for by the exporter (*Philippine Yearbook*, 1992).

3. This section draws heavily on the study undertaken by Tiukinhoy (1991). Observations were derived from the results of the survey of MEPZ workers and firms undertaken in February 1990. The survey covered zone firms which had been in operation for a full year as of July 1989. A stratified random sampling procedure was applied to select sample workers.

**References**

Abella, M. (1988), 'Emigration and Return Migration Policies: Sending Country Perspectives', paper presented at the Seminar on International Migration Systems Processes and Policies, International Union for the Scientific Study of Population (IUSSP).

Abrera-Mangahas, A. (1989), 'Response to New Market Opportunities: The Case of Overseas Employment Sector', *Working Paper Series*, 89–11 (Manila: Philippines Institute of Development Studies (PIDS)).

Alburo, F., C. Bautista and M.S. Gochoco (1992), 'Pacific Direct Investment Flows into ASEAN', *ASEAN Economic Bulletin*, 8(3) (March).

Aldaba, R. (1994), 'Foreign Direct Investment in the Philippines: A Reassessment' *Research Paper Series*, 94–10 (Manila: Philippine Institute of Development Studies).

Austria, M. (1994), 'Textile and Garment Industries: Impact of Trade Reforms on Performance, Competitiveness and Structure', *PIDS Research Paper Series*, 94–06 (Manila: Philippine Institute of Development Studies).

Bautista, R., J. Power and associates (1979), 'Industrial Promotion Policies in the Philippines' (Makati: Philippine Institute for Development Studies).

Edgren, G. (1990), 'The Challenge of Human Resource Utilization', in *Employment Challenges for the 90s*, International Labour Organization–Asian Regional Team for Employment Promotion (Bangkok).

Intal, P. (1994), 'Changing Comparative Advantage and Interregional Trade Expansion in Asia and the Pacific: The Case of the ASEAN-4', paper presented at the ESCAP/UNDP/APDC Regional Seminar on Changing Comparative Advantages and Interregional Trade Expansion in Asia and the Pacific (21–23 December) (Kuala Lumpur).

International Labour Organization (1990), 'Employment and Manpower in the Philippines: A Sectoral Review Report (Manila: ILO).

Lamberte, M. (1994), 'Managing Surges in Capital Inflows: The Philippine Case', *PIDS Discussion Paper Series*, 94–20 (Makati: Philippine Institute for Development Studies).

Lamberte, M. *et al.* (1993), 'Decentralization and Prospects for Regional Growth (Makati: Philippine Institute for Development Studies).

Lapid, D. (1994), 'Appliance Industry: Impact of Trade Reforms on Performance, Competitiveness and Structure, PIDS Research Paper Series, 94–05 (Makati: Philippine Institute for Development Studies).

Manasan, R. (1988), 'A Review of Investment Incentives in ASEAN Countries', *PIDS Working Paper Series*, 88–22 (Makati: Philippine Institute for Development Studies).

Medalla, E. (1990), 'Assessment of Trade and Industrial Policy, 1986–1988',

*PIDS Working Paper Series*, 90–07 (Makati: Philippine Institute for Development Studies).

Medalla, E. *et al.* (1994), 'Catching up with Asia's Tigers: A Call for a More Effective Philippine Industrial Policy' (Makati: Philippine Institute for Development Studies).

Mercado, R. (1986), 'A Study of the Effects of Tariff Reform and Import Liberalization in the Textile Industry, *Tariff Commission PIDS Joint Research Project Staff Paper Szeries*, 86–14 (Makati: Philippine Institute for Development Studies).

National Economic Development Authority (NEDA) (1994), *A Framework for agro-industrial Restructuring for Competitiveness in the Philippines* (Manila).

Soriano, Ma. C.G. (1992) 'Philippine Structural Adjustment Measures', Working Paper Series No. 92–10 (Makati, Philippines).

Tiukinhoy, A.C. (1992), 'Employment and Industrial Relations Conditions in the Mactan Export Processing Zone', Pre-final draft submitted to the Institute for Labor Studies – Department of Labor and Employment (ILS-DOLE).

World Bank (1993), *The East Asian Miracle: Economic Growth and Public Policy* (London and New York: Oxford University Press).

World Bank (1995), *World Development Report* (New York: Oxford University Press).

# An Employer Response

Francisco R. Floro

In revisiting the postwar circumstances of Philippine economic growth and development, Orbeta and Sanchez's chapter reiterates what has already been accepted as gospel truth in policy circles. While neighbouring countries laid the foundations for outward-looking economic development, the economics of import-substitution in the Philippines was deeply entrenched throughout the postwar period. In the 1980s, it became apparent that sustainable growth could be attained only through a complete reversal of the prevailing inward-looking strategy. The social and political cost of structural reform, however, was prohibitive as a combined result of political and economic instability in the Philippines and the volatility of the global economy following the two oil crises.

## STRUCTURAL REFORMS

In the past, there have been many unsuccessful attempts to implement structural reforms in the Philippines. According to the ILO, the failure of these was largely due to (a) their predominantly deflationary nature; (b) the direct negative effects of some macroeconomic policies on the welfare of low and middle income groups; and (c) corruption, inefficient tax collection and economic mismanagement.

The current adjustment programme calls for bold and fundamental reforms that seek to break the stranglehold of an entrenched inward-looking and import-led economic structure. Until recently, reforms merely paid lip service to an export-led strategy; the current reforms, however, are expected to maximize employment generation over time and to complement scarce domestic resources with external capital. These reforms involve a comprehensive liberalization programme covering trade, industry, finance and agriculture; privatization of public sector activities and assets; deregulation of industries such as telecommunications, shipping and banking, air and land transport; and the decentralization of authority and funds to local governments.

The government recognizes that structural reforms of such magnitude will have short-term costs. Workers will lose jobs, especially those in highly protected and inefficient industries which may be unable to cope in a liberalized environment. Food prices may rise as the peso depreciates, hurting the poor more than anybody else. Thus, and this constitutes a major departure from previous adjustment programmes, the government is determined to address the short-term costs with the forceful provision of specific safety nets to those who would be hurt most by the structural changes.

For the first time, the government consulted and involved both the employers and the workers who would be directly and profoundly affected. In January 1994, a tripartite agreement on structural reforms was signed by leading representatives of employers, labour and government, which forged commitments between sectors and created a mechanism with which to monitor the effects of these reforms.

## THE INFORMAL SECTOR

In spite of economic vicissitudes, and perhaps as a result of the poor employment performance of the formal sector, the dynamism and magnitude of the informal sector in the Philippines distinguishes it from neighbouring countries. The Philippines Chamber of Commerce and Industry (PCCI) estimates that as much as 40 per cent of GNP is contributed by the informal sector – which includes establishments which do not pay taxes because they are too small. Furthermore, the PCCI estimates that the 1994 official growth rate of GNP should be revised upwards to 7.5 per cent. In the same vein, official figures on overseas contract workers (OCWs) and their remittances are likely to be underestimated by at least 50 per cent because they fail to include illegal migrants and the informal remittance delivery system outside the official banking system. Appropriate methodology should be developed to catch informal activities in official statistics and measure their contribution to national income. Attention should be given to their activities in macropolicy formation.

## OVERSEAS CONTRACT WORKERS

Concerning the issue of OCWs, the Philippines has not been the only major labour exporter in East Asia. In the early stages of development, Thailand, Malaysia and Indonesia also experienced a substantial exodus of contract workers of various skill levels to the Middle East, Japan, Singapore, Taiwan and Hong Kong. In fact, it was South Korea, with the active intervention and support of its government through the Korean Overseas Employment Development Board, that perfected the technique of overseas service contracting and project contracting during the construction boom in the Middle East. Between the mid-1970s and early 1980s, 100 000–300 000 highly trained and disciplined Korean workers were deployed in the Middle East. Combining advanced technology with the skills of the workers, large Korean contractors were able to compete with Western multinational corporations. During this period, South Korea earned up to US$ 10 million annually in foreign exchange receipts.

Some lessons can be drawn from the experiences of these countries. First, for developing countries, overseas employment is traditionally seen as an outlet for surplus labour, providing a safety valve to reduce the pressure on the limited labour-absorptive capacity of the domestic economy. The pressure becomes non-existent once a state of full employment within the country is attained, invariably as the result of sustained high growth rates. Malaysia, for example, has now become a labour-short economy and has become the focus of massive regional labour migration flows, especially from Indonesia and the Philippines. Thailand is also experiencing labour shortages in certain sectors. For some developing countries like the Philippines, overseas employment can be seen as a short- to medium-term strategy for reducing local unemployment.

Second, overseas employment may serve as a catalyst in the transfer of technology. Workers employed abroad may upgrade their skills and be exposed to new technology. The opposite has been true, however, in the Korean model,where Korean firms brought with them their own skills and technology. As the Philippines seeks to attain world competitiveness and to develop a world class labour force, its labour force will have to master the latest technologies, one way to do this is through overseas employment.

Third, overseas employment is also a significant source of foreign exchange reserves, which is important if not essential for economic growth.

Fourth, the social costs of labour migration are high as contract workers are separated from their families and home, and have to adjust to different cultures. In addition, they are sometimes abused or mistreated. These costs are difficult to quantify, but nonetheless, have to be addressed in the policy discussion, including through bilateral initiatives, preferably with ILO intervention.

## REGIONAL COOPERATION

Growth triangle initiatives are another instance for cooperation across nations. For many years Mindanao, the second largest island in the Philippines, has been known as the Land of Promise. While it is rich in natural resources, it has remained a backward and relatively under-developed region compared with the Northern island of Luzon, where Metro Manila is located. One of the reasons for its laggard development is distance. The air distance from Davao City, the biggest city in Mindanao, to Manila is as far as going to Hong Kong, and as costly. Freight costs between the two cities are as much as between Honolulu and Manila. Since most shipments have to be routed through Manila, freight costs reduce the global competitiveness of goods produced in Mindanao. Given this situation, Mindanao saw an opportunity to accelerate the development of trade through the East ASEAN Growth Area (EAGA), which links it with countries that are closer geographically and even culturally. While trading activities between the partners have already begun, the formal establishment of the EAGA will institutionalize the interdependence of these trading partners. It is hoped that with strong private sector initiatives and government support, the necessary infrastructure will be put in place, concomitant with increasing trade and investment flows and labour mobility.

## THE GARMENT AND ELECTRONICS INDUSTRIES

Concerning the impact of FDI, the chapter's focus on the electronics and garment industries in the Mactan Export-Processing Zone (MEPZ) limits its conclusions. In spite of the lack of data on the destination of recent direct investment flows in the Philippines, it is common knowledge that much of the newer FDI flows are destined for other areas outside the traditional export-processing zones (EPZs), such as the CALABAR region, the Subic Bay Freeport, and other industrial parks in strategic areas in the country. For example, the umbrella organization of semi-conductor companies in the Philippines, SEIFI, with a membership of 45 corporations employing approximately 8000 workers, has only ten of its members located in the EPZs, and only about 10 per cent of its membership is unionized.

In addition, the study on the garment industry operating within the MEPZ cannot capture the complexities of the industry in the country and its role in promoting exports. The main feature of the garment industry in the Philippines is its layer of subcontracting arrangements from foreign subsidiaries to principals, subcontractors, middlemen, and homeworkers, to whom most of the piecework, which is defined in the Philippine Labor Code as 'industrial homework', is consigned. This structure of subcontracting has a high labour-absorptive capacity and provides employment for hundreds of thousands of households.

## LABOUR STANDARDS IN EPZs

Finally, the chapter assessment of the working conditions in EPZs does not reflect the most recent developments and seems to be out of touch with the law and practice of labour relations in the Philippines. Freedom of association, the right to form, join or assist a union, the right to collective bargaining, the right of concerted action including the right to strike, are all guaranteed by the Constitution and implemented by the Labour Code, and operate throughout the entire jurisdiction of the Philippines, including the EPZs.

While the study may have found a low level of unionization in the MEPZ, the opposite is true of the Bataan EPZ (BEPZ), which is a hotbed of union activity reflecting a variety of viewpoints and representing 98 per cent of the workers. On two separate occasions during the 1980s, the BEPZ was paralyzed when its entire work force, numbering 24 000, walked out of their jobs and staged a zone-wide strike that lasted several days.

In fact, the law on unfair labor practice acts, which was patterned after similar legislation in the USA, is unheard of in the rest of the ASEAN countries. This law makes an employer's act of omission or commission against the exercise of the political and economic rights of workers and unions illegal and subject to sanctions. This law contributes to the adversarial orientation of labour relations in the Philippines. In addition, there are no wage restrictions in the EPZs. Minimum wage legislation enacted in the past and the wage orders now issued by the Regional Tripartite Wages and Productivity Boards apply with equal force in the zones as in the region where they are located.

# A Worker Response

Andres J. Dinglasan

Two important points have had a great impact on the Philippine trade union movement, the outmigration of workers and the proliferation of export-processing zones (EPZs). One effect of the tremendous outmigration of workers to other countries, particularly in the Middle East, is that it has robbed the trade unions of a great potential for organization, and rendered them unable to protect the labour force against human rights abuses. Outmigration has imposed a deep social cost on the social life of the Filipino family, often resulting in failed marriages and broken homes because of long traumatic separations. The jobs overseas will not always be there. The trade unions, together with the government and the private sector, recently initiated a new and vigorous tripartite strategy to fast track economic development so that workers can work in their own country where they belong.

The trade union movement is not respected in the special economic zones (SEZs) such as the Mactan EPZ (MEPZ) and the Canita EPZ. Although there is no law prohibiting the organization of unions, it is well known that one of the benefits enjoyed by foreign investors is an unwritten assurance by the zone administrators, backed by political leaders of the province, that labour disputes will rarely occur in the EPZs because unionization will be made difficult.

As a member of the trade union congress and as a practitioner in labour relations, I would like to present some ideas in dealing with the challenges of the future of our country by way of complementing the recommendations of the Orbeta and Sanchez's chapter. The Philippines is committed to the AFTA and the APEC and has ratified the Uruguay Round of the GATT and is now a member of meet the challenges of free competition in the world market. But globalization is now a reality. It is a force that should motivate the workers, the employers and the government to be active players in the world market in order for the country to survive. How should the Philippines then respond to the challenge of globalization?

In the next two decades, it is projected that six of the world's ten biggest economies will be found in Asia: China, Japan, India, Indonesia,

254

the Republic of Korea and Taiwan, (POC). The remaining economies in the region are likely to be grouped as follows:

- Small industrial economies: Malaysia, Singapore and Hong Kong
- Big industrializing economies: the Philippines and Vietnam
- Other developing countries: Bangladesh, Pakistan, Sri Lanka, Myanmar, Laos and Cambodia.


## CONSEQUENCES FOR THE ECONOMY

The ascent of the 'seven giants' will have several consequences for the Philippine economy.

### Industrial Relocation

Industrial relocation will take place as certain industries become expensive to operate and uncompetitive in their old locations. For example, tool and die making in Japan and Taiwan are locating in such countries as Malaysia, Indonesia and the Philippines in order to take advantage of lower costs. Small-scale industrial production for labour-intensive activities such as leatherware and specialized gift items – for example, music boxes which are popular in Japan and Hong Kong – are also being relocated.

### Food Production

Food production will increasingly be passed on to countries lower on the industrial ladder. This is essentially because industrialization encroaches on the farmlands, raising the actual costs of production, which are also raised by the lack of availability of farm labourers.

### Upscale Products

Increased demand for upscale products including special food items, jewelry, wines and other trappings of a higher standard of living may not be met by what is available in the domestic market. This will result in increased imports. Even China, with its huge population and *higher per capita* incomes, cannot cope with the increase in the demand for pork.

**Tourism**

The demand for tourism will increase significantly as the large middle class seek new travel destinations and place a premium on vacations. Points north of Metro Manila are highly accessible to tourists from China, Taiwan, South Korea and Japan, while Mindanao is a more proximate destination for tourists from India, Indonesia and Malaysia.

**Service Exports**

Service exports, including the export of manpower, will continue to offer attractive business opportunities. Data encoding, engineering design and contract packaging will be distinctive areas of interest in the long term. Factory workers, building maintenance personnel, office workers and household workers will be highly coveted in the giant economies.

## LONG-TERM DEVELOPMENT EFFORTS

In this broad setting, the Philippines should apply two general criteria in selecting the manufacturing industries and activities in which to concentrate long-term development efforts.

- Industries where there is a shift from the lower end labour-intensive activities to the middle range technologically advanced activities
- Industries which have linkages with the rest of the economy and that are characterized by upgraded skills and technologies that are easily transmitted.

In other words, the economy must emphasize the high value added component, away from sweatshop, technology-freezing types of activities.

**Comparative Advantage**

There should be a dynamic sense of the country's comparative advantages. These should be designed, planned and defended, and not left to be dictated by other economies. The Philippines must launch offensive strategies to establish competitive technologies, factories and workers. As a matter of policy, the country should pass on lower end, low range activities to countries that are at lower levels of development. It should not stay within the current structure of low labour cost industrial activities.

## Education and Growth Targets

To be able to move up the industrial ladder requires an emphasis on (1) making structural changes in education; (2) shifting growth targets and policy attitudes; and (3) designing market-driven approaches to regional development.

Changes in education are urgently needed to prepare the cultural environment for industrialization. The population must experience the disciplines of an industrial society and upgrade its general skill level. Community based groups should be involved in implementing aggressive growth enhancing measures. Policies in general must demand more discipline, reward entrepreneurship, penalize luxurious consumption, and encourage free competition. Regional development must respond to market signals coming from the Asian economic giants and small industrialized markets within the region. Mindanao should be operated as an export-oriented production base, linked to India, Singapore, Malaysia, Indonesia and even Australia. The northern Luzon region should be developed in conjunction with the markets of China, Taiwan (POC), Hong Kong, Thailand, Vietnam and South Korea.

## Engineering

In these three major adjustments, the focus should be on developing a viable and competitive engineering sector. This can serve as its growth flagship, a major source of new opportunities and competitive strategy into the long-term future. Science and technology must be central to the educational system. Metal processing skills must be popularly cultivated; it should be a priority to encourage small and medium-sized enterprises (SMEs) to get into the metal production business and to integrate with bigger engineering projects with strong backward linkages. The establishment of regional industrial belts in this sector, taking the necessary precautions in terms of protecting the environment, may be viable. Enlarging the tool and die-making industry can serve as the initial stage of a massive increase in the domestic production of metals, machinery and equipment.

## INFORMAL SECTOR EMPLOYMENT STRATEGY

In the rural sector, strategies to regenerate depleted resources should designed so as to absorb excess labour. Reforestation, for example, is a labour-intensive activity that can be undertaken on a large scale. Tree farms using species that have a high energy content and are harvestable within two or three years could also be mixed with long-gestating hardwood varieties. Off-farm manufacturing activities can provide the impetus for diversification into crops that can be processed for urban markets. In certain cases, the presence of overseas workers abroad can serve as an entry point for the promotion of exports of food products. Backward linkages with farmers can be significant, especially where high value crops are involved.

In the urban sector, the promotion of home based production activities should take more innovative directions. For example, abundant small business loans available through informal and semi-formal conduits will not directly generate employment unless the major bottleneck, that of the lack of viable small business ideas, is tackled. This is the key problem to solve. A system of business advisory services operated by entrepreneurial talents or retired business executives should be introduced to promote small entrepreneurs.

## AGRO-BUSINESS STRATEGY

Another strategy would be to focus on the area of agro-based industrialization. This would involve a specialization in high value crops intended for relatively small but profitable market niches. Farm production offers many possibilities. Fruit and vegetables, as well as high grade nuts, aquaculture products like crab and grouper, and processed products from these raw materials should be on the priority list. For example, the demand for cocktail preparations of nuts is increasing; basic production and packaging can be done in the Philippines. Stamping the words 'distributed by Hong Kong' would double the perceived market value of the products. Many snack food items can follow this model of contract processing.

At the farm level, intensive gardening approaches and large farms operated by cooperatives can form the core of high value crop production for the accessible upscale markets of Hong Kong, Taiwan, Singapore and Japan. These initiatives have to be supported by better post-harvest technologies and facilities, however, which also have to be integrated into the three fundamental strategies. Modern farming methodologies and 'back-to-the-farm' educational components can be introduced on a larger scale. Targets in terms of higher farm productivity, which leads directly to higher farm incomes, can be the motivating force for rural families who directly network with dynamic production and marketing rural cooperatives. Regional food production programmes should also be modified along the lines of market determined demand opportunities.

## CONCLUSIONS

In sum, the Philippines must revise and programme its comparative advantages over the long term by:

- Integrating with the markets of big economies
- Recognizing its competitors and the rules of the competitive economic game
- Focussing on the development of engineering industries
- Encouraging food processing industries development and downstream, complementary modernized farm production
- Restructuring and refocussing education
- Setting higher quantitative and qualitative standards for business performance
- Developing regions on the basis of these key criteria.

# 9 Labour, Labour Markets, and the Economic Integration of Nations

Anil Verma

## INTRODUCTION

World trade has had an enormous impact on the way we live. Trade has expanded to cover almost every corner of the earth and continues to grow at a rate that is touching even the most insulated people in significant ways. Classical economic theory holds that trade occurs when there is a mutual advantage to trading and its result is to make all the partners better off. Much of the evidence in the Post-Second World War era when trade barriers were gradually falling, is supportive of the classical Ricardian view that nations are better off with more rather than less trade. However, when we begin to examine the lives of people affected by trade at a more disaggregated level, a complex reality with mixed results begins to emerge. A nation as a whole may be better off but trade creates winners and losers. New jobs are created and as a result, some people acquire new skills while other jobs disappear and those people holding them at the time, discover that there is no demand for their skills. In some places, with rising prosperity attributable to trade, worker organizations make gains for their members while in other places competitive advantage is created by suppressing worker voice and representation.

The chapters in this volume have sought to develop a better understanding of how conditions in the labour market are affected by increasing trade in the East Asia and South-east Asia (ESEA) region. According to classical economics, increasing trade results in greater integration of product and factor markets. In the area of labour, it implies that labour markets of the trading countries will become increasingly integrated with each other. The many aspects of labour market integration are addressed throughout this volume. Does integration lead to gradual improvement in the conditions of workers or does it lead to a 'race to the bottom'? Does trade and integration of economies lead to better voice for workers or to a disempowerment in the work-place?

There is a normative premise behind this volume: unless labour markets also benefit from increased trade, we will not all be better off. In fact, the growing consensus which has led to the rapid expansion of the freer trade regime in the 1980s and the 1990s, will be increasingly undermined if more and more workers discover that they are worse off as a result of trade. Trade, like all other systems, has both positive and negative outcomes. If we want to enjoy the fruits of greater economic integration of nations, we will have to ensure a smoother integration of labour markets as well. The unanticipated and negative effects of trade on labour markets will have to be managed through selective application of public and business policy. In this respect, nation-states and firms are not hapless bystanders who need to accept passively the market outcomes of a free trade regime. Both states and firms can respond in a variety of ways to ensure that market outcomes serve both efficiency and equity interests.

In this concluding chapter, we develop a conceptual framework for understanding the effects of increasing trade and economic integration on labour market outcomes at aggregated and disaggregated (firm) levels. This framework is then used to explore policy options for government, business and labour. The evidence presented in other chapters is used selectively to highlight various arguments. The last section discussed the implications of these policy choices for the dilemmas created in labour markets as a result of increased trade and economic integration.

## CONCEPTUAL FRAMEWORK

There is no consensus among theoreticians and practitioners on the effects of trade and economic integration on labour markets and, consequently, on our lives. Several competing views are apparent in the literature. Three such views are discussed here briefly in order to provide a context for discussing the results of this study. The first of these views, that of comparative advantage, comes out of the classical economics tradition best enunciated by Ricardo (1772–1823). The second is a critical view that has its roots in the Marxian geopolitical theory of domination and colonialism. Lastly, we discuss the more current view of competitive advantage best enunciated by Porter (1980, 1990).

**The Classical View**

The law of comparative advantage suggests that nations trade in goods that they can produce cheaply. Over the course of history, this idea has mostly translated into trade in the natural endowments of a nation. Thus, countries with large ore deposits or forests or arable land would sell minerals or paper products or agricultural produce. Countries with surplus labour and correspondingly low wages would compete on the basis of low labour costs while those with a shortage of labour would employ machines to produce cheaply. Although this view has seen considerable modification over the years because of its inadequacies, it still retains significant explanatory power in describing the patterns of global trade.

Given our perspective of economic development, this view states that as trade increases between nations with complementary goods, products and factor prices will rise where they are lower and fall where they are higher until prices become level. At this point, the comparative advantage to trade disappears. In the context of developing nations, this view does not fully explain the past experience. To fill the gaps, a more critical view has been developed.

**The Critical View**

Many development economists have held that since successful economic expansion requires large amounts of capital of which poor countries have very little, capital-rich countries can and should play a lead role in promoting growth. Developing countries ought to open up their economies and adopt investor-friendly policies to attract foreign investment. This will promote growth, create jobs- and increase purchasing power which, in turn, will lead to increased savings and domestic pools of capital to sustain growth. This school of development has attracted considerable following in the last two decades from governments and international institutions such as the World Bank and the International Monetary Fund (IMF). A number of countries in the ESEA region have embarked on a foreign investment-driven export-led growth strategy (Kuruvilla, 1995; Kuruvilla and Arudsothy, 1995; Verma *et al.*, 1995). Some countries have ridden more successfully on export-led growth to raise domestic demand and purchasing power. Others have been less successful.

The critical view suggests that the classical scenario of product and factor prices levelling out among trading partners in a simplistic one.

In trading relationships in practice, some nations (typically the rich ones) are dominant players dictating terms to lesser (i.e. the poorer) nations (see Table 9.1). These terms are often designed to retain an advantage for the dominant partner. Thus, despite increasing trade the junior trading partner finds it difficult to raise living standards and escape poverty.

This view is prompted by the history of trade under colonial rule over the last 200 years. The colonizing power would create a vertically integrated market in which the colony supplied inexpensive raw materials, creating mostly low wage, low skill jobs. The raw materials were processed to add value almost exclusively in the (typically) European countries which were industrializing their own economies during the greater part of the nineteenth century and the first half of the twentieth century. Value adding activities created new skills, technologies and high wages in the colonizing economies while the colonies remained relegated to performing low skill, low wage jobs in undiversified economies that relied almost exclusively on primary industries (e.g. agriculture, mining, forestry, fishing, etc.) dependent on natural resources such as land, minerals, forests or water. While this view may not provide the sole explanation for the lack of industrialization in the colonized countries, it helps link some patterns of trade to unfavourable outcomes in the labour market.

Selected evidence presented in earlier chapters is supportive, at least in part, of the critical view. Japan's investment in the region has been much more in low wage, labour-intensive industries compared to its investments elsewhere. The pattern of this investment is driven primarily by Japanese needs rather than by needs of the recipient countries. Moreover, the sources of comparative advantage in the recipient countries are transitory. The recipient countries have few options as they court foreign investment. The global commodity chains also illustrate the power relationship among capital-rich and capital-poor countries. The buyer-driven chain concentrates most of the market power in the industrialized countries. As manufacturing shifts to lower wage countries, the producer appears to have less power within the chain to direct its own development.

Gereffi in Chapter 2 notes that it is very hard for most developing countries to move up the ladder in terms of export roles with greater control and market power. In Thailand, the inflow of foreign investment has led to hyperurbanization of Bangkok while the rest of the country is mired in poverty. New wealth is increasingly concentrated in a few hands while the poor are marginalized. In the Philippines,

*Table* 9.1  Critical and differentiation views of trade and labour markets

| | Investment flow | Domestic purchasing power | Trade patterns | Intra-Asia trade | Industry | Firm | Labour market integration | Labour standards |
|---|---|---|---|---|---|---|---|---|
| Critical view: 'Economic colonialism' | From rich to poor countries | Low and stable | High wage countries dominant | Low | Low skill industries in poor countries, High skill industries in rich countries | Research and Development, marketing structural planning in high wage countries, manufacturing in low wage countries 'Captive production' | Vertical | Race to the bottom |
| Differentiation view: 'Multiple nodes of economic power' | Multidirectional | Increasing | Multidirectional trade | High | Industry distribution based on specialization | Integrated operations in several countries specialized by product groups and global product mandates | Horizontal | Gradual leveling of standards |

foreign investment has led to repetitive, low skill, low wage jobs with little or no skill acquisition or upward mobility. Few of the garment and electronic industries set up with foreign capital have enough backward or forward linkages with local industry. A similar picture emerges from Chapters 5 and 6 on growth triangles in this volume.

## The Differentiation View

The differentiation view has been best articulated by Porter (1980, 1990) in his treatment of competitive advantage. This view suggests that advantage in trade need not come only from natural endowments. Such competitive advantage can be created by combining various inputs to provide products and services that are differentiated from their competition in quality, service, or price. Its implications are that every country can choose to specialize in certain market niches and become world-class competitors in those niches. Thus, the global economy can have multiple nodes of economic power rather a small group of economic superpowers dominating the marketplace.

Differentiation requires that firms (and countries) develop unique advantages by developing skills in certain areas of competence. Thus, skill development, a labour market activity, is central to the idea of differentiation. The Porterian vision would see horizontally integrated labour markets in which no single country in the region would dominate. Hypothetically, Singapore would sell, say, pagers to the Philippines and buy computer printers in return. For such development to occur, firms investing in the region would develop skills within the firm with investment in training while the state would build a public infrastructure for education. Over a period of time, firms would move to higher value added products that require higher skills. This scenario is likely to be feasible only if firms investing in the region take a longer-term view.

A handful of countries in the region have followed this path which lends credibility to this view. The examples which stand out are Singapore (Chew and Chew, 1995), Taiwan (Lee, 1995), and South Korea (Park and Lee, 1995). In each of these cases, a partnership between public and private investment in skill development was set up alongside incentives to attract foreign investment. Successive waves of investment were directed at higher value added production for which a well educated and trained work-force was made available. Skill development was also accompanied with the development of a local economy for services and component manufacturing. This allowed the foreign firms to develop backward and forward linkages with the local economy.

Although the details across these three countries vary, their overarching message reinforces the validity of the differentiation view.

There is some evidence in this volume, however scant, that the differentiation vision may have begun to take shape in the ESEA region. East and Southeast Asian economies are becoming more closely integrated largely as a result of Japanese overseas direct investment (ODI) and related trade (see Watanabe, Chapter 4 in this volume). The rapidly expanding market, the labour shortages in the region and the continuing appreciation of the yen have shifted the patterns of ODI away from Europe and North America to concentrate more heavily in the ASEAN countries. Watanabe suggests that some of the current Japanese ODI is directed at promoting intra-regional horizontal rather than vertical division of labour as evidenced by greater local sourcing of parts and services. Chapter 1 by Bloom and Noor in this volume shows that intra-regional trade has grown faster than inter-regional trade. This trend may be indicative of some horizontal integration, although this is not true of all intra-regional trade.

The most telling signs of the development of a differentiation process in a developing economy is the growth of a local infrastructure for skill development as well as for supplying parts and services. In some export-processing zones (EPZs), industrialization often takes the form of a large industrial park surrounded by a rural area. Workers are often bused in because there is little or no local transport services. There are no schools or colleges offering night classes for workers to upgrade their skills. The firms typically compete on the basis of price, so they have little incentive to offer extensive training. If workers lose their jobs, there is little alternative employment in the local economy. On the other side, if the investment in the industrial park were matched by a parallel development of the local economy and services, it would signal that the area was able to pursue a differentiation strategy for sustained growth.

## ECONOMIC GROWTH AND LABOUR MARKET INTEGRATION: A SYNTHESIS

It can be argued that we are still in the early stages of the development of a global free trade regime. Hence, not all of the effects of a free trade regime are fully observable yet. However, this collection of chapters presents sufficient evidence to begin an assessment of some of the effects of trade on labour market outcomes and to ask what role business and public policy can play in ensuring that efficiency goals do not overwhelm equity outcomes. We offer four generalizations on the basis of evidence presented in this volume.

## Greater Economic Integration is Leading to Greater Labour Market Integration

Present-day patterns of trade are leading to greater economic integration of all parts of the world but especially within ESEA. Throughout this volume we see evidence of greater trade and integration. Three specific pieces of evidence can be cited: first, the growth of intra-Asia trade; second, the growth of global commodity chains (GCCs); and third, Japanese direct investment in the ESEA region.

Bloom and Noor in Chapter 1 examine the growth rates of exports to suggest that while the integration between ESEA and the rest of the world has been quite swift the integration within ESEA has been even faster. Intra-regional exports during 1979–91 grew at an average annual rate of 12.2 per cent whereas inter-regional exports grew at only 9.4 per cent. Thus, in terms of trade growth, ESEA countries outperformed non-ESEA countries with the growth ESEA's intra-regional trade outpacing the growth of its inter-regional trade, which implies even faster integration within ESEA that between ESEA and the rest of the world.

By examining the growth of trade in terms of changes in its distribution among country groups, Bloom and Noor find that from 1979–1981 to 1990–2, ESEA countries increased their share of world exports from 15 to 22 per cent. This growth outpaced the increase in the share of world GNP by ESEA which increased from 17 to 22 per cent. Finally ESEA exports going to ESEA countries during this same period increased from 33 to 41 per cent. Further, the rapid growth of trade between Hong Kong and China and of exports from Japan to Hong Kong, Korea and Taiwan account for 41 per cent of the growth in intra-regional trade.

On the labour market side, intra-regional labour mobility in ESEA, although not a large share of the total labour force, contributed significantly to annual labor force growth in the labour-receiving countries. Documented migrants accounted for approximately one-third of labour force growth in 1991 (Bloom and Noor, this volume). For the labour-sending countries outmigration reduced labour force expansion by about 13 per cent between 1990 and 1991 which helped to even out the supply of labour across countries within ESEA.

Gereffi's study of the development of global commodity chains (GCCs) in Chapter 2 is an excellent description of the manner in which re-source complementarity is playing a role in globalization of produc-tion in certain industries such as garments. A high wage country such as the USA specializes in garment designs and market research; the middle end work involving new production technologies and supply of quality textiles may come from a medium wage country such as Tai-wan; at the production end are lower wage countries such as India, China or, still further down the wage spectrum, Bangladesh or Myanmar.

The GCC framework encompasses several features of global capi-talism and integration of national economies. First, the governance struc-ture of GCCs allows the coordination of transnational production systems either through producer-driven chains or buyer-driven chains. In pro-ducer-driven chains (PDCCs), transnational corporations control the production system including backward and forward linkages. This type of governance structure is most often found in technologically-inten-sive industries like airplanes, computers, cars or machinery. Buyer-driven commodity chains (BDCCs) are found in labour-intensive, consumer goods industries like garments, footwear and electronics. They are characterized by a decentralized production network in a variety of exporting counties typically in the Third World because of the labour intensity of production. The companies involved are marketers who rely on tiered networks of overseas production contracts to perform specialized tasks. Those countries that operate in BDCCs deal with competition from low cost suppliers by developing a triangle network. In the network manufacturers from lower wage countries are used as middle-men in obtaining production of their goods from low wage countries.

### Labour Market Outcomes Under Greater Economic Integration are Mixed – There are Both Positive and Negative Outcomes

Since the 1970s an export-oriented economic structure has developed throughout the world in general, and in the ESEA region in particular. Despite the growth in trade, most developing nations have not been successful in exploiting the backward and forward linkages requires to capitalize on the new system. As a result there is an uneven distribu-tion of economic advantages between regions due to globalization.

In terms of the models outlined earlier, it is the appearance of sec-ondary conditions in the labour market and inadequate responses from business and government that often underlie the uneven gains in de-velopment. An illustration of this phenomenon is the so-called 'growth triangles' (GT). Because of its limited size and scope, GTs provide laboratory-like conditions under which development processes can be examined in greater detail. Chapter 6 outlines many of the reasons why the GT concept makes sense: resource complementarity; limited impact on national economies; and limited free trade. GTs allow national governments to limit political risks associated with unfettered free trade and yet benefit from free trade under controlled conditions.

Manufacturing industries within GTs are a paradigm for shaping development. As industries become globalized and producers in different parts of the world are more tightly linked, the pace of change quickens and exporters have shorter periods to exploit their competitive advantages. Thus, the manufacturers are always looking for the low wage advantage and are attracted to GTs for this reason; they expect to see wages remain low and stable. This is sometimes the case but if wages rise, GTs must move toward higher value added products within a certain period of time or else economic growth may be short-lived as globalized manufacturers shift operations to new areas.

As Skeldon shows in Chapter 5, Hong Kong has shed employment in low wage, labour-intensive industries which have been migrating to the coastal provinces in China. Meanwhile, the Hong Kong economy has created substantial new employment in higher wage, higher skilled service occupations. The shift from manufacturing has created rising educational and skill levels. With more workers going on to higher levels of education, the overall labour force participation rate has declined, further tightening the labour market and driving up wages. Moreover, with increasing levels of education, workers are less willing to undertake low paid and manual employment.

The outcomes of growth triangles are clearly mixed. On the labour market side, the success of SIJORI has created many of the problems described as 'secondary conditions' (Verma *et al.*, 1995). Higher wages have attracted legal and illegal migration from other parts of Malaysia and Indonesia. Many workers in the zone remain locked into low wage–low skill jobs and are unlikely to develop better skills. The skill development infrastructure is poor. Continued inflow of Singaporian capital is dependent upon availability of cheap labour. Should wages and working conditions improve rapidly without commensurate increases in skills and productivity, the capital would go elsewhere leaving workers with little or no future.

Chapter 6 by Tang and Thant and Chapter 5 by Skeldon have described what appears to be successful experiments in regional economic development. However, unless the problems of labour market integration are addressed effectively, it is unlikely that the strategy can be sustained. While there is no single answer, it would appear that any attempt at an effective solution must contain some of the following elements: gradual expansion of the zone; development of a skill infrastructure; mechanisms for worker voice; and a local infrastructure for a service economy.

The success of Thailand, like most of the countries in the ASEAN area, is due to the country abandoning the import-substitution (IS) policy in exchange for policies that will attract FDI. The IS strategy presented a number of obstacles for development in Thailand. Most notably, instead of decreasing imports it actually increased imports because of a lack of intermediate and capital goods. This strategy also promoted a local market with a skewed distribution of income and it encouraged hypergrowth in the Bangkok region while leaving the rural areas in virtual poverty. The promotion of large-scale manufacturing through FDI did not generate high employment because it was not labour-intensive (Charoenloet, Chapter 7 in this volume).

In the Philippines, FDI resulted in division of labour characterized by assembly line jobs with little or no skill acquisition or upward mobility, insecurity of jobs, no unions and a very well defined gender division of labour (Orbeta and Sanchez, Chapter 8 in this volume). Further, there are very few backward linkages with the domestic economy in either the garment or the electronics industry, both of which have been recipients of large FDI flows. This is mainly due to the protective advantage given to imported raw materials which makes them cheaper relative to domestic materials.

The dominant role of Japan in driving growth in ESEA is well documented by Watanabe in Chapter 4. Despite Watanabe's optimism about Japan's ability to spur sustainable growth in ESEA, there are dissenting views. Nomura (1995) argues that both history and politics will conspire to keep Japan from doing any more than subcontracting low end production to their Asian neighbours. According to this view, a number of security issues remain unresolved in the region that will keep closer relations from developing between Japan and some of its neighbours. It is also argued that negative attitudes in both Japan and overseas about quality of production in ESEA still present a formidable obstacle to better horizontal integration between Japan and its neighbours.

Overall, the evidence in this volume suggests that vertical integration of product and labour markets is well under-way in the ESEA region but that many problems remain in the process of moving towards horizontal integration of labour markets.

## Economic Growth in Many Developing Regions of ESEA can be Short-lived, with no Lasting Benefits for the Local People and their Economy

The GCC paradigm for globalization of some industries described by Gereffi in Chapter 2 underlines the dangers for some developing economies should they fail to develop a strategy for skill and wage upgrading. There is always a country or region where wages are relatively lower and some industries, particularly garment and electronic assembly, will always be prone to moving down the chain if local labour market conditions change.

Chapters 8 by Orbeta and Sanchez on the Philippines and Chapter 7 by Charoenloet on Thailand confirm on a national scale what we have learned from the whole volume at a more aggregated level. The Philippine picture is somewhat optimistic in terms of future growth but the authors note that much of this integration with the world economy is vertical in nature. Charoenloet clearly illustrates the persisting problems in the labour market despite rapid economic growth in the past twenty years. It is suggested that the pace of economic growth is potentially threatened because of lack of attention paid to labour market planning in the past.

The employment performance of the Philippine economy has been very weak with most workers (45 per cent) still employed in agriculture. The manufacturing sector has declined and the service sector has absorbed surplus labour. High fertility rates and political instability during the 1980s have pushed unemployment rate to very high levels. To cope with the over-supply of labour the government began to develop mechanisms for exporting labour. The push for overseas contract workers (OCWs) is due to the poor performance of the economy and the increase in the education of workers. Huge numbers of OCWs moved to the Middle East and more recently to the Asian countries. Currently the export of professional workers outperforms the export output of blue-collar workers.

State policies helped encourage foreign firms to set up in the Philippines by giving them advantages like the establishment of special export processing zones (EPZs), tariff exemptions for importing raw materials and the exemption from labour legislation like minimum wage; most firms, however, pay wage rates required by law in these special economic zones (SEZs). The lack of unions in the SEZs helps present the area as a showcase of harmonious industrial relations relative to other EPZs.

The resurgence of FDI in the region should continue. Because of this the economy should grow and blue-collar OCW should decline even further as the wage advantage will not sufficiently cover the social costs. Professional workers, on the other hand will continue to work abroad even if the domestic economy continues to improve. This is mainly due to high wage differentials between the professional and technical workers domestically and abroad. Further, the comparative advantage for labour costs domestically will soon be lost. Thus, the government must push for higher value added products. One way this can be accomplished is to make the acquisition of new technology rewarding for the private sector. This is particularly important since the opportunity for skill upgrading and upward mobility in assembly-type production activities is insignificant in the SEZs.

In Thailand, one consequence of export-led growth is that wealth is increasingly concentrated in the hands of few. This is evident in the hyperurbanization of Bangkok and the marginalization of the poor. In addition, the country has witnessed a rise of the informal sector which is not regulated by laws. The informal sector employs over 4 million workers and consists of such professions as street vendors and garbage collectors. These workers have few, if any unions to represent them, and Lack of representation leads to further marginalization of these workers. Permanent employment is also on the decline and short-term employment has become more prevalent in textile, hotel, food and beverage industries, in particular. The abolition of temporary employment has been attempted by the government, but it remains an important strategy for employers to lower costs and create flexibility of employment. Privatization is also becoming a major public policy issue in Thailand. The state enterprise unions were abolished in 1991 which allowed the implementation of the privatization programme. This move weakened the position of the labour movement significantly.

**To Sustain Economic Growth, a Policy of Open Trade and Free Markets needs to be Combined with a Labour/Social Policy Aimed at Improving Worker Skills and Providing Workers with Voice in the Work place**

Gereffi in Chapter 3 explains that countries are connected to GCCs through the goods and services they supply to the world economy. They develop trade linkages in one of five major export roles: primary commodity export, export processing assembly, component supply sub-contracting, original equipment manufacturing (OEM) and original brandname manufacturing (OBM). As you move up the list each type of exporting is more difficult to establish. Currently, East Asian NICs are concentrating on component supply subcontracting, OEM and OBM while most of the countries in Southeast Asia and Latin America are involved in the first three types. There is also a typical sequence of export roles. Countries usually begin exporting primary commodities and then turn to staple consumer items like textiles, garments and foot-wear. Then countries can either fill OEM orders or they can make component parts to be exported for finished assembly abroad. Finally a country may begin to export OBM production, the highest level of export strategy.

It can be argued that the experience of the East Asian NICs sug-gests that a diversified array of backward linkages is essential in mov-ing toward the more complex component supply, OEM and OMB export roles. Some East Asian NICs have been successful in upgrading their export industries in large measure because of their highly efficient networks of suppliers for intermediate goods and components.

The opportunities for developing economies depends on the kind of export role they are able to assume and their ability to move to a higher value product. Both technological advance (in the form of physical capital) an organizational learning (in the form of human capital) are required to sustain industrial development. Progress requires a dynamic enterprise base, supportive state policies, and improving skills and higher wages in the work force. For too many nations in the developing world, reaching the status of core countries is an ever-receding frontier, com-plicated by a growing technology gap and a constantly changing inter-national environment.

The success of some ESEA nations prompted the World Bank to identify the key strategies used by these countries to sustain growth and development. These include: an orientation to markets outside its borders, macroeconomic stability, and investing in people (Leipziger and Thomas, 1993; World Bank, 1993).

Growth driven by rich (high wage) countries, GTs and export-driven industrialization are all viable strategies for attaining high rates of growth. However, if these rates of growth are to be sustained these must be more meaningful improvement in the lives of people affected. Countries exporting capital must sooner or later begin to source more value added products locally. Governments need to develop skill-building infrastructure and firms need to recruit and develop local skills.

Export-driven growth must lead to rises in domestic purchasing power.

In the next ten years, Thailand may be expected to phase out the traditional labour-intensive industries – textiles, garments, shoes, etc. – because they will soon lose their current competitive advantage due largely to lower wages. Thailand will either shift production out or introduce technology to secure manufacturing by moving to higher value added products. Such a move up the value chain will require a commensurate improvement in skills of the work-force. The current development efforts in exported-oriented structure have not contributed to skill development because of their need to keep labour costs low. Currently the Thai labour force lacks skilled labour and 80 per cent of the workers in manufacturing have only elementary education. The role of government is very important in investing in training and development, to develop labour legislation and to ensure that the infrastructure development continues.


CONCLUSIONS

The evidence in this volume suggests that the growth in trade linkages has led to greater integration of labour markets in the ESEA region. Any change in local labour market conditions such as wages, working conditions, new labour legislation, etc. can be expected to have an effect on all the other labour markets in the chain. For example, a debate in Thailand over raising the minimum wage will have to consider the opening up of Vietnam for foreign investment. Whether these linkages will lead to 'better' outcomes in the labour market such as improved wages, safety, etc. or whether it will lead to a 'race to the bottom' will depend on a host of public and private policies.

Verma *et al.* (1995) suggest that a less developed country begins the growth process by creating some initial conditions conducive to investment (see Figure 9.1). In human resource terms it may translate into low wages and, possibly, low unionization. These advantages attract initial investments and businesses can make money by arbitraging these labour market conditions across markets where wages are higher. As investment increases over time, the initial labour market conditions inevitably change. There are pressures on wages to rise and growing demands for unionization and collective bargaining. These may be called 'secondary conditions of the labour market' because they follow the initial spate of investment.

The result of secondary conditions developing in the labour market

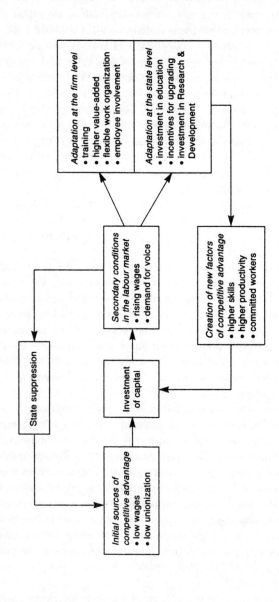

*Figure 9.1*  Economic growth and human resources

Reproduced with permission from Anil Verma, Thomas A. Kochan and Russell Lansbury (eds) (1995). *Employment Relations in the Changing Asian Economies.* London: Routledge.

may be to reduce the initial advantage that attracted new investment in the first place. The secondary conditions present the state with a critical juncture in the development process. The state appears to respond in two ways. The first is to undertake a series of measures that would maintain the advantages of the initial conditions. These policies may include wage controls and suppression of unions and collective bargaining. This is presently most evident in Malaysia and Thailand (Frenkel, 1993). The second response is to adapt to the secondary conditions, a process in which firm-level responses are as significant as state-level policies. Some of the ways in which adaptation in human resource terms occurs are to link wages to productivity and to upgrade skills by investing in training and education. In a virtuous cycle, businesses upgrade skills to increase value added production which makes them more profitable, and hence, they are able to pay higher wages to their workers (Birdsall and Sabot, 1995).

At the firm level, greater training, more performance based pay (as opposed to seniority based pay), flexible work organization, and greater employee involvement in the production process, would lead to conditions conducive to greater value added production. At the state level, incentives for firm-level training, creation of a training fund at the national or sectoral level, and productivity-driven wage policy are some of the ways in which governments have responded to the secondary conditions. It may also include a variety of ways in which the state could provide greater voice. The state may coopt and include unions in national policymaking (Singapore) or provide greater freedom after a period of suppression (Korea and Taiwan) (Frenkel, 1993). These adaptations essentially create new factors of competitive advantage leading to further investment and growth.

An important theorem of the adaptation process is that public and private investments in skills must complement each other for sustained growth. In the absence of a public infrastructure for education and a reliable supply of educated workers, businesses will be hesitant in making new investments or in upgrading existing operations. On the other hand, education alone will not guarantee upgrading to higher value added production. The firm must invest in a variety of on-the-job skills such as problem-solving, interpersonal skills, and functional skills. Thus, the state is not only responsible for investing in a public skill development infrastructure but also for ensuring that private firms make commensurate investments in training.

Although the two responses appear to be alternatives, in practice, a government may choose to follow a bit of both. In the case of Korea, the government pursued both responses for a number of years. In Singapore, the union was not suppressed in the same way but its independence was compromised when it was coopted into the state policymaking process. In Malaysia, unions are independent but the labour laws are restrictive. The pursuit of both responses best illustrates that a simple link between labour suppression and economic growth can not be drawn. It is not clear if any of these economies would have been as successful if they had only pursued the first response (i.e., labour suppression) without the adaptation response to secondary conditions. Thus, our evidence suggests that the success of these economies can not be explained purely in terms of labour suppression, as has been argued by Deyo (1989) and others. Freeman (1993) has also argued that labour suppression alone is an inadequate explanation for the economic success of East Asian economies.

To end, we should note that there is substantial social and cultural resistance to globalization because of uneven effects within and between countries. Moreover, globalization is not inevitable. Its foundations are both political and economic and thus of questionable stability should a majority of people fail to prosper from it. Developing nations face radical transformation of their industry from low wage industries to higher value added and more technologically sophisticated manufacturing and service industries. The initial sources of competitive advantage in activities such as export processing are transitory. No country can afford to rely on such low value added activities for sustained growth. The ultimate goal for national policy as well as for partners in international trade should be the development of skills of a people so that they can enjoy the fruits of modern times – health, education, leisure, and a chance to be creative and productive.

**References**

Asian Development Bank (1992), *Key Indicators of Developing Asian and Pacific Countries* (London: Oxford University Press).
Birdsall, N. and R. Sabot (1995), *Virtuous Circles: Human Capital, Growth and Equity in East Asia* (Washington, DC: The World Bank).
Chew S. and R. Chew (1995), *Employment-Driven Industrial Relations Regimes: The Singapore Experience* (Aldershot: Avebury).
Deyo, F.C. (1989), *Beneath the Miracle: Labour Subordination in the New Asian Industrialism* (Berkeley and Los Angeles: University of California Press).
Freeman, R.B. (1993), 'Does Suppression of Labour Contribute to Economic

Success? Labour Relations and Markets in East Asia' (August), prepared for the World Bank (mimeo).

Frenkel, S. (ed.) (1993), *Organized Labour in the Asia-Pacific Region* (Ithaca NY.: ILR Press).

Kuruvilla, S.C. (1995), 'Economic Development Strategies, Industrial Relations Policies and Workplace IR/HR Practices in Southeast Asia', in K.S. Wever and L. Turner (eds), *The Comparative Political Economy of Industrial Relations* (Madison WI: IRRA)

Kuruvilla, S.C. and P. Arudsothy (1995), 'Economic Development Strategy, Government Labour Policy and Film-level Industrial Relations Practices in Malaysia', in A. Verma, T.A. Kochan and R.L. Lansbury (eds), *Employment Relations in the Changing Asian Economies* (London: Routledge).

Lee, J.S. (1995), 'Economic Development and the Evolution of Industrial Relations in Taiwan, 1950-1993', in A. Verma, T.A. Kochan, and R.D. Lansbury (eds), *Employment Relations in the Changing Asian Economies*, (London: Routledge): 88-118

Leipziger, D.M. and V. Thomas (1993), *The Lessons of East Asia: An Overview of Country Experience* (Washington, DC.: World Bank).

Locke, R., T. Kochan and M. Piore (eds) (1995), *Employment Relations in Changing World Economy* (Cambridge, MA: MIT Press).

Nomura, M. (1995), 'The Asian Markets and the Difficult Position of Japan: Political Economy of Asia', paper presented at the Meeting on Regionalization and Labour Market Independence in East and Southeast Asia (23-26 January) (Bangkok, Thailand).

Ogawa, N., G.W. Jones, and J.G. Williamson (eds) (1993), *Human Resources in Development along the Asia-Pacific Rim* (London: Oxford University Press).

Park, Young-bum and M. Lee (1995), 'Economic Development, Globalization, and Practices in Industrial Relations and Human Resources Management in Korea', in Verma, Kochan and Lansbury (eds) *Employment Relations in the Changing Asian Economics* (London: Routledge).

Porter, M.E. (1980), *Competitive Strategy* (New York: Macmillan).

Porter M.E. (1990), *The Competitive Advantage of Nations* (New York: Macmillan).

Rana, P.B. and N. Hamid (eds) (1995), *From Centrally Planned to Market Economies: The Asian Approach*, vol. 1 (Hong Kong: Oxford University Press).

Thant, M., M. Tang and H. Kakazu (eds), *Growth Triangles in Asia: A New Approach to Regional Economic Cooperation* (Hong Kong: Oxford University Press).

Verma, A., T.A. Kochan and R.L. Lansbury (eds) (1995), *Employment Relations in the Changing Asian Economies* (London: Routledge).

World Bank (1993), *The East Asian Miracle: Economic Growth and Public Policy* (London and New York: Oxford University Press).

# Index

*Notes*: figures and tables (indicated by page numbers in *italics*) are only indexed when separate from the relevant text; contributions to this volume are shown in **bold** type.

Switzerland 95, *96, 101–3*

Taiwan (POC)
agriculture 200
apparel industry 66, 68–76
*passim*, 78, 79, 86
capital–labour ratio *29*
commodity chains 66, 68–76
*passim*, 78, 79, 81–7 *passim*,
106–7
economic growth 46, 154–5
electronics industry 68, 81–6
*passim*, 95, *96, 101–3*, 104–7,
108–9; home-grown 104–5,
106–7, 108–9, 119, 120;
linkages and technology
transfer 111, 113, 114
employment in Japanese
affiliates 139, *140*
engineering skills 118
export specialization 49
FDI by 23, 100, 119, 147, 206, 210;
in coastal China 169–70, 184
FDI in, by Japan 99–100, 131,
*134*, 138
government policies 74, 75,
108–9, 120
labour costs: low 69, 79, 116–17;
rising 58, 74, 100, 108–9
labour shortages 191
migration to *21*, 22, 251
original brandname manufacturing
(OBM) 63, 64, 65
original equipment manufacturing
(OEM) 61, 62, 68, 106–7
trade: exports 47, *48*, 49, *50–1*,
66, 68–76 *passim*; inter- and
intra-regional 26, *28*, 29; with
Japan 138, *139*
*see also* Southern China Growth
Triangle
Tang, M. and Thant, M. 269–70
**Recent Development of Growth
Triangles and the Implications
for Labour Mobility in
Asia** 174–93
Tanzania *48, 50–1*
Tatung 106, 107
tax incentives 154–5

technology transfer
electronics industry 106, 111–12,
113–15, 120
and overseas employment 251
Thailand 219
Techtrans 112
TECO 106, 109
Teledyne *100–2*
Texas Instruments *101–3*, 105,
113–14
Textile Institute, Thailand 217
textiles and clothing *see* apparel
industry
Thailand 70, 74, 199–223, 270
agricultural sector 199, 200,
204, 205
balance of payments crises 201,
203
Board of Investment 200, 204
capital–labour ratio *29*
Code of Investment 204
collective bargaining 202–3, 212
commodity chains 68, 86
comparative advantage 199,
208–9, 210, 274
democratization 202–3, 209
development: export-oriented
industrialization 203–4, 272;
import substitution
industrialization 200–3;
industrialization policy 200–2;
and non-wage labour 206–8;
stages of 214–15
economic growth 203–4, 221
education 211, 220, *225*, 274
electronics industry 68, 86, 95–7,
*101–3*; MNEs in 95–7, 99, 104,
111, 112, 121
employment 202, 205, 207–8,
209, 212, 218; flexibility 207–8,
212; in Japanese affiliates *140*,
141; of women 205, 209
environmental degradation 212
exports 47, *48*, 49, *50–1*, 204;
apparel 68, 70, 72, 73, 204
FDI in 25, 100, 199, 202, 204,
206, 210; by Japan 99–100,
131, 134, *135*, 138, 210
GDP *181, 225*